# THE HATFIELD & MCCOY FEUD AFTER KEVIN COSTNER: RESCUING HISTORY

## Mr. Tom E. Dotson

ISBN-13: 9781484177853
ISBN-10: 1484177851
Library of Congress Control Number: 2013908314
CreateSpace Independent Publishing Platform
North Charleston, South Carolina

For the love of my life—Patricia.  Fifty-two years and counting.

"The past was erased, the erasure was forgotten, the lie became the truth."
— George Orwell, 1984.

# CONTENTS

# OVERVIEW

There was an election on Blackberry Creek, in Pike County, Kentucky, on August 7, 1882. In a drunken brawl, three sons of (Randolph) Ran'l McCoy, Tolbert, Pharmer and Bud McCoy, knifed and shot Ellison Hatfield. The following day, Ellison Hatfield's brother, Anderson, known as "Devil Anse," leading a group of about twenty kinsmen and employees of his timbering business, took the three McCoys from the Kentucky law officers and transported them to West Virginia. When Ellison died a day later, the Hatfields brought the three McCoys back across the Tug River to the Kentucky side, tied them to paw paw bushes and executed them.

As Ellison Hatfield was considered a splendid man by people on both sides of the Tug River--Hatfield, McCoys and others--there was no effort to arrest or try the Hatfields for the lynching.[1] No newspaper anywhere referred to these events as part of a *feud*, and nothing was published in any newspaper about *feud* events in the Tug Valley[2] until January, 1888.

Nothing at all happened between the two families from the paw paw killings until the fall of 1886, when Jeff McCoy, a cousin of the three McCoys killed in 1882, was shot and killed by Cap Hatfield, son of Devil Anse. McCoy, who was wanted for murder in Kentucky, was arrested by Hatfield in West Virginia and shot while escaping from custody.

After another year of peace, the Pikeville power structure,[3] in an effort to force Devil Anse to sell the five thousand prime coal-bearing acres he owned on the West Virginia side of the Tug, organized a posse. The posse, less than a quarter of whom were McCoys, illegally invaded West Virginia, capturing six of the Hatfield cohort and killing two. Responding to the incursions of the Kentucky posse into West Virginia, on January 1, 1888, a group of men who were relatives and/or employees of Devil Anse raided the home of Randolph (Ran'l) McCoy. The raiders burned the home, killed a son and a daughter of Ran'l McCoy and beat his wife. No other killings occurred between the families of Ran'l McCoy and Devil Anse Hatfield.

Four weeks later, amid a firestorm of newspaper coverage, Devil Anse sold his five thousand acres to a speculator and left Tug Valley. The feud ended when Anse sold his land.

In January, 1888, having never reported a feud in Pike County before, several large newspapers, including three from New York, sent reporters to Pikeville, Kentucky. The articles they wrote made the Hatfield and McCoy feud the most famous of all the American feuds, even though its death toll was far smaller than several other such conflicts.

Some writers went all the way back to the Civil War to include the killing of a McCoy Union soldier by Confederate Hatfields as the beginning of the feud they created while others dated it from a lawsuit over a hog in 1878.

All of them filled up the quiet years with fabricated tales of violent events which either never happened or which had nothing to do with the two families. Many of the tall tales were told to the reporters by the people in the valley. Several books followed during the next ninety years, all of which adopted most of the yellow journalists' tales as history.

In 1988, Professor Altina Waller did the first real historical study of the feud, placing the events in their economic and political context, and refuting the stereotypical savage hillbilly.

The success of the highly fictionalized Kevin Costner TV special in 2012 brought forth an avalanche of feud-related books, two of which became best-sellers. Those books, by Lisa Alther and Dean King, both claim to be history, while adopting and even embellishing the tall tales of the yellow journalists.

This book attempts to refute the pseudo histories and set the historical record straight.

1  While lynching is usually thought of as a hanging, it actually means any extra-legal execution. According to the Tuskegee Institute, there were 113 lynchings in 1882, with 64 of the victims being White. The McCoys represented less than five percent of the White victims, but no one knows any of the names of the other 61.

2  When I speak of "Tug Valley," I mean that part of the drainage area of the Tug River from the mouth of Pond Creek—across from Williamson, West Virginia—to the Virginia border.

3  The Pikeville elite had the support of the Governor, who wished to deflect attention away from the ongoing feuds in Kentucky onto the West Virginia Hatfields.

# PREFACE:

The Hatfield and McCoy feud is *a story* that has become an *industry*. The participants in the industry, like their counterparts in other industries, seek growth. The growth needed to expand the revenue of the industry cannot occur unless the story itself grows. This growth is possible — and is occurring as I write — only because *the feud is a story* and not history.

The feud story, as it has been told from the time of the 1888 newspaper reporters to the 2013 book by Dean King, is *not* a true story. It is not true, because it is built upon a false premise. This premise is stated early in the Dean King book, in his Prologue, where he says of the people of the Tug Valley: "...the bloodthirst in their veins worked on them like spring..."

Then he writes of: "...their inescapable urge to behold a man hang by his neck."[1] King makes these atrociously false judgments of Tug Valley people at the beginning of his book, then spends the bulk of the following four hundred plus pages trying to prove it, by gathering up almost every tall tale told over the last century and a quarter, while ignoring almost entirely the factual record.

The facts belie King's assessment from the start. There was not a single documented case of murder in the Tug Valley before the Civil War. For fifteen years after the war, there was peace in the valley, broken by the killing of Bill Staton in 1880, after a new generation of landless young men reached manhood. How does King derive "bloodthirst" from a record like that? "Bloodthirst in their veins" denotes an inborn defect of character that can never be overcome. One of King's favorite yellow journalist "sources," T.C. Crawford admitted in 1888, after all the killings associated with the "feud" had occurred, that the murder rate in the valley was no greater than in other "more civilized states,"[2] yet King says our forefathers had a "bloodthirst." King is wrong, as we shall see.

To his second charge, I answer: As a boy, I talked to more than twenty people who were old enough to remember the hanging of Ellison Mounts. Not one person I talked to on Blackberry Creek went to the hanging of Ellison Mounts. Furthermore, not one person I talked to even knew anyone who saw the hanging. No one on Blackberry Creek, where most of the "feud" happened, had King's "inescapable urge to behold a man hang by his neck."[3]

With the History Channel now running a reality show which claims that the feud is one hundred fifty years old and still counting, one might think the growth has reached its limit — but it hasn't. The feud story can grow continually, limited only by the imagination of the story-tellers.

I have both Hatfield and McCoy blood, although not directly from either Ran'l McCoy or Devil Anse Hatfield. One of my maternal great, great grandfathers was the Confederate veteran, Uriah McCoy. He was Ran'l's first cousin and also a brother of Ran'l's wife, (Sarah) Sally. Neither Uriah nor his son Asa, who was my great grandfather, was ever involved in the feud. Preacher Anderson Hatfield, first cousin once removed to Devil Anse was my great-great grandfather on both sides. I was born and raised about a mile from the spot where Ellison Hatfield was killed, and about four miles from where the three McCoy boys met vigilante justice.

The first question most people ask when they learn that I have both Hatfield and McCoy blood is, "Which side are you on?"

I confound most of them when I answer: "I'm with the majority." The Pareto Principle, also known as the 80-20 rule, states that 80% of the effects come from 20% of the causes. Anyone who has worked in an office knows the general validity of the principle, since 80% of the work in most offices is done by 20% of the people.

The Pareto Principle was definitely at work in the Hatfield and McCoy troubles. There were about sixty males over the age of fourteen in each of the two families in the 1880 Census but the largest number of men of either name that was ever involved in a feud incident was nine. There was never an event in the feud — not even the climactic Battle of Grapevine — that involved as many as 20% of *either* family.

Therefore, if one is a descendant of either of these Tug Valley families, the odds are at least four to one against that person being the descendant of a feudist.

In fact, since eight McCoys were witnesses against Paris McCoy at his 1880 trial in Logan, and eight Hatfields were witnesses against the Hatfields tried in Pikeville in 1889, the odds that today's Hatfield or McCoy is descended from someone who took the opposite side are roughly the same as the odds that he or she is descended from a feudist.

All of my Hatfield and McCoy ancestors were among the great majority who elected not to participate in the feud. Those members of the eighty percent are libeled by the recent supersizing of the feud story, which melds them into the tiny percentage who engaged in violence. Thus we see the descendants of Uriah McCoy presented in a television reality show as potential feudists who may erupt in violence at any minute, when Uriah, himself, was never involved in any of the feud violence.

The feud became, for a while, more history than a story in the 1980's, with the book by the historian, Altina Waller— but that period has now ended.

The 2012 Kevin Costner film, which was a great drama but terrible history, signaled the end of the feud as a subject for serious historical inquiry and breathed new life into the *story* of the feud. The story grew with the Lisa Alther book, *Blood Feud*, which followed in the wake of the movie. Ms. Alther entitles the introduction to her book, *Murderland*. That title is a good indication of the validity of the tale that follows.

The 2013 book by Dean King, *The Feud*, is an exponential expansion of the feud story, which, of course, brings with it a similar expansion of the feud industry. It is amazing to see someone writing what he purports to be history, while citing as factual proof the writings of nineteenth century newspaper reporters who were demonstrably in error in many, if not most of the factual statements they wrote. King obviously thinks that the uncorroborated word of a yellow journalist is the stuff of which real history is made. By regurgitating most of the tallest tales from 1888 forward in a book that has been stamped as history by the media complex, King has set real history back to where it was at the beginning of the twentieth century.

With several Kentucky feuds ongoing at the same time as our feud, involving more people-- including high county office holders--resulting in much higher casualties than our feud, why has the Hatfield and McCoy feud received more publicity than all the other feuds combined? In the three years preceding the inauguration of Governor Simon B. Buckner, in August, 1887, the feud in Rowan County claimed more than twenty lives. A few days before he was sworn in there was a battle in the streets of the county seat of Morehead that involved more than sixty fighters and claimed four lives with several more wounded.

Within days of his inauguration, the governor took steps which reignited a "feud" that had been dormant for five years and led directly to the illegal raids by his Kentucky posse into West Virginia kicking off the most violent phase of the Pike County conflict. Why did he do this?

Within weeks of this re-ignition of our feud, New York newspapers sent their reporters to Kentucky. They ignored the much larger and bloodier feuds ongoing elsewhere in Kentucky and went directly to Pikeville and Logan, from whence they returned to their city bases and emitted a string of columns that grossly exaggerated the events in Tug Valley, thus becoming the original *supersizers*[4] of our feud. Why did they do this? This book will attempt to give the answers.

The two best-selling books that followed the TV movie, like most previous books on the feud, are largely fable, legend and fiction. I hope to prove it by showing that much of what has been written is either illogical, impossible, or is in conflict with the evidence.

The Hatfield and McCoy feud is probably unique among all the events in history in that writers of feud-based fiction are more constrained than are writers of feud history. The good fiction writer is always careful to avoid writing something that is patently impossible. A fiction writer would never say that twelve hundred people regularly attended a church in an isolated mountain hollow that had only two dozen members. Dean King, writing a *"True Story"* of the feud, can say that and still have reviewers from prestigious media organs laud his factual accuracy.

The New York newspapermen wrote in 1888 with the sure knowledge that, with the exception of a small group of professional historians, none of their readers would check their facts. Today's feud industry writers obviously count on the same thing — but they are wrong. With the modern miracle of the internet, one does not have to be a professional historian to be able to expose many spurious "historical" facts.

If I have more to say about some writers than about others, it is because they wrote more fiction and sold it as history.

This writer presumes that most readers have either seen the Costner movie, or have read at least one of the many books that tell the feud story. If not, then an occasional look at the time line and the maps should help the reader follow along

---

1  King, Dean, The *Feud*, 3.

2  Crawford, T. C., *American Vendetta*, 7-8.

3  The only person I ever talked to who was at that hanging was a woman who lived on Johns Creek at the time of the hanging.

4  Mr. Ryan Hardesty invented the term "supersizer," to identify writers who fill books with folklore, legend and outright lies about the Hatfield and McCoy feud and call it history.

# THE FEUD ON THE MAP

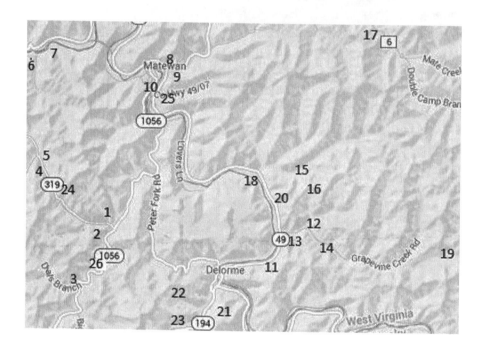

Feud map legend:

1. Preacher Anse Hatfield home. Hog trial held here, 1878.
2. Ellison Hatfield killed here, August, 1882.
3. Three McCoys taken from custody of law officers by Wall and Elias Hatfield, August, 1882.
4. Ran'l McCoy home place. Author's sister lived here in mid-1950's.
5. McCoy family cemetery-- Calvin McCoy's stone. Author's wife grew up next door

6. Aunt Betty Blankenship McCoy's house, where Roseanna sought refuge.
7. "Hog Floyd" lived here, just across the ridge from Ran'l McCoy.
8. Anderson Ferrell home, where Ellison Hatfield died. Town of Matewan is here now.
9. Old schoolhouse where the three sons of Ran'l McCoy were held prisoners.
10. Paw-paw grove where the three McCoys were executed, August, 1882.
11. Devil Anse lived here, on the old Cline home place.
12. Grapevine Creek. Cap Hatfield lived here.
13. Battle of Grapevine fought here.
14. Grapevine Creek. Johnse and Nancy McCoy Hatfield lived here.
15. Thacker Creek. Jim Vance home.
16. Jim Vance killed here, January, 1888.
17. Mate Creek home of Ellison Hatfield.
18. Jeff McCoy killed here, November, 1886.
19. Beech Creek home of Wall Hatfield.
20. Elias Hatfield home.
21. John Dils owned land here.
22. Asa Harmon McCoy killed here, January, 1865.
23. Devil Anse terrorized Unionists in this area during the Civil War.
24. Jim McCoy home.
25. Asa McCoy home. Asa and Jim sat here while Jim's brothers were slain across the river.
26. This author born and raised here.

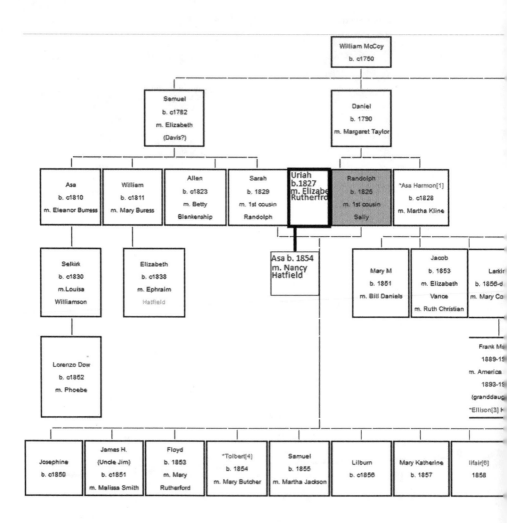

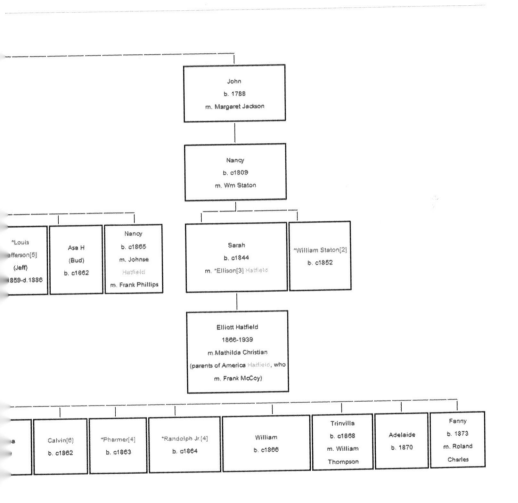

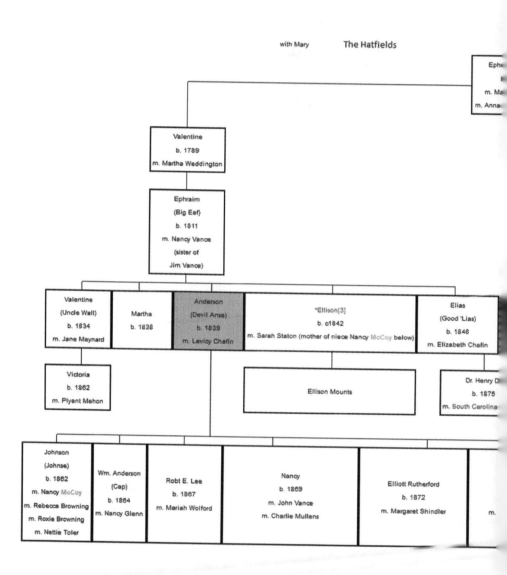

with Mary        The Hatfields

Eph...

m. Ma...

m. Anna...

Valentine
b. 1789
m. Martha Weddington

Ephraim
(Big Eaf)
b. 1811
m. Nancy Vance
(sister of
Jim Vance)

| Valentine (Uncle Wall) b. 1834 m. Jane Maynard | Martha b. 1838 | Anderson (Devil Anse) b. 1839 m. Levicy Chafin | *Ellison[3] b. c1842 m. Sarah Staton (mother of niece Nancy McCoy below) | Elias (Good 'Lias) b. 1848 m. Elizabeth Chafin |

Victoria
b. 1862
m. Plyant Mahon

Ellison Mounts

Dr. Henry D...
b. 1875
m. South Carolina...

| Johnson (Johnse) b. 1862 m. Nancy McCoy m. Rebecca Browning m. Roxie Browning m. Nettie Toler | Wm. Anderson (Cap) b. 1864 m. Nancy Glenn | Robt E. Lee b. 1867 m. Mariah Wolford | Nancy b. 1869 m. John Vance m. Charlie Mullens | Elliott Rutherford b. 1872 m. Margaret Shindler | m. |

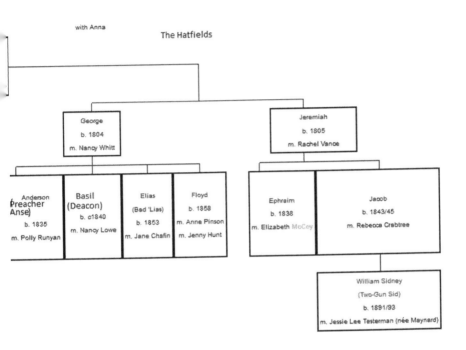

with Anna

The Hatfields

George
b. 1804
m. Nancy Whitt

Jeremiah
b. 1805
m. Rachel Vance

Anderson
(Preacher Anse)
b. 1835
m. Polly Runyan

Basil
(Deacon)
b. c1840
m. Nancy Lowe

Elias
(Bad 'Lias)
b. 1853
m. Jane Chafin

Floyd
b. 1858
m. Anne Pinson
m. Jenny Hunt

Ephraim
b. 1838
m. Elizabeth McCoy

Jacob
b. 1843/45
m. Rebecca Crabtree

William Sidney
(Two-Gun Sid)
b. 1891/93
m. Jessie Lee Testerman (née Maynard)

Elizabeth
b. 1875
m. John Caldwell

Elias
b. 1878
m. Peggy Simple

Detroit
(Troy)
b. 1881
m. Pearl

Joseph
b. 1883
m. Grace Ferrell

Roseda
b. 1885
m. Marion Browning

Willis Wilson
b. 1888
m. Lakie Maynor
m. Ida Chafin

Tennyson
(Tennis)
b. 1890
m. Lettie Hunter
m. Sadie Walters
m. Margaret

# INTRODUCTION

The Oxford Dictionary defines a feud as "a state of prolonged mutual hostility, typically between two families or communities, characterized by violent assaults in revenge for previous injuries. Dictionary.com defines feud as "a bitter, continuous hostility, especially between two families, clans, etc., often lasting for many years or generations."

The conflict between the families of Ran'l McCoy and Devil Anse Hatfield during the last half of the nineteenth century fits neither of these definitions. The actual record of violent conflict between the two families is scant, indeed, consisting only of the arrest of Johnse Hatfield and the ensuing confrontation between the Anse Hatfield family and two members of the Ran'l McCoy family when Johnse was freed from arrest (the only such armed confrontation other than the New Year's raid during the entire period); the murder of Ellison Hatfield and the execution of his killers two days later and the raid on the McCoy home on New Year's Day, 1888.

Everything else in the feud stories, apart from those four incidents, is either part of the larger conflict involving the Pikeville elite, involves people other than the immediate families of Ran'l and Devil Anse, or is filler material consisting of folklore or figments of the writers' imaginations.

The conflict in Tug Valley was never referred to in the press as a feud until January, 1888, the month in which the last episode occurred.

The New Year's raid, being a reaction to the raids by the Phillips posse, was clearly connected to the larger conflict, but, since it involved only members of the Devil Anse Hatfield cohort and the family of Ran'l McCoy, it is part of the Hatfield and McCoy feud.

1

The only way one can come up with a scenario that fits either Oxford's "state of *prolonged mutual* hostility" (emphasis mine), or Dictionary's "*continuous hostility*, especially between two families, clans, etc., often *lasting for many years or generations*" (emphasis mine), between clans led by Randolph McCoy and Devil Anse Hatfield, is to invent it. That is exactly what Costner's writers do in the film — and what most writers have done in the books on the feud.

As the feud supersizers have gone to such lengths recently, with their tales of company-sized invasions of Logan, thriving whorehouses in remote mountain hollows, etc., I think it behooves us to require proof for any claimed Hatfield and McCoy feud event other than the ones noted above. We should require the person telling the tale to first produce evidence that the event happened, then show proof that the families or close associates of Devil Anse and Ran'l McCoy were involved before they can claim that it is part of the Hatfield and McCoy feud.

Devil Anse killed Ran'l McCoy's three sons in August 1882, and you can't get any more hostile than that. The problem is that there is absolutely no hard evidence that Devil Anse had anything near a feuding hostility toward Ran'l McCoy between that time and the revival of the conflict by the Kentucky authorities in 1887. Then the hostility was mutual for several weeks, until Anse capitulated and moved away from Tug Valley.

*The Louisville Courier Journal*, whose editor, Henry Watterson, was a crusader against feud violence, carried dozens of articles about the many feuds occurring in Kentucky during the 1880's. After reporting Ellison Hatfield's death in 1882, the paper reported no further violence in Pike County until January, 1888. In fact, "the feud" ended the same month it was first called a feud by *any* newspaper.

One of the New York newspapermen, T.C. Crawford, actually agrees with me on this. Crawford wrote: "For five years, there was nothing more than ordinary neighborhood quarreling. Murders which were committed during those years...were incidental killings, which had no relation to the great feud."[1]

After referring to a *great feud* here, Crawford later wrote: "Much more importance has been attached to this petty war than it really deserves."[2] These two statements show that Crawford, having never visited Pikeville, did not really perceive the existence of a feud, even after visiting Logan and Devil Anse in his home.

Cap Hatfield's grandson, Coleman Hatfield, in cooperation with the historian, Robert Spence, wrote the 2003 book, *Tale of the Devil.* Hatfield clearly recognizes the fact that there was no feud during the years following the events of August, 1882:

"Between 1882 and 1886, it seemed that there was no "feud" in the sense that there was a vendetta in the eastern Kentucky meaning of the word, as in Rowan and Breathitt and other counties. Until journalists began trying to piece together the tale of the Hatfields and McCoys, the semi-comic episode of the pig trial and the failed romance of Johnse Hatfield and Roseanna McCoy appeared to be events without consequence. The serious trouble was the killing of Ellison Hatfield and the vengeful killing of Tolbert McCoy and his brothers."[3]

Hatfield and Spence are saying that prior to the visit of Cap Hatfield and Tom Wallace to the Daniels cabin in the fall of 1886, the only feud incidents took place in a three-day period, August 7-9, 1882. Most of the events included in the feud story are simply the result of what Hatfield and Spence referred to as *piecing the tale together.*

When I deny the existence of a Hatfield and McCoy feud, I am in good company. Neither of my great-great grandfathers, Uriah McCoy and Preacher Anderson Hatfield recognized such a feud. My great grandfather, Asa McCoy, was a partner in real estate with Devil Anse Hatfield during the 1880's.

Despite the fact that a feud, as defined in the dictionary, did not exist between the Hatfields and the McCoys in the 1880's, I will discuss a Hatfield and McCoy feud, solely for the sake of communicating with the reader. The deaths of nearly a dozen people in a little more than a decade arising in connection with a conflict between two families is feud enough for most people, although the connection is tenuous at times.

There was a larger conflict which resulted from the change from a subsistence farming economy to an economy based on the extraction of the natural resources of the mountains. This change resulted in a large number of young men coming of age with no economic prospects, due to a lack of land to support them as subsistence farmers, and to the large-scale takeover of the resources of the mountains by outside capitalists. This led to friction between the modernizers, including the local elites who saw an opportunity to capitalize on the wealth of their neighbors and men like Devil Anse Hatfield, who wanted to retain local and family control of the land and its resources.

This conflict continued until the inevitable capitulation of the locals. Devil Anse Hatfield was one of the last to capitulate, and his resistance to the powerful economic forces bearing down upon the Valley is the real reason that he became a nationally known figure in his own lifetime. His war-time exploits and his participation in a few of the events that form the feud story are just eruptions within that larger conflict.

Writers call it *The* Hatfield and McCoy Feud, but all agree that the Kentucky leadership for the last and bloodiest phase did not come from Ran'l or any other McCoy, but, rather from the Pikeville elite. Like the movie scriptwriters, they all agree that Perry Cline was the leader and Frank Phillips the enforcer. I say that both of those men were subordinate to their foster-father, Colonel John Dils, during the feud's last bloody phase.

In the first phase of the feud, of the twenty men indicted for the murders of the three McCoy boys, only seven were Hatfields. Of nearly forty identifiable members of Frank Phillips's posse in the second phase of the feud, only nine bore the name, *McCoy*. How then do the writers come up with a Hatfield and McCoy feud? Well, they simply treat a plethora of fables, rumors, and folklore as historical fact.

The name of our feud is much too short. During the time our feud happened, Rowan County, Kentucky, had its *Tolliver-Martin-Logan feud*, and Breathitt County did them one better with its *Hargis-Cockrell-Marcum-Callahan feud*. If Breathitt County can have a four-name feud, why can't Pike, a much larger county, have a five-name feud?

If we called our feud the *Hatfield and Dils-Cline-Phillips-McCoy feud*, then we could bring in all that happened from the raid on John Dils's store in 1862, in which Devil Anse probably participated, until Ellison Mounts was hanged in February 1890. As we can't change the name of the feud at this late date, we will discuss the Hatfield and McCoy feud, bearing in mind that the trouble between the Hatfields and the McCoys occurred within the context of the larger conflict.

Although Colonel John Dils is not mentioned in the movie, I consider him the most important person on the Kentucky/McCoy side of the feud. John Dils was not physically present at the election on Blackberry Creek in 1882 when Ellison Hatfield was killed; however, he was definitely there, in the mind of Devil Anse in the aftermath of the Election Day fight. John Dils is the key to the answer to the question: "Why did Devil Anse take the three McCoys away from the Kentucky law and take them to West Virginia, and then later execute them in Kentucky?"

When Devil Anse executed the three McCoy boys on the river bank in 1882, he was acting out of the sure knowledge that his brother's killers would not receive their just desserts in a Pikeville court, largely controlled by his old war-time nemesis, Colonel John Dils. The actual behavior of Devil Anse, over his entire lifetime, belies the notion that he was a man who preferred extralegal solutions to problems. He was involved in nearly two dozen lawsuits, many of which were initiated by him, and he complied with the decision of the court in every case.

Given Devil Anse's record, I think it very unlikely that he would have resorted to a lynching of the killers of Ellison if he had reason to believe that the McCoys would receive a fair trial. Even the McCoys knew that a trial of Ellison's killers in Pikeville would be a farce. Truda McCoy said the McCoys were not worried about the prospects of Tolbert, Pharmer, and Bud in a Pikeville trial because they knew as well as Anse knew that no Pikeville jury would convict a McCoy for killing a West Virginia Hatfield.[4]

When the Hatfield gang burned Ran'l McCoy's home, slaughtered two of his children, and maimed his wife, it was a reaction to the unbearable pressure being brought to bear on the Hatfields by the Dils/Cline/Phillips gang in Pikeville. The last bloody phase of the feud was, in part, a continuation of the Civil War. Three-fourths of the Pikeville gang who invaded West Virginia had no connection to Ran'l McCoy.

I contend that apart from the killing of Bill Staton, which I deny was actually part of the feud, and that of Ellison Hatfield,[5] the larger conflict between the Pikeville elite and Devil Anse Hatfield was a contributing factor in all the other killings. This larger conflict had roots reaching back to the Civil War, but the war was a facilitator and not a cause of the feud.

The feud was a creation of the big city newspapers. The immediate purpose for its creation was to devalue the people and thereby facilitate the transfer of ownership of the wealth of the Valley to the same big city financiers who controlled those newspapers. The ultimate purpose was to transform the independent mountaineers into docile and willing wage workers. This transformation was abetted by the state governments and the elites on both the state and local levels, who hoped to profit by the transformation.

Because they refused to look at the larger picture, including the activities of the elites on the state and county levels, the writers for Costner's film, like the writers of feud books, had to come up with something to fill in all the dead time in the story. This they did on a grand scale, resulting in the distorted history that permeates the minds of the public today.

The newspaper reporters, Spears, Howell, Creelman, Crawford, et. al., were sent to Tug Valley to report on a feud. Upon arrival, and after cursory questioning of the persons involved *on one side only*, the reporters saw that they had a killing on Election Day, 1882, a retaliatory lynching two days later, followed by five full years during which nothing that was documentable as feud-related violence happened. Being very good writers, and having heard the front-porch tales told to them by Perry Cline and others in Pikeville, they had little trouble coming up with enough feud incidents to fill the five year gap. Then they worked backward to either the 1878 hog trial, or, in some cases to the 1865 killing of Asa Harmon McCoy, and created what has been the Hatfield and McCoy feud story ever since. As Coleman Hatfield wrote, they "pieced the tale together."

This means that, from a public information standpoint, our feud was born supersized! Most of what was written in 1888 was untrue, so the story of "the feud" was a monster at birth.

The mass media has sustained the gross caricature of the feud for a century and a quarter. When the *Washington Post* reported the death of Jim McCoy on September 7, 1929, it said: "With his death passes the last picturesque active figure of any feud which has marked Kentucky Mountain battling in the last 50 years. The Hatfield and McCoy Feud cost nearly 100 lives."

The *Post* was obviously unaware that the very picturesque and active Cap Hatfield was still alive, and the total death count was a dozen, at most.

When the *New York Times* reported the death of Cap Hatfield on August 23, 1930, the *Old Gray Lady* went the *Post* one better with: "He was the eldest of the thirteen children of Anderson (Devil Anse) Hatfield, chief of the clan and its leader throughout the forty-eight years of the feud. More than 100 men, women and children of the two families were slain in the battles, which raged in Logan and Mingo Counties, West Virginia, and Pike County, Kentucky. It was said in those days that whenever a McCoy head showed out of a window a Hatfield gun would bark; whenever a Hatfield gazed from his home at the surrounding hill country a McCoy gun would bark."

I know that the forgoing paragraph reads like *The National Enquirer*, but it was, in fact, the nation's newspaper of record, *The New York Times*. When the *Times* reported the death of the last surviving son of Devil Anse fifty years later, it still had a decades-long war with a hundred casualties. The *Times* and the *Post* agreed that the dozen actual victims of the conflict actually equaled a hundred, but they disagreed on whether the feud lasted forty-eight or fifty years.

The supersized feud monster has been nourished by almost every author since the original newspaper midwives. Truda McCoy, writing what she called *The McCoys: Their Story,* was a modern supersizer, but L.D. Hatfield was worse and G. Elliott Hatfield the worst — until the two big sellers that have emerged in the wake of the Costner movie.

Lisa Alther, the novelist who emitted her "history" immediately in the wake of the movie, said of McCoy: "she wrote an account that reads like a novel — *and is probably about as reliable as one.*"[6] Ms. Alther was, of course, right about Truda McCoy, but the same criticism is valid for her own fictional history and for all the other supersized "feud histories." All their books—except for the books by Altina Waller and Otis Rice-- read like novels, complete with descriptions of what people wore, how they walked, what they thought and what they said. The 2013 *True Story,* by Dean King, contains scores, if not hundreds of quotations attributed to people who have been dead for a century or more, with no foundation for the quotations.

After stating early on that Truda McCoy's book is "probably about as reliable as a novel," what does the novelist, Alther do? Why, she cites that "unreliable" source *one hundred and two times* in her footnotes!

With one hundred and two citations of Truda McCoy in one hundred forty-seven pages of feud-related text, it is clear that this author can't write two pages without falling back upon a book she says is no more trustworthy on historical fact than a novel. And she touts her book as *non-fiction!*

In spite of its fictional content, Truda McCoy's book is a valuable resource on the feud, containing much material not available anywhere else. The caveat applies here, that we should look very closely at any writing based on the relationship of the writer to the feud participants. Applying the tests of what fits the characters, and what makes contextual sense, there are many things of value in Truda McCoy's book-- especially in the notes by the editor, Leonard Roberts.

Although it is sometimes obscured, purposefully or not, the mindset of the Ran'l McCoy family of the feud era is in McCoy's book.

Except for the notes of editor Roberts, I would use Truda McCoy's book for historical matter only when she either criticizes McCoys or compliments Hatfields, or where there is confirmation from other sources.

We have had a century and a quarter during which the early writers cited the yellow journalists, because they represented the oldest and nearest to the events' sources. Then the writers who followed with books in succeeding years cited the earlier books, because they were then accepted as standard. This brought us to where we are now, with many of the events which constitute the received history being simply a daisy chain leading back to the original yellow journalists, who based most of what they wrote on unsubstantiated tales they heard during brief visits to the Valley. The culmination of it all is King's 2013 book which, in four hundred thirty pages, gathers almost all of the tallest tales from previous writers, including especially the yellowest of the yellow journalists,[7] John Spears, and presents this conglomeration as *The True Story*.

Luckily for the discerning reader, the supersizers frequently employ the *big lie* technique, making some of the most egregious whoppers easy to spot. King's aggregation of fantastic yarns featuring a beating of two women with several hundred blows from a three-pound bludgeon which both survived; an ambush with seven mountain sharpshooters spraying a fusillade of bullets from an ambush only thirty feet off the road with no fatalities, and a whorehouse in an isolated mountain hollow doing a booming business cannot be sold to erudite readers as *The True Story*. When he says that one hundred armed McCoys descended upon the tiny village of Logan in 1880,[8] or that eight hundred horses were tied up outside a tiny mountain church house,[9] or that 1200 people regularly attended a church that had only about 25 members,[10] he relieves his more intelligent readers from the work of checking sources, simply because the tale is incredible on its face.

Likewise, no thinking reader will accept as anything other than fantasy King's claim that someone made the thirty mile trip from Pikeville to Blackberry Fork between the time court adjourned in the afternoon and sunset,[11] or that two mountain hunters repeatedly missed a man while shooting at him with Winchester rifles at a distance of only a few yards.[12]

Discerning readers of King's book are fortunate that there are dozens of these tales which are so outrageously exaggerated that they are easily ignored, without the necessity of even researching them. Glowing reviews from prestigious organs like the Wall Street Journal and the Boston Globe lauding this aggregation of yarns as history fool only the gullible. Anyone who believes that twelve hundred people attended a mountain church with twenty-five members is a likely prospect for a peddler of beach-front property in Arizona.

As I attempt to interpret what happened in Tug Valley over a century ago, there will be times when, of necessity due to sparse records, I will be giving an opinion, and not writing history. When I have proof, I will show it. When I don't have proof, then what you are reading is speculation. But it is speculation by someone who grew up among people who lived during the feud, and who has studied the area and its history for over half a century. When I rely on my personal memory, I am being honest, but I am subject to the common human failings with regard to memory.[13] No one's memory is as good as a written record for the historian, and that includes the historian's own memory.

Nothing in this book will conflict with the known documentary evidence, as so many of the tales of the supersizers do. This is not, however, the *True Story* of the Hatfield and McCoy feud, because no one has the complete *True Story*. It is my best effort to interpret the events of the feud era in a way that makes sense for future serious students, and especially for my grandchildren. I hope that it will also be a lesson to students of history in how *not* to do historical research.

This book will disappoint any reader who is looking for more excitement — more blood and gore — than was found in the last feud book the reader has read. What I do promise is that it will be almost as much fun as reading tall tales of make-believe events, because we will be deconstructing the tall tales and outright lies that form the bulk of feud lore. We will see that many of the tales are ludicrous from the bottom up, having no basis in reality. Other feud yarns sold as history will be shown to conflict with the meager hard evidence that exists.

When there is a solid basis for stating something as a fact, it will be so stated. When an opinion is being offered, it will be clear to the reader that it is an opinion. It will be opinion honestly arrived at after sixty years of study, beginning with talking with people who were alive at the time of the major events, and continuing through a long lifetime of reading almost everything ever written on the subject.

You will not learn who the winner was because there was no winner. You will not learn which side was in the right because both sides were in the wrong. You will learn that there was a lot less fussin' and fightin' than the popular *True Stories* tell you, but there was a lot more of the really important things, such as politics, economics, war and peace than you will get from a rehash of the old folk tales and newspaper lies usually peddled as feud history.

I approach the feud in a way that only one previous writer does. In *Feud: Hatfields, McCoys and Social Change in Appalachia, 1860–1900*, Altina Waller develops the same basic premise as I do. This book will try to build upon the foundation laid by Waller, especially as it relates to the involvement of the Pikeville elite and the connection between outside capital and "the feud," bringing forth new evidence not previously examined.

After Professor Waller's book was published in 1988, we enjoyed a generation of partial relief from the terrible stereotypes manufactured by the yellow journalists of the late 1800s and perpetuated in several tales masquerading as history. The movie and the Alther book in 2012, followed by the Dean King book in 2013, take us back to square one, and with the entire media complex on the side of sensationalism, we have our work cut out for us.

Not only have the scriptwriters and authors taken our ancestors back to being perceived by non-Appalachians as bloodthirsty and amoral people, but King has brought it up to the present by claiming that he was shot at in the Valley on two occasions, while researching his book. He says:"I can attest to *the continuing feroc-ity of the neighborhood."*[14] (Italics mine)

Tall tales to titillate an audience are not the exclusive province of Appalachian story-tellers and nineteenth century reporters. King wrote that he was in the Tug Valley in the summer of 2009, accompanied by two forest rangers and his 16-year-old daughter, and was "the second chronicler of the feud to be warned off with rifle shots while researching the story."[15] Then he says he was in the same place again in the spring of 2010, at which time, "a hidden marksman began firing a pistol into the water dangerously close to us."[16]

Well, we must at least credit the man with nerve-- he is shot at with a rifle in 2009, and less than a year later he is back at the same place again, only to be shot at with a pistol. If he went a third time, they'd probably use BB guns — or slingshots.

While King's second foray into the wilds of Thacker showed that he had nerve, the fact that he took his sixteen year-old daughter back to the same spot where she had been shot at several months before showed that he was derelict in his duty as a father. No Hatfield or McCoy of the late nineteenth century would have exposed his daughter to such danger.

These episodes were a godsend to Mr. King. His superior writing skills, coupled with his willingness to say anything that is titillating, no matter how fantastically inaccurate, would have insured the financial success of his book. The claim that he twice came under fire in gathering the material for his book has undoubtedly boosted his sales substantially. It is an advantage he has over all previous writers:

Charles Mutzenberg did his original research during the 1890s, when all the feudists who survived the feud were still alive. He visited Tug Valley several times, yet he couldn't boast to his readers that he was due combat pay.

John Spivak, the novelist, did field research in the Valley several times during the 1920s, when all the men who riddled the Baldwin-Felts thugs with bullets in Matewan were still alive, but he was not fired upon once, even though he was from New York--and communist to boot!

Virgil Jones spent many days in Tug Valley during the 1940s. He was on Blackberry Creek on several occasions and spent many hours talking to my Uncles, Jeff and Ransom Hatfield, yet Jones could not boast of coming under fire.

Shirley Donnelly visited Ransom and Jeff in 1955. I saw the West Virginia car while delivering papers and asked Uncle Ransom the next day who his visitor was. He got a big laugh out of telling me about talking to "A boy named Shirley." Donnelly talks about his visit with the Hatfield brothers in his little book.[17] Donnelly also tells of visiting the haunts of the West Virginia Hatfields, right in the ferocious neighborhood where King had two brushes with death,[18] but Donnelly never had to dodge bullets.

Lisa Alther at least drove through the mountains, but given her description of her thoughts about a pistol she saw on a billboard,[19] her mind might have been so concentrated on other things that she could have been shot at without realizing it happened.

King says, "We beat a hasty retreat up the riverbank," so he clearly means that the two rangers retreated with him. Thus we are to believe that two West Virginia forest ranger — armed, uniformed law enforcement officers with the power of arrest — simply beat a hasty retreat when shot at in broad daylight.[20]

King has an even greater advantage over me than he has over all those earlier writers. I spent my first eighteen years in that "ferocious neighborhood," and was never shot at a single time!

The apparent failure on the part of some Tug Valley people to realize that they and their ancestors are being insulted by these recent writers is very disheartening.

The Hatfield and McCoy feud is preeminent in the public mind only because of the extensive nationwide newspaper coverage it received in 1888–90. The National Archives' *Chronicling America* project and the University of Kentucky's *Kentucky Digital Library* contain a handful of reports on the 1882 events involving only the Hatfields and McCoys, but they have many hundreds of articles from 1888–90, covering the period when no one even claims that Ran'l McCoy was leading the Kentucky forces.

Our feud received so much more publicity than other bloodier and longer feuds for one reason only: The Hatfields and McCoys owned land under which lay some of the richest deposits of bituminous coal in the world, and the moneyed interests in the East, who also controlled the newspapers, wanted that land. Making the people of Tug Valley appear to be uncivilized and less than human to newspaper readers across the country made it more palatable to steal their coal riches. During 1887–88 (what Professor Waller calls the second phase of the Hatfield and McCoy feud), pressure was put on Devil Anse Hatfield specifically because he held five thousand acres located right in the heart of the *billion-dollar coal field*.

This period featured the Pikeville elite against the Hatfields and their West Virginia cohort, with Ran'l McCoy only tangentially involved. This bloodiest and most publicized part of the feud had nothing to do with hogs or love affairs. It happened only because there was enmity dating from the Civil War between John Dils and Devil Anse, and there was a contest for five thousand very valuable acres involving Dils, Perry Cline, and Devil Anse Hatfield, dating back to about 1868. It all occurred in the context of a concerted effort on the part of modernizers in the two state capitals and in the county seats to clean up the feuding image of the mountaineers.

These modernizers were contending with a force even more formidable than the mountaineers' vaunted independence, and that was the ongoing effort of Eastern financial moguls to use their newspapers to paint the mountaineers as semi-savages who probably deserved to be robbed of their mineral wealth. This book deals with those realities.

1  Crawford, T.C. *American Vendetta*, 16.

2  Crawford, 69.

3  Hatfield and Spence, *Tale of the Devil*, 128.

4  McCoy, Truda, *The McCoys*, 76.

5  I would argue that economic conditions had a significant influence here, too, as all the grown sons of Ran'l McCoy were farm laborers or share croppers, with dismal economic prospects due to lack of sufficient land available for the burgeoning population.

6  Alther, Lisa, *Blood Feud:* The Hatfields and the McCoys: The Epic Story of Murder and Vengeance. Guilford, Lyons Press, 2012, xvi.

7  The Free Dictionary defines 'yellow journalism' as: "Journalism that exploits, distorts or exaggerates the news to create sensations and attract readers."

8  King, Dean, *The Feud*, 85.

9  King, 89.

10  *Ibid.*

11  King, 125.

12  King, 150.

13  My memory is aided by notes I wrote in 1952-55, after I read the Virgil Jones book.

14  King, Dean, *The Feud*, 377, n. 21.

15  King, xii.

16  King, 377, n. 21.

17  Donnelly, Shirley, *The Hatfield-McCoy Feud Reader*, 23-4.

18  Donnelly, 24-5.

19  Ms. Alther said the depiction of a revolver on a billboard reminded her of an erect penis with the trigger-guard a testicle hanging below it. Alther, Lisa, *Blood Feud*, 229.

20  King goes into much more detail in describing his second penetration of the wilds of Tug River. This time the timid rangers are identified by name and the shooters were using pistols instead of rifles — which I don't understand; if they couldn't hit King with a rifle in 2009, why in thunder did they think they could hit him with a pistol the following year? Of course it could mean only that there were two separate groups of shooters.

In this second foray into the wilds of Thacker in the spring of 2010, the marauders were riding an ATV, what we call a "four-wheeler" in the hills. The author says the mysterious riders "...were peering at us from the riverbank, far enough away to be out of hailing distance but close enough for them to get a good look at us..." Now, after getting a good look at the foursome, which included two uniformed officers and a teen-aged girl, what did the nasty descendants of the feudists do? Why they opened fire on them!

King says that before shooting at him, the shooters (he uses the plural but does not tell us how many shooters there were) "drove to a collection of houses upriver." As the Google map shows, there are four houses and two mobile homes upriver within sight of the creek mouth. So we are being told that these shooters sat in someone's backyard, less than a hundred feet from a house, and opened fire on two law officers and two out of state visitors.

King was not at all deterred by the posting of the Google satellite view or by the postings by locals attesting to the accuracy of the maps and what I said about them. Several days later, in a chat on Good Reads with some of his fans, King repeated the story, this time embellishing it by bringing in the illegal drug trade. When one of his fans asked him if he encountered any roadblocks during his research, he said: "Well, the first time in, I actually got shot at, but I was later told that was because I was too near somebody's marijuana patch, something I never confirmed!"

# CHAPTER 1.
# OF CLANS AND CLAN LEADERS

If I say that there were two clans, Hatfields and McCoys, in Tug Valley and that they were led by Devil Anse Hatfield and Ran'l McCoy, I would find almost universal agreement — but we would all be wrong! The primary definition of a clan is a group defined by kinship and descent. Neither Devil Anse nor Ran'l McCoy was ever the leader of a kinship group larger than their immediate households, and neither of them was always able to control even that restricted group.

## Devil Anse Hatfield

Devil Anse Hatfield is known to the entire English-speaking world as the leader of *the Hatfield clan*, but he was never the leader of such a clan. There were sixty-one Hatfield males aged fifteen years and above in Tug Valley in the 1880 Census, and Devil Anse never had as many as ten of them following him in any of the events commonly referred to as feud events.

Devil Anse had support from his younger brother, Elias, at the time of the 1882 killings, but Elias was not active in any feuding after August, 1882. He removed himself from Tug valley and relocated to Logan town after the New Year's raid, where he became a Republican and a Methodist and raised a son who became West Virginia's youngest governor.

Anse's older brother Valentine (Wall) was with him during the August, 1882 troubles, but he, like Elias, was not involved in any feuding afterwards. He surrendered himself to the Kentucky authorities when the second phase of the feud heated up, telling the world that the murders were committed by his brother Anse and a few bad apples associated with his brother.

One could make a good argument that the involvement of both Wall and Elias in feud events resulted from their loyalty and devotion to their brother, Ellison, and not to the leadership of Devil Anse. Although I cannot prove it, that is what I believe. Furthermore, Anse's two youngest brothers, Smith and Patterson, never had anything to do with the *troubles*.

The second definition of *clan* in Webster's is: "a group united by a common interest or common characteristics." By this definition, Devil Anse was a clan leader, as he was the leader of his timber business, and the bulk of his followers in the feud actions were employees, tied to him by economic ties, and not by blood only. He also possessed an uncanny ability to make friends across family and party lines. This knack for forming lasting friendships served him better than his prowess with a Winchester in his mature years.

Devil Anse was indeed an alpha male and a leader of men. He was chosen by the men of his company in both the Virginia State Line and the 45th Battalion as 1st Lieutenant. Since the men elevated an illiterate man to that position, it is quite likely that had he been able to read and write, he would have been elected Captain. A Captain would have to be able to communicate in writing with his superiors, and since Devil Anse could not do that, a First Lieutenancy was the ceiling for him. But insofar as the feud is concerned, he only led part of his immediate family, and some men who depended upon him for their livelihood as employees of his timber operation.

In reality Devil Anse Hatfield, the man, was a much larger figure than simply Devil Anse the feudist. He was a legend in his own time and remains one today. Devil Anse, an illiterate backwoodsman, later became the friend of generations of politicians of both parties and started and ran a successful timbering business. He was also a moonshiner, war-time bushwhacker and, on one occasion, the leader of a lynch mob.

Devil Anse Hatfield's notoriety was largely won for him by his sons, who participated in the killing of six McCoys and at least seven non-McCoys during their lifetimes. Some writers meld the majority non-McCoy victims in with the minority of the sons' victims who were McCoys; it's one of the favorite ploys of the feud supersizers. Some feud books have scores of pages devoted to the escapades of the sons of Devil Anse in which even the feud supersizer doesn't even claim a connection to any McCoy, much less to the purported clan leader, Ran'l McCoy.

If someone wanted to write a book devoted to proving that Anse's brothers, Wall and Elias were right when they said that "Anse had some bad boys," well, there's plenty of material out there. Scores of pages about Elias's 1899 shooting of a West Virginia timber man, Cap's1896 Matewan shootout with the Rutherfords, and Troy and Elias's deadly 1911 turf war with a competitor in their booze business in Boomer hardly belong, however, in a "True Story" of the Hatfield and McCoy feud.

His friends, both then and now, accentuate the positives in Devil Anse, while his detractors clamor about his failings. He was undoubtedly a good man to have as a friend or neighbor, but he was also a vengeful killer at best, and a cold-blooded murderer at worst. The man and the legend now meld into a blurred image.

Altina Waller is probably correct in finding evidence of alienation from his father in Anse's boyhood. The fact that Ephraim Hatfield left Anse no land cannot be glossed over. Neither can Anse's failure to name one of his sons for his father, as most mountaineers of that era did. Shorter than his brothers and father,[1] the dark-eyed and rather homely Anse might have felt out of place around his tall, blue eyed and handsome brothers and his tall, blue-eyed father.[2] Estrangement from his father probably contributed to Anse's drive to excel in everything he undertook, from hunting, riding and shooting to business and politics.

Dean King's renaming of the people involved in his *"True Story,"* did not reach Devil Anse, although he came close. King tells the unsubstantiated story of Devil Anse receiving a piece of the rope used to hang Ellison Mounts in a mail package addressed to Devil

Anse Hatfield, saying: "Some say the package, addressed to "Devil" Anse Hatfield, was what gave him his nickname. Others say he already had it."[3]

This produces the bizarre result where a man who says he has done four years of intensive research doesn't know whether or not Anderson Hatfield was called "Devil Anse" before February, 1890.

With a few key strokes, anyone can find the contemporary newspaper articles on the West Virginia Archives web page and see one article from the year before in the Wheeling Intelligencer, which has a *headline* that says: "Devil Anse Tells the True History."[4]

King also appears to be unaware that T.C. Crawford, the *New York World* reporter that he cites many times as a factual source in his book, referred to the man as "Devil Ance" (sic) more than a year before the purported receipt of the rope package. Crawford misspells "Anse," as he also misspells most of the other names, but what do you expect from a man who spent only a few days talking to people in Logan County who wouldn't give him either facts or opinions,[5] and who wrote the book in three hours?[6]

I am personally very pleased that Anse held onto his moniker in the King book, because the feud story would lose much of its flavor without the Devil on the scene.

Although Devil Anse Hatfield accomplished far more than would normally be expected of an illiterate mountaineer, the legend is much bigger than the man, and it is still growing!

## Randolph "Ran'l" McCoy

Ran'l McCoy, like Devil Anse, is commonly referred to as a clan leader. The average reader or viewer believes that there was a McCoy clan in the Tug Valley, and that Ran'l was the leader of that clan, because writers continue to say so. They believe it, despite the plain words of Truda McCoy, the McCoy family historian, that Jim McCoy, Ran'l's eldest son was "the leader of the clan, as well as the bravest..."[7]

Jim McCoy might well have been the bravest of the McCoys, but he never assumed the position of a feuding clan leader. His only feuding was his riding with the Frank Phillips' posse for a month in 1887-8.

Ran'l had problems, but he was not a coward. Real courage is shown under fire and, in the only feud-related incident where Ran'l faced enemy fire he acquitted himself well. During that attack on his home, Ol' Ran'l set a record for most Hatfields shot by anyone in a single day that stood until an Italian bootlegger tied it in 1911, by shooting two of Devil Anse's sons in Boomer, West Virginia.

The only record I have seen of Ran'l McCoy ever taking a leadership role in anything was his 1861 appointment by the county court as the road surveyor for his branch of the creek, up to the gap of the mountain. Whether Ran'l successfully fulfilled those duties is not known, but we do know that there were several county court orders in 1880 which cited Ran'l for failing to do the work required of him on the road across his property, and ordering him to either do the work or appear in court to show cause why he had not done the work.[8]

There is also a record of a lawsuit charging Ran'l and his wife, Sally, with malicious gossip, in 1862.[9] Their cousin, Pleasant McCoy, accused them of falsely telling folks that he, Pleasant, had engaged in an illicit love affair with his cow. To the novelists who write "true stories" of the feud, the alleged bestiality is important. What matters to the historian is that *it was Ran'l McCoy* who was sued for allegedly falsely accusing his cousin, Pleasant, of pleasuring himself with a bovine lass. If Ran'l was engaged in malicious gossip about his McCoy relatives in 1861 that might help to explain why not one of them, outside his own sons, rallied to Ran'l's side twenty years later.

Nothing in Ran'l's background prepared him to be the leader of a clan, and he never was the leader of a clan, as Truda McCoy clearly stated. Furthermore, there is no evidence that Ran'l McCoy ever aspired to be the leader of a clan. The record plainly shows him to have been a man of fierce loyalty to his family, who, although he retained his deep enmity toward Devil Anse and his sons for decades, never made any real attempt to assert leadership of the McCoy clan. He harangued the county law enforcement officials for years following the 1882 murders, but this is understandable. He was the father of three sons who had been lynched, and he persisted in demanding that the Pikeville officials bring the killers to justice.

As a reasonably intelligent man, he surely knew as he neared the age of sixty that he was not a man who could inspire others to follow him into a war against the most feared man in the Valley. Although he kept the embers glowing during the quiet years after 1882, by repeatedly travelling to the county seat of Pikeville to seek redress through the county law enforcement apparatus, he was involved in violence only during the 1888 New Year's raid on his home. Apart from that night it was, for Ol' Ran'l, a war of words.

If the Pikeville power structure, under the control of Colonel Dils, had not decided in 1887 to go after the five thousand acres owned by Devil Anse, there would have been no invasion of West Virginia, no New Year's raid, no hanging of Ellison Mounts, and, therefore, no feud. The record shows that Ran'l McCoy had very little to do with what happened in 1887-8. Governor Simon B. Buckner, who was convinced by the Pikeville elite that by going after the West Virginia Hatfields he could divert the attention of nation's financiers away from his Kentucky feuds ongoing at that time, was a much more important personality in the second and most violent phase of "the feud" than was Ran'l McCoy.

Many writers have said over the years that Ran'l was hampered by the fact that there were so many more Hatfields than McCoys that he would have always been outnumbered, no matter how well he did in recruiting supporters among his kinsmen. That is categorically false. The 1880 Census shows exactly the same number — forty — of McCoy males over age fourteen in Pike County as there were Hatfield males over fourteen in Logan County. Ran'l's problem was not a lack of potential support, but, rather, a lack of either the will or the ability to gain that support.

The question of Ran'l's clan leadership was settled forever for me when I visited the Dils cemetery back in the 1960's. When I inquired, I was told that Ran'l McCoy was, indeed, buried there, but no one knew where the grave was located! As I had visited the graves of dozens of my McCoy relatives which were marked with headstones, I knew that if Ran'l were really the leader of the McCoy clan at any time, there would have been a marker on his grave fifty years after his passing, but there was no marker.

I have been told recently that there was a piece of native rock with an "M" on it marking Ran'l's grave at the time I looked for his marker. That may well be true, but if I had seen such a marker I would have assumed that it was for one of Dils's slaves, or one of the free Blacks who worked in his tannery, and not for the leader of a large and powerful clan.

Leonard Roberts, editor of Truda McCoy's book, visited Dils cemetery a decade after I visited and he said that none of the McCoy graves was marked.[10]

Despite Ran'l's obvious shortcomings, the Costner movie goes overboard in trashing him. He was undoubtedly affected by his wartime stay in Camp Douglas prison and the grievous losses he suffered in the feud, but he was neither the religious nut he is depicted as being early in the movie nor the God-cursing drunk seen later.

The extremely harsh treatment of Ran'l McCoy in the movie has given rise to a reaction from some McCoy descendants. In an effort to counter the Costner movie's inaccurate portrayal of Ran'l, they are attempting to construct an equally fictitious clan leader, who was brave, charismatic and nearly sinless. I call them "The Randolph McCoy Cult." Ask one of them to show evidence that Ran'l McCoy ever led anyone anywhere at any time, and the conversation will quickly deteriorate into name-calling.

Given recent developments, it is apparent that the process will never end. I recently saw a video on YouTube, featuring some McCoy descendants, who said that they were producing a documentary, which would finally tell the McCoy side of the story, which they adamantly claim has *never been told*. The size of the market for the fabrications of the feud industry is hinted at by the fact that the documentary's producers claim to have raised nearly two hundred thousand dollars in donations from people who don't know that the McCoy story has been told. The sky's the limit for someone who can con the smart ones.

When three of the four reporters who reached a national audience in 1888, Charles Howell of the *Pittsburgh Times*, James Creelman of the *New York Herald* and John Spears of the *New York Sun* spoke *only* to the McCoys, and the fourth, Crawford of the *New York World,* painted the Hatfields and their Logan neighbors as uncivilized and amoral, it is hardly credible to claim that the McCoy side was not fully told in 1888.

From the descriptions of people who knew him, it is apparent that Ran'l McCoy suffered periodically from depression after his war-time experience, and it worsened as he aged. Charles Howell, who interviewed him in 1888 and wrote a very sympathetic report, said that he was "a man who had been bent and almost broken by the weight of his afflictions and grief."[11]

Virgil Jones said of Ran'l, after the move to Pikeville: "The women were silent...but the wails of the father (Ran'l) were uncontrolled. He moved about the streets, a broken old man, talking freely about the attack, cursing the Hatfields..."[12]

Truda McCoy, who knew him personally, said, "He went about the streets of the town dazed by his traumatic experience of that night, muttering and relating it time and again."[13] McCoy makes it clear that Ran'l harbored a decades-long hatred, approaching the level of obsession, for Devil Anse Hatfield, and everyone I talked to as a youngster affirmed that. Whether jealousy for Devil Anse's success in the same business that Ran'l and his father failed in was a major factor[14] is an open question, but I believe it played a signifi-cant part in forming Ran'l McCoy's mindset.

The depiction of Ran'l in the movie is grossly distorted on both ends. He was not the pious, Bible-quoting religious fanatic we see in the years leading up to the feud. There weren't any of those in that valley at that time. The evangelical preachers had not yet been brought in by the town elites to tame the natives,[15] and the hyper-Calvinism of the Primitive Baptists expounded by Preacher Anse Hatfield, was probably the only theology Ran'l knew.

The doctrine, in a nutshell, was that everyone was born destined either for Heaven or Hell, and there wasn't a damn thing anyone could do to change it. A person's time of death was determined before he or she was born. This was, of course, not conducive to docile and compliant behavior, and it is the reason men like John Dils financially supported Methodist and Missionary Baptist preachers after the war.[16] It is also why Stonewall Jackson could sit astride his horse, Little Sorrel, at the front of his division in battle with sublime indifference to the bullets whizzing past his head.

During the time Ran'l is depicted in the movie as a pious pain in everyone's neck, most church services in Tug Valley were attended mainly by old men and the womenfolk, while the men of virile years spent the time in other activities. The biggest annual event among the Primitive Baptists was the yearly meeting of the Association, which involved a summer gathering of all the churches in the Association at one church for all-day meetings on Saturday and Sunday. There were hours of preaching and singing and dinner on the ground.

While the old men and the womenfolk were thus employed, the younger males would be in a large field nearby, drinking, arguing, and fighting, and trading knives, guns, and horses. This activity was known as the *horse-swapping*, and its location was called *the swapping grounds*.

Although it cannot be proved, it is much more likely that during the Annual Association Meeting — called the "So-say-shun" colloquially — Ran'l McCoy was at the horse-swapping while Sally was at the services.

Truda McCoy, who knew Ran'l McCoy, described his religious convictions: "He had a standard of right and wrong — a code which he lived by. He believed in God and the Devil... Sure, he was religious in his way, but not to the point where he would let a damn Hatfield walk all over him and take it lying down."[17]

Ran'l's views on the finer points of doctrine are illustrated by a conversation Truda McCoy says took place between Ran'l and Sally after the hog trial:

Ran'l: "I hope they (the pigs) die of cholera."
Sally: "It's a sin to wish anything like that."
Ran'l: "Sin, hell!"[18]

On the other hand, there is absolutely no evidence supporting the movie's depiction of the aging Ran'l as a hopeless drunk, who openly cursed God. He might have tried the patience of his neighbors and ferry customers with endless talk about his troubles with the Hatfields,[19] but he was not a raving lunatic, as depicted in the movie.

As one studies the history of the feud, it becomes apparent that Ran'l McCoy had a feuding mindset, while Devil Anse did not. His enmity toward Devil Anse Hatfield probably started with envy of Devil Anse's business success early in the post-war years, and gradually grew, becoming an obsession when his three sons were killed in 1882, and continuing for the remainder of his life. As his kinswoman and historian, Truda McCoy said, "God forgives...but Ranel McCoy was not so lenient."[20]

This statement by a kinswoman who knew Ran'l personally is a classic description of the mindset of a feudist. While his mindset never drove Ran'l' to violence, it led him to keep the pot stirred during the five quiet years following the deaths of his three sons, which paved the way for the violence of the bloody "second phase" brought on by the Pikeville elite in late 1887.

While no moral blame can be laid on Ran'l for his frequent trips to Pikeville during the five "quiet years "to urge the county authorities to pursue the Hatfields, it is quite likely that he regretted those trips for the last twenty-six years of his life. How much of the tragedy in his life was his own fault can be debated, but the tragedy was real. He, more than any other character in the story, represents the humanity of us all.

I spent an entire summer with my McCoy grandparents after I had read the Virgil Jones book, *The Hatfields & the McCoys*, and never succeeded in getting Grandpa — a grand-nephew of Sally McCoy and a cousin of Ran'l McCoy — to say more than a single sentence in response to any of my questions.

When asked about Ran'l McCoy, he said, "Nobody paid Ran'l no mind." When I learned later that Grandpa's own father, Asa McCoy — a partner in real estate with Devil Anse — sat on his front porch with Jim McCoy, Ran'l's eldest son, and heard the shots that killed Ran'l's three sons just across the river from him, I understood the reason for Grandpa's cryptic remark about Ran'l.

Several Blackberry men remembered crossing the river to Pikeville on the ferry operated by Ran'l McCoy, but they never saw him anywhere else. Other than being the father of the three young men murdered on the river bank in 1882, and the two victims of the New Year's raid, Ran'l McCoy figured minimally in the history of Blackberry Creek.

Grandpa was in his mid-twenties when Ran'l died, and his only memory of Ran'l was riding the ferry with him once or twice. This was all any of the several people I knew who remembered the New Year's raid, and who were young adults at the time Ran'l operated the ferry in Pikeville, remembered about the purported clan leader. Neither my grandfather nor anyone else I ever knew attended the funeral of Ran'l McCoy.

## Preacher Anse Hatfield

Preacher Anse Hatfield was the only legitimate clan leader in Tug Valley during the last quarter of the nineteenth century. He was also a preacher in the Primitive Baptist church, the elected justice of the peace, and the undisputed leader on the Kentucky side of Tug River. The following photo shows what a real clan gathering looks like, as the Kentucky Hatfield clan gathered for the patriarch's seventy-fifth birthday. No comparable photograph featuring either Devil Anse or Ran'l McCoy exists anywhere.

**(Photo owned by Ron G. Blackburn)**

Preacher Anse also served briefly in the war, under Colonel John Dils. The record shows him a member of Company E of the 39th Kentucky. This company was raised in Pike County. The record shows that he enlisted in October, 1862, and was captured on January 15, 1863. He was obviously paroled immediately, because there is no record of him being in a POW camp.[21]

Preacher Anse also had some difficulty leading all of his immediate family all the time. Although Preacher Anse was licensed to preach in 1868, his wife, Polly did not join the church until 1892.

---

1 Most writers say that Anse was six feet tall, but his military record lists him at five feet six. A careful study of the various photographs that exist leads me to believe that he was taller than the army says he was. He appears to have been about an inch or two short of six feet. My estimates are just that—estimates. There is no real proof, one way or the other.

2 While no photograph of Ephraim, father of Devil Anse, exists, the army record shows him six feet tall, with blue eyes. Ellison Hatfield is listed as five feet-ten, with blue eyes. I believe, based on photos and descriptions by people who saw him, that Ellison was six feet tall, or maybe an inch or so above that. Again, this is my opinion only. Osborne and Weaver, *The Virginia State Rangers and State Line*, p. 200.

3 King, *The Feud*, p. 397, n.6. King fails to explain how a piece of mail, presumably seen only by Devil Anse and his immediate family could possibly cause people throughout the country to start calling him "Devil Anse."

4 http://www.wvculture.org/history/hatfieldmccoyarticles.html

5 Crawford, T. C. *American Vendetta*, 9.

6 Crawford, 1.

7 McCoy, Truda, *The McCoys*, 215.

8 *County Court Order Book I,* Pike County Courthouse.

9 *Pleasant McCoy v. Randolph McCoy and Wife*, January 22, 1862. Kentucky Department for Libraries and Archives.

10 McCoy, *The McCoys*, 230, n. 18

11 Rice, Otis, *The Hatfields and the McCoys,* 73.

12 Jones, Virgil, 99.

13 McCoy, *McCoys*, 215.

14 Waller, *Feud*, 56-7.

15 Waller, 162.

16 Waller, *Feud*, 162.

17 McCoy, *McCoys*, 19.

18 *Ibid*,

19 McCoy, *The McCoys*, 215.

20 McCoy, *The McCoys*, 38.

21 Preston, *Civil War*, 441.

# CHAPTER 2.

# HOW LEGENDS AND LIES BECOME HISTORY

Legends and lies become history by sheer repetition. Most of the incidents that are part of the accepted history of the Hatfield and McCoy feud never happened. Some of them can be traced to folklore, some come to us from the yellow journalists from New York and other major cities and the others are later inventions. Stories written by big city reporters after brief visits to either Logan County or Pike County have been recycled over and over by feud writers until they now have the stamp of history on them.

Chief among the original supersizers were John Spears, of the *New York Sun,* Charles Howell, of the *Pittsburgh Times* and T.C. Crawford of the *New York World.* Spears made a trip to Pikeville and Tug Valley that year and wrote a series of articles for his paper. You can find them on the Library of Congress's *Chronicling America* website. Spears aggregated his articles into a forty-four page book on the Feud, published that same year, called: *The Hatfields and the McCoys: The Dramatic Story of a Mountain Feud.* Note that this novelist said that he said he was writing *A Dramatic Story.* You can get it on Kindle for only ninety-nine cents.

Spears, whose knowledge of the feud did not even extend to the proper spelling of most of the names, is the most cited writer in Dean King's "*True Story*" of the feud,[1] receiving some sixty-six mentions. This is compared to a handful for the premier historian of the feud, Altina Waller  You might think that if Spears' forty-four page book merits more than one citation per page in a "*True Story*," it must be chock full of feud facts — but you would be wrong. Spears starts right off on page one with the statement that Floyd Hatfield, of hog trial fame, was Devil Anse's *brother* (he was a cousin), and that the feud started when the pigs were taken.[2] He then says that the Hog trial judge was Matthew Hatfield, *not* Preacher Anse Hatfield.

Spears says that he, Spears, saw with his own eyes, the seven-year-old son of Johnse and Roseanna in Ran'l McCoy's home in 1888. Spears wrote that when the Hatfields staged the News Year's raid on the home of Ran'l McCoy,[3] Johnse Hatfield shot into the bed where his seven year old son was sleeping, narrowly missing killing his own child.[4] No such child ever lived!

While much of the manufactured history that appears in the early newspaper articles came from tales spun for the reporters by the locals themselves, there was also a fair amount of fabrication by the reporters.

Spears refers to Ellison Hatfield as *Deacon* Hatfield, telling the outrageous tale that Ellison Hatfield was a deacon in Preacher Anse's church.[5] I think *Deacon Ellison* is Spears' own creation, based upon another Hatfield who was, indeed, called *Deacon*. That was Basil Hatfield, brother of Preacher Anse and sheriff of Pike County at that time. I think Spears heard the name, and then confused the two men as he hurriedly composed his reports. I do not think that he concocted the character out of whole cloth.

Spears said that Tolbert McCoy tried to collect $1.75 from *Bad* Elias Hatfield on Election Day, 1882, because he "wanted the money to buy moonshine with."[6] This is in line with what every other writer has said, and it is supported by the 1880 census which shows Tolbert McCoy as a farm laborer, living and working on a neighbor's farm.

Then, only ten pages later, Spears says that Tolbert was a wealthy timber merchant, who left his wife an estate that was so complicated that it required several lawsuits to settle.

The common thread running through all the manufactured tales in the supersized versions of the feud is that they make the men involved appear either bloodthirsty or stupid, or both. If Tolbert McCoy was a rich man, who started a fight with the town drunk over a pittance, then he was bloodthirsty. If Devil Anse did not realize that he could send a man to hide in the woods near Ran'l McCoy's house and assassinate him easily and instead conducted an elaborate espionage effort to learn when Ran'l would be traveling down the road so he could set up an ambush, then Devil Anse was stupid. John Spears presents both Hatfields and McCoys as stupid, bloodthirsty, or both throughout his writings.

Spears says that Paris and Sam McCoy ambushed and killed Bill Staton *in Kentucky*, and were tried *in Kentucky*,[7] when both events actually occurred in West Virginia. It is easy to see why no legitimate historian ever used Spears as a source.

By ignoring the serious historical research of Waller, while seeking to change history to fit the garbled writings of the newspaper reporter, Spears, Dean King has done significant harm to feud history. As King is a gifted writer who has the ability to make his book a best-seller, it will be years—possibly a generation—before the history is reclaimed, but someone has to start sometime.

Because no legitimate historian has used Spears as a source for historical fact, King claims that he *discovered* lost Spears articles, saying, "This article and two others about the feud by Spears that appeared on the same page *had been lost to feud historians* until now."[8] (Italics mine) He says this with full knowledge that the articles mentioned have been available in the Library of Congress for over a century, and were actually available on the LOC website *Chronicling America*, at the time he wrote this. The Spears articles were "lost to feud historians" only in that historians ignored them.

Theron C. Crawford scored a major scoop for the *New York World* by penetrating the mountain fastness to the lair of the Devil himself. His descriptions of the town of Logan, its citizens and the Hatfield family are the basis for all the hillbilly stereotypes that follow. Crawford's tale of drunken *orgies in the courthouse* in

Logan[9] did far more to establish the image of the toothless and dissolute hillbilly than Al Capp's *Lil' Abner* could ever do. Crawford's opinion of Devil Anse's wife, Levicy, whose well-thumbed Bible — complete with her margin notes — is still available for inspection, is especially repugnant. Crawford said that she "had no more idea of right and wrong than a mastiff dog."[10] King repeats that calumny in his book.

Spears' short book was re-issued in the wake of the Costner movie. Crawford's *An American Vendetta* is being re-issued in 2013.

When a writer is accepted as a historian, his or her product is then accepted as history. The writer may glean "facts" from legend, folklore, old front-porch tales, or the writer's own imagination, but it becomes gospel when it is recycled through the pen of the "historian." The story may have originally been considered folklore by its originator and by the people who first heard it, but it is transformed into history by the "historian."

Most people who have read books and seen movies on the feud know a lot more about the filler material than they know about the history. Unless they have read Professor Waller's book,[11] they know practically nothing about what I consider the most important aspects of the feud, which are the economic and political forces influencing the key players at the time of the feud.

Coleman Hatfield and Robert Spence called their book *The TALE of the Devil*. (Emphasis added) They did not call it *The True Story of the Hatfield and McCoy Feud*. It is the family lore of the Hatfield family, and is so labeled by its authors.

Truda McCoy called her book, *The McCoys: Their Story as Told to the Author by Eyewitnesses and Descendants*. She did not call it *The True Story of the Hatfield and McCoy Feud*. It is the family lore of the McCoy family, and is so labeled by its author.

Does this mean that these two books are of no value to real historians? Of course not. To the discerning reader, they impart rare glimpses into the mindset of the families. When there is independent corroborating evidence for something reported by Coleman Hatfield or Truda McCoy, their writings add valuable detail. When they write something that is either flattering to the other side, or critical of their own side, it can generally be accepted as factual.

As both books are replete with historical inaccuracies, they cannot be considered good independent sources for historical fact. Truda McCoy had Johnse Hatfield in jail ten years too early, along with the other Hatfields who were rounded up in 1887-8, and she had Wall Hatfield imprisoned and dead before the time he was actually arrested.

Coleman Hatfield, grandson of Cap Hatfield, in his *Tale of the Devil*, has Floyd Hatfield (of hog trial fame) living in West Virginia, and the trial presided over by a justice named Stafford,[12] when in fact it was really held in Kentucky, before Preacher Anse Hatfield. This shows that the best of the feud descendant writers are on thin ice when they leave the area of their expertise. Hatfield and Spence are weakest when describing Kentucky events, where they are depending upon secondary sources.

Truda McCoy, a McCoy by both blood and marriage, who personally knew the Ran'l McCoy family, has Johnse and Roseanna contemplating a trip to Williamson, West Virginia, several years before the town was even laid out.[13]

The two books are not equally bad as histories; *Tale of the Devil*, while containing a few reports relating to Kentucky events that can be traced back to the 1880s newspapers, avoids most of the huge whoppers we find in other books by descendants and gives valuable insights into the Hatfield family.

Truda McCoy gives us a unique insight into the McCoy clan, but she buried the McCoy story in one of the largest collections of tall tales written before Dean King's "*True Story.*"

One distinction that I make between the two family books is that Tale of the *Devil* is pro-Hatfield, while *The McCoys* is anti-Hatfield. Coleman Hatfield writes nothing disparaging about the McCoys, but shades much of the history in favor of his family. Truda McCoy reams the Hatfields unmercifully, while also ripping into some of the McCoys—especially Ran'l.

Some writers pick and choose items from the family story books and state them as historical fact, referring their readers to the family stories for substantiation. Others go to ridiculous lengths to establish their own bona fides based on kinship to the "feudists." Lisa Alther tells us that one of her grandfather's brothers' daughters married a man whose grandfather was a cousin to Ran'l McCoy, as if that makes her fictionalized version of the feud more credible.[14]

I claim no such advantage; I hope to write a factual book in spite of my blood and geographical relationships to the people and events involved.

Readers of *The Tale of the Devil* who are sufficiently astute to doubt that Paul Bunyan picked his teeth with saw-logs and Pecos Bill rode around atop a tornado recognize right away that the tale of a scrawny fifteen year old Devil Anse kicking a huge bear in the ass and driving it up a tree is not historical fact.

Hatfield and Spence make it clear that the story of the youthful Devil Anse's bear hunt is a *tale*. It is referred to as a *tale* twice in the introductory paragraph. The authors even disclose that the tale is a composite of two tales, originating with two different family members. One of the sources is given as Cap's wife, who wasn't even born at the time of the adventure, and the other is Devil Anse, whom the authors say loved to tell tall tales to his visitors, children and grandchildren.[15]

*Tale of the Devil*, is the Hatfield side of the story, and many events are slanted that way. Some events are incorrectly recounted In *Tale of the Devil* to make the Hatfields look better, but it has much less actual supersizing than do the other two major books by descendants, Truda McCoy's *The McCoys*, and G. Elliott Hatfield's *The Hatfields*. Although the books by Hatfield and McCoy descendants are, for the most part, enjoyable reading, the facts are notoriously wrong in almost all of them. A Hatfield is a good source for a Hatfield story, and a McCoy is a good source for a McCoy story, but for history, only Altina Waller and to a lesser extent, Otis Rice[16], are dependable sources.

Now comes a twenty-first-century "historian," King, who starts his book off in chapter 1 with the tale of Devil Anse, as a fifteen-year-old, kicking a *colossal* bear in the ass and running it up a tree.[17] Presenting what might be the tallest of all the tall tales that Devil Anse was famous for telling as history is in direct violation of his pledge "to correct the record, to deflate the legends, check the biases, and to add or restore accurate historical detail."[18]

King purports to know what Devil Anse wore, what he carried, and even what he thought and said as he conquered the giant bruin back in 1854. The tale has words enclosed within quotation marks, wherein King purports to know what was said in the deep woods of West Virginia more than a century and a half ago.

The tallest of the tall tales from the New York reporter, John Spears, is also reproduced and will be covered later in detail. King, who promised in his Author's Note to "Deflate the legends," includes in his book the tallest tales of most previous writers.

I think that there ought to be a rule that requires any writer of a future *"True Story"* of the feud to use the most entertaining of the tall tales of any writer he cites.

Truda McCoy says that Wall Hatfield was a bootlegger, and a sly one old Uncle Wall was. So sly was Wall that he built a house that reached across the state line between Kentucky and West Virginia. When the Kentucky law raided Wall, he simply transferred his inventory to West Virginia, and vice versa. Since the border between the two states is the Tug River for its entire length, Wall must have lived in a structure the likes of which has never been seen, before or since Wall's time. No one, except for Truda McCoy, has ever reported the existence of any building, residential or otherwise, that spanned the Tug River. Future *"True Story"* writers who wish to use Truda McCoy as a stand-alone source of historical fact should be required to use the tale of Wall's humongous bootlegging joint.[19]

Truda McCoy's counterpart on the Hatfield side is G. Elliott Hatfield, who's *The Hatfields*, was published about the same time as Truda McCoy's book. Of course, Dean King cites G. Elliott Hatfield as a factual source several times. After all, a writer can always say he was quoting a direct descendant of the Hatfields if he is questioned about any of the whoppers he gets from *The Hatfields*.

Dr. G. Elliott Hatfield has two tales in his book each of which is so outrageously funny that I couldn't choose between them. I congratulate King for choosing one of them for his "True Story."

King chose not to use G. Ellicott Hatfield's account of the shooting exhibition he witnessed. It probably would have been better than the one he chose, as it would have made a great scene in King's upcoming television series. Hatfield has a note following his account of the shooting exhibition, wherein he says: "As a lad of 8, the author, who was reared by his grandparent, observed this episode. He has in his possession the Smith and Wesson revolver his father used. Virgil C. Jones, p. 11, relates a similar shooting match."[20]

Hatfield wrote: "First a silver dollar was tossed in the air, three shots exploded as one, completely demolishing the coin."[21]

Whew! I've seen synchronized swimming, which is amazing, but synchronized shooting is an art with which I am entirely unfamiliar. The good Dr. Hatfield says he saw it with his own eyes, but I am dubious, to say the least. Shooting a coin in the air has been part of the routine for exhibition shooters for more than a century. I have personally witnessed such an exhibition, so I know it is possible, but I have never seen or heard of three experts firing simultaneously at the same coin, with all three bullets hitting the coin and completely demolishing it.

We all know that meteor strikes somewhere on the earth are not all that rare, but what about two meteors striking the same spot at the same time? What about three?

If you think the Doc is pulling your leg with this tale, hang on, because it gets better. Hatfield continues: "Next a tin can was tossed up. This time two loud explosions were heard, resulting in six neat holes in the can. The three brothers' shots had been so perfectly synchronized that each punctured the can with both their shots."[22] He is telling us that he saw with his own two eyes, three men shoot twice at a flying can, and all three fired each shot within a nanosecond of each other, and all six shots hit the can.

Even with the pulling of all the triggers at precisely the right time, the variation in the powder loads of the cartridges would preclude the bullets reaching the target simultaneously. To top it all off there is the little matter of distance, since each shooter would have to be exactly the same distance from the can when the shots were fired. If a reader believes this pistol shooting story, which appears in Chapter 1 of *The Hatfields*, he should have very little trouble believing the rest of the book.

I don't want to be too hard on a man who is no longer around to defend himself, but I just simply don't believe G. Elliot Hatfield saw what he reports. If he saw three men shoot twice each at a can and "...each punctured the can with both their shots," then he would have seen *twelve* holes in the can, and not the six he reported. Yes, he is right about six neat holes, but he fails to report the six jagged holes where the bullets came out.

I think Hatfield perceived the need for some support for this tall tale, so he says in his note that Virgil Jones "relates a similar shooting match."[23] Yes, it is similar, but there is a big difference, in that the feat Jones reports is definitely within the realm of the possible. Jones says that an unnamed mountaineer gave a demonstration to two men from the U.S. Geological survey wherein the mountaineer shot twice at a half-dollar in mid-air, hitting it both times.[24] This feat, unlike Hatfield's synchronized shooting, has been accomplished by many professional touring trick shooters.

G. Elliot Hatfield's book, like many others, claims to be history, but reads like a novel. When Hatfield tells us what Frank Phillips and Nancy McCoy were thinking and saying at a dance, he is writing fiction, not history.[25] When Dean King gives us the actual words Anse or Wall spoke while hunting in the woods as teenagers, he is writing fiction, not history.[26]

Hatfield, a kinsman of Devil Anse and a man with academic training, was an egregious supersizer. His book reads like a novel in many places, such as where he is describing what happened at the schoolhouse where the three McCoys were held after the killing of Ellison Hatfield: "When Carpenter, *again feeling the urge to sing*, started out with 'Nearer My God to Thee,' Johnse *turned sullenly* to him *with an ugly look*."[27]

How can a writer know ninety years later what Charlie Carpenter was singing or the expression on Johnse Hatfield's face? Unless someone who was there told him, he can't know, and if he says he knows, he is writing fiction.

Hatfield writes that, while looking sullenly at Carpenter, Johnse said coldly: *"Them McCoys has enough to think about without listening to yo'r songs."*[28] He gives us a footnote to back up what Johnse said. Now, you would expect a man who was descended from the Hatfields, and whose life overlapped Devil Anse's by more than two decades to say in that note that he heard Johnse's words from someone who was there in the schoolhouse that night and heard Johnse say it, wouldn't you? If so, you could hardly be more wrong. The footnote Hatfield gives is to a book called *The Devil's Brigade*, a fictional work by John Spivak, in 1930.[29] Spivak was born in New Haven, Connecticut in 1897. At the time he wrote the book he was living in New York and was a writer for the Communist Party's "Daily Worker."

Hatfield, a contemporary relative of the feudists, cites a *novel* by a New York communist as a source for a Hatfield quote! I was tempted at that point to lay the book aside, but I forced myself to read the rest of it.

After telling us about the Hatfield clan's stupendous skill with a pistol, Hatfield does a one-eighty and says that when Pharmer McCoy shot Ellison Hatfield, Elias Hatfield took the gun from McCoy, and fired at Pharmer's head from point blank range. He was so close that Pharmer's face and neck were powder-burnt — yet he missed him! Then, to top it off, he says that Elias fired five more times, so close that each shot powder-burnt Pharmer,[30] missing him all five times! Firing a pistol so close[31] to a man's head that many times and missing him every time is almost as incredible as three men hitting a tossed coin simultaneously.

Holes in a tin can are not the only things Dr. Hatfield has trouble counting. Remember he said that Elias shot at Pharmer and missed. Then he says he fired five more times, which makes a total of six shots fired at Pharmer, using a six-shooter that Pharmer, a second or so ago had used to shoot Elias' brother. He stops at the seventh shot from the six-shooter, saying that "another pull at the trigger brought only a dull click."[32]

Hatfield's last note to his Chapter 7, which describes the action at the 1882 election where Ellison was killed, says:"*The Spivak Papers* are followed closely in this narration.[33] Hatfield is telling us that he, a grand-nephew of Devil Anse, is getting his description of the most important single day in the feud from a New York novelist!

Having opened his book with the fantastic tale of the shooting exhibition, Hatfield closes it with the equally fantastic tale of "The Battle of the Devil's Backbone," between Cap Hatfield and a posse following Cap's escape from the Williamson jail. Hatfield says that there were over a thousand men in the Mingo county posse.[34] As the posse approaches the Devil's Backbone, which Hatfield places on Beech Creek, they are joined by none other than Ran'l McCoy, who, according to G. Elliott, knew every inch of the territory. How this could be when Ran'l had almost surely never been there in his life is not explained. Nevertheless, Ol' Ran'l, now seventy-two years old (Hatfield said he was nearing eighty), wearing a coonskin cap and toting an ancient muzzle loader, joined in the attack on the Devil's Backbone.[35] Why Ol' Ran'l opted for an antique muzzle loader instead of the Winchester Calvin used in the New Year's fight is not explained.

The battle climaxed with two huge dynamite explosions, blowing the entire top of the mountain off. There was so much rock and earth displaced by the explosions that the material slid all the way down the mountain and diverted the creek.[36] (We are not told who got the coal uncovered in this first-ever mountaintop removal operation in West Virginia.)

Cap survived the assault and escaped. Ol' Ran'l also survived, but not before Cap scored a near-miss, cutting the squirrel's tail off Ran'l's cap.[37] How Ran'l's coonskin cap had a squirrel's tail dangling from it and not a raccoon's tail is not explained. Dean King incorporates this fantastic tale almost in its entirety in his "*True Story.*"[38]

It is obvious that King set out to demolish the work of Altina Waller, whose book set the feud in the proper economic, social and political context. Waller based her history on years of research of original documents in the various courthouses, personal, business and public archives, and census reports, giving scant notice to front porch tales and the sensationalist reportage of the newspapers of the feud era. On the Facebook "*Real Hatfields, Real McCoys, Real Feud, Real Matewan*" page, on May, 29, 2013, quoted with permission of the owner of the page, King makes this clear: "There is very little evidence to show a direct link of economics on the events of the feud as Waller tries to do."

If there really is *"very little evidence to show a direct link of economics on the events of the feud,"* then the Hatfield and McCoy feud is the only significant multi-year event in history that occurred in an economic vacuum.

This was a decade during which an entire generation of Appalachians was growing up in numbers too great for the land to accommodate as subsistence farmers. Many of these young people were taking up timbering or moonshining — or simply leaving for points west. Furthermore, the moguls of international finance were flooding the hills with land-buying agents, who scooped up the land and mineral riches of the locals. Yet King says that economics had nothing to do with the feud and that the legitimate historian, Waller, was mistaken in her effort to explain the feud in that context.

For a full exposition of how it came about that so many episodes of sporadic violence in Appalachia are referred to as "feuds," see the chapter Waller wrote in *Appalachia in the Making*, in 1995. In this essay, *Feuding in Appalachia: Evolution of a Cultural Stereotype*, Professor Waller traces the evolution of the term "feud," and explains how it came to be applied to Appalachian violence.[39]

Dr. T.R.C "Bob" Hutton's 2009 Vanderbilt PhD thesis, *Bloody Breathitt*, soon to be published as a book, also shreds the "blood feud" thesis. Professor Hutton's work shows that the Breathitt County violence, long ascribed to the extreme family loyalty and lawlessness said to be hallmarks of the Southern hillbilly, was actually political warfare.

Hutton wrote: "Feud, and all it entailed, was a device of depoliticization, obscuring or removing the political implications of political violence...Feud, not as an event or type of social relation but as an imprecise, misleading descriptor of violence, distorted the larger meaning of violence in Breathitt County."[40]The same analysis applies in spades to the conflict in Pike County.

To sensationalist writers, from the yellow journalists of the late nineteenth century to Alther's 2012 *Blood Feud* and King's 2013 "*True Story*," the history of Tug Valley during the 1880s is a collection of senselessly violent episodes occurring in an economic and political vacuum and bereft of any influence by outside forces. That Tolbert McCoy was an intelligent, good-looking man with no economic prospects when he started drinking moonshine on Election Day, 1882, is not relevant to the purveyors of legend as history. The fact that Dils and Mayo in Kentucky and Nighbert and Sergeant in West Virginia were swooping down on Devil Anse's inestimable underground riches in his five thousand acres in the heart of the billion dollar coal field means nothing to them.

Even though the New York newspaper reporters cranked out their stories within days after only a few days in the hills, King treats them as history.[41] Crawford was the fastest writer of all, saying in his preface that *most of his book was dictated within three hours* of his return to New York.[42]

Crawford undoubtedly has the record for speed in writing a *classic*. It probably takes a modern "feud historian" the greater part of a month to agglomerate enough of the old yarns and fables to produce a modern "feud history."

In citing the yellow Journalists of the 1880s, King frequently interjects his own inventions among the "facts" he derives from the yellow journalists in such a way that it is almost impossible to distinguish between the inventions of the newspapermen and those of King himself.

Relating Crawford's October, 1888 visit to Logan, King interjects into the narrative, "Logan Courthouse, though small, boasted a newspaper — the Logan Democrat."[43] King says that, in spite of the fact that Crawford, wrote in the report King quotes: "There are no newspapers circulated throughout the district."[44] Crawford was right and King is wrong; the first newspaper in Logan County, the Logan Banner, published its first issue several months after Crawford's visit.[45]

Other feud writers who have been ignored by historians because of their factual errors are also prominent in the citations in the "True Story." Jean Thomas,[46] who wrote about the feud in her 1940 book, Big Sandy is another cited source. Thomas begins her section on the feud, entitled Romeo and Juliet, by saying that Devil Anse served in the Confederate army and Ran'l served the Union. Despite the fact that both men served the Confederacy, first in the Virginia State Line, then in the 45th Battalion, Virginia Infantry. She says that whenever they met, "the very sight of the blue and the gray aroused animosity."[47]

Thomas has more drivel in her "history:" She has Devil Anse living on Peter Creek, in Kentucky, when he actually lived in West Virginia every day of his long life.[48] She has the hog trial held in a blacksmith's shop, when it was actually held in the home of Preacher Anse Hatfield.[49] Her list of attendees at the trial includes names that do not appear in the 1880 census for the area.[50]

Like all other purveyors of tall tales as history, from Spears to King, Thomas claims to know details that she did not know — and could not possibly know — and includes dozens of direct quotations that she could not possibly have a basis for quoting.

Thomas had Alifair McCoy fifteen years old at the time she was killed, when she was actually twice that age.[51] Remarkably, she has Calvin McCoy, who was killed along with his sister, Alifair, during the New Year's raid, surviving the raid and burying his slain sister.[52] This aggregation of errors by Jean Thomas is the very first source for King, in Chapter 1.

Approximately fifteen million people have seen Kevin Costner's movie, The Hatfields & McCoys. Those people will always think that Randolph McCoy became deeply angered at Devil Anse Hatfield when he watched Devil Anse desert the Confederate Army, and that was the germ for the "Hatfield and McCoy Feud." The hopelessly garbled "history" of Lisa Alther's Blood Feud, which followed closely in the wake of the movie made it worse. Then, in May of 2013, King's egregiously distorted and exaggerated *"True Story,"* made a shambles of the history of that era in Appalachia.

---

1 King, Dean, *"The Feud: The Hatfields & McCoys: The True Story*, New York Little, Brown and Company, 2013.

2 Spears, A *Mountain Feud*, New York, Current Literature Magazine, 1888. 1.

3 Spears, *Mountain Feud*, 4.

4 Spears, 28.

5 Spears, John R. *Mountain News Getting*, New York Sun. Quoted by Dean King in The Feud, 89.

6 Spears, John, *"A Mountain Feud,"* 7.

7 Spears, 2.

8 King, Dean, The Feud, 360, n. 2.

9 Quoted in King, Dean, *The Feud*, 262-3

10 Quoted in King, *The Feud*, 268.

11 Waller, Altina, *Feud: Hatfields, McCoys, and Social Change in Appalachia, 1860-1900.* University of North Carolina Press, Chapel Hill, 1988.

12 Hatfield and Spence, *Tale of the Devil*. Chapmanville, Woodland Press, 2012, 108–09.

13 Truda McCoy, *The McCoys* Pikeville, Preservation Council Press, 1976, 42.

14 Lisa Alther, *Blood Feud*, xii–xiv.

15 King says in his Note 3 on page 352 that his bear tale "is *adapted* from Coleman C. Hatfield and Robert Y. Spence, *The Tale of the Devil.*" This means that an *adaptation* of a combination of two tales, by two different tellers, is presented to King's readers as *history!*

16 Rice does not conflict with the written record, but he sometimes uses sources that a historian should not use as a factual basis, such as newspapers and family stories.

17 King, Dean, *The Feud: The Hatfields and the McCoys: The True Story*, 15-20.

18 King, xii, xiii.

19 McCoy, Truda, *The McCoys*, 101.

20 Hatfield, G. Elliot. "The Hatfields." 175, n.6.

21 Hatfield, 9.

22 Ibid.

23 Hatfield, G. E., *The Hatfields*, 175, n.7.

24 Jones, V. C., *The Hatfields & the McCoys*, 11.

25 Hatfield, *The Hatfields*, 123-5.

26  King, Dean, *The Feud,* 19.

27  Hatfield, The Hatfields, 58.

28  *Ibid.*

29  *Ibid.*

30  Hatfield, *The Hatfields,* 52.

31  Experts say that powder-burning is restricted to about six inches from the end of the barrel. *Stippling* — tiny deposits of unburned powder — occur within about thirty inches, but the book clearly says "Powder-burn."

32  ibid

33  Hatfield, *The Hatfields,* 177.

34  Hatfield, *The Hatfields,* 164.

35  Hatfield, 164.

36  Hatfield, 168.

37  Ibid.

38  King, pp. 317-320.  After more than three pages of this spurious tale, King says that the explosion part may have been exaggerated, because someone showed him "The Devil's Backbone," and it was undamaged by explosion.

39  Waller, Altina, *Feuding in Appalachia: Evolution of a Cultural Stereotype,* in *Appalachia in the Making: The Mountain South in the Nineteenth Century.* Chapel Hill, University of North Carolina Press, 1995.

40  Hutton, T.R.C., *Bloody Breathitt: Power and Violence in the Mountain South,* (PhD. Thesis) Vanderbilt University, 2009, pp. 5-6.

41  King cites the old journalists over two hundred times as support for his "history."

42  Crawford, T.C., *American Vendetta,* 1.

43  King, *The Feud,* p. 262.

44  Crawford, *American Vendetta,* 83.

45  Waller, *Feud,* 145.

46  Jean Thomas also wrote an article on *"The Hatfield and McCoy Feud"* for the May 12, 1944 issue of *Life Magazine.*  In that article she says that Lark McCoy attacked a gang of forty Hatfields and killed fourteen of them.

47  Thomas, Jean, *Big Sandy,* 177.

48  Thomas, Jean, 179.

49  Thomas, Jean, 181.

50  Ibid.

51  Thomas, Jean, 224

52  Thomas, Jean, 226.

# CHAPTER 3.

# TALL TALES FROM THE HOLLOWS TO HOLLYWOOD

It took me many years to accept the fact that much of the worst writing about my own people came not from the fevered minds of big city newspaper reporters, or from starving novelists trying to make a buck by writing "history," but rather from us! In their efforts to poison the atmosphere surrounding the trials of the Hatfields and to enlist the support of the state government in their move to strip Devil Anse from his land, the Pikeville elite spun for the visiting reporters many fantastic tales about the evil of the West Virginia Hatfields. The Louisville Courier Journal and other large Kentucky papers enthusiastically grasped the opportunity to deflect the onus of feuding onto another state.

When the New York and Pittsburgh reporters came to Pikeville, Cline, Ferguson and others gave them the same tales about the perfidious Hatfields, and they ran with the stories. Little did the Pikeville crowd know that the stories would paint all of Appalachia — not just the Hatfields — with the same savage brush.

Of course Perry Cline heard many of the same stories growing up on Grapevine Creek in West Virginia that Truda McCoy and I heard growing up in Pike County. Many of these stories had no connection whatsoever with "the feud" itself, but Cline and others in Pikeville adapted the tales to Tug Valley personalities and spun them for the visiting big city newsmen. Many of those tales showed up in the newspaper articles about "the feud." They continue in the "histories" being written today.

Except for the raids into West Virginia by Frank Phillips' posse in 1887-8, all the documented events connected to the feud occurred in Pike County, Kentucky. Only about a quarter of the posse were from the Tug Valley area. There were more of the wealthy members of the Pikeville elite in the posse than there were McCoys. The feud story, like the Phillips posse, was largely made in Pikeville. With the exception of the whoppers in the books by descendants, and a few modern inventions, such as Dean King's tale of a bounty hunter reading his rights to Devil Anse in the woods in Logan County, almost all of the unsubstantiated tales of feud violence can be traced to the 1888 writings of big city newspaper men.

King's primary sources are John Spears of the *New York Sun*, T.C. Crawford of the *New York World* and Charles Howell of the *Pittsburgh Times*. The critical question is: "From whom did the reporters get their 'facts?'"

It is noteworthy that none of the reporters attributes a single one of the stories to a person who was involved in the purported activities. None of the stories is attributed to a person who even lived in Tug Valley at the time. T.C. Crawford explains the dearth of information from Valley residents, when he reported that "even the best people of the community...will not furnish a scrap of information or give even an opinion."[1]

If the people in the community would not give the reporters even a scrap of information, then where did the stories come from? As it is not reasonable to believe that the reporters concocted the stories out of whole cloth, then the necessary conclusion is that they heard them from someone in Pikeville, or copied them from another reporter who heard them in Pikeville.

I do not believe that John Spears manufactured his tale of Johnse Hatfield shooting into the bed where his seven year-old-son was sleeping. I am sure that someone — most likely Perry Cline — told him the story. Spears says that he saw the son of Johnse and

Roseanna in Ran'l McCoy's home.[2] I am sure that someone — most likely Cline — pointed to Melvin, the son of Tolbert McCoy, and told Spears that the boy was Roseanna's son.

The closest Spears comes to attributing a story to anyone is when telling about the romance between Johnse and Roseanna, he says he is giving the words of "a lawyer in Pikeville who was familiar with the story."[3] The lawyer referred to was none other than Perry Cline.

As T.C. Crawford visited only Logan County West Virginia, it follows that his own recounting of feud events in the first four chapters of *American Vendetta* comes from the other reporters who had visited Pikeville and had written their stories several months before Crawford went to Logan. Crawford says that he dictated that part of his book in three hours, immediately after returning to New York. As we saw earlier, Crawford found no feud in his visit to Logan; therefore he must have had the Spears and Howell articles in front of him as he dictated his first three chapters, which closely follow the story as told by Spears and Howell.

Every feud writer since 1888, from Mutzenberg in 1899 to King in 2013 has had access to those 1888 newspaper articles. The Hatfield and McCoy feud as it exists in the literature--with the exception of Altina Waller's book — was to a large extent made in Pikeville, in 1888. The Pikeville stories, manufactured for the purpose of scandalizing the West Virginia Hatfields, actually stereotyped all of Southern Appalachia in the minds of newspaper and book readers from 1888 forward.

When Truda McCoy told the tale of the hillbilly hooker, Belle Beaver of Happy Hollow, she was writing a story that had been told on Appalachian front porches for decades. Belle was no more real than were Pecos Bill or Paul Bunyan, but she was part of our oral heritage.

Belle Beaver, the lead character in dozens of bawdy tales, is a generic rendering of Belle Brezing, the Lexington, Kentucky madam who was probably the most famous woman in Kentucky at the time Truda McCoy was compiling her book. Madam Brezing catered to the blue-bloods associated with the Bluegrass horse industry. Her fame was such that when her house was razed in 1973, more than thirty years after her death, the individual bricks were sold as souvenirs. Madam Brezing is generally acknowledged to have been the basis for Margaret Mitchell's bawdy-house owner, Belle Watling, in *Gone with the Wind*.

I heard many variations of the Belle Beaver tales on various front porches and around many campfires decades before Truda McCoy's book was published in 1976. McCoy knew she was telling a tall tale when she included Belle Beaver in her book, but, since it was used to show the moral shortcomings of Johnse Hatfield, she obviously saw no harm in it. Truda could have done it to entertain the unwashed multitude, knowing that astute readers would recognize the alliterative names for what they were — fiction. But she was wrong.

Belle Beaver shows up, big as life, in the 2103 "*True Story*" by Dean King. King makes Belle and her busy cathouse in the holler just as real as Annie Oakley or Bonnie Parker. Is Belle Beaver is part of King's commitment to "deflate the legends and restore accurate historical detail?"[4] King does make one concession in that he admits that he does not know even the approximate location of Happy Hollow. He says it's real, but he just doesn't know where it is.[5]

Truda McCoy is not the only feud descendant who introduced folklore into history, only to have modern "historians" cite it as real history. My cousin, L.D. Hatfield, is a repeat offender. Hatfield's tale of Bud McCoy, son of Asa Harmon McCoy, greasing his boots with the brains of Jim Vance, which was part of my own family lore, is one example of a totally false tale included in Hatfield's *True Story of the Hatfield and McCoy Feud*.[6]

The biggest yarn that L.D. Hatfield spun in his little book is the one about Abner Vance, the grandfather of Jim Vance and the great-grandfather of Devil Anse Hatfield.

In Hatfield's yarn, Abner Vance was a Baptist Preacher, who killed a man named Lewis Horton after the man debauched Vance's daughter, and insulted the old man when he returned the wayward lass to her home. In reality, Vance killed Horton because the man had testified against Vance's interests in a court case.[7]

Hatfield says that Vance shot Horton in the head from one hundred seventy-five yards. According to the evidence he was shot just under the shoulder blade from less than forty yards.

Hatfield says that Vance went on the lam to Tug Valley for several years, where he accumulated several thousand acres of land, which he divided among his kin upon his death. In reality, Abner Vance was listed as a laborer when he appeared at trial. Abner Vance accumulated absolutely nothing after he shot Mr. Horton, with the possible exception of lice and bedbugs, as he spent every single day from his crime until his hanging in jail. The man who is said to have owned thousands of acres of land was actually listed as a "laborer" at his trial, and was unable to come up with enough assets to post the bond for his daughter, who was charged with him as an accessory.

Abner Vance killed Lewis Horton in September, 1817, and was hanged for the crime in July, 1819, *having spent every day of the interim in jail.* He was tried twice, as the appeals court overturned his original conviction because the trial judge erred in unfairly denying Vance an insanity defense. Retried on a plea of insanity, Vance was found to be sane and sentenced to hang.

L.D. Hatfield could reproduce the old front porch tale of Abner Vance in his book seventy years ago, knowing that no one would take the trouble to go to Virginia and consult the court records. Modern "historians" do not have that advantage of writing for an uninformed readership--thanks to the internet-- but they do it anyway.

Lisa Alther, in her "non-fiction" book *Blood Feud*, has the Vance yarn.[8] As one should expect, Dean King could not resist such a juicy bit of folklore, and he has the tale in his 2013 *"True Story."*[9]

King says: "He had shot Horton, a doctor, for an affront of a sexual nature to his daughter and fled to the west. After many months on the run in the wilds of the Tug River Valley, he had returned to face the charges against him, hoping for leniency given the circumstances."[10]

King says that before meeting his fate, Vance parceled out the land he had claimed during his months on the lam in Tug Valley to his children, and "They went there to start a new life."[11]

After reading the book three times, I still shake my head in disbelief. The man says he is going to deflate the legends and restore accurate historical detail, and then he starts the book off with a wild yarn I heard on Pa-Paw George's front porch sixty years ago, and wrote off as a fable. Then he follows it up immediately with the tale of Devil Anse, as a mere stripling of a lad, kicking a colossal bear in the ass and driving it up a tree.[12]

For this, King is feted as a feud expert and a historian.

Anyone with web access can simply go to Google and type in "Abner Vance" and find on the first page of results, http://tgv7. tripod.com/index-12.html which refutes King's Abner Vance yarn in detail. The public loves a good story, even if they are being lied to. Very few give a damn about truth in history, but I wrote this book anyway.

L.D. Hatfield was a story-teller--his book's title notwithstanding.[13] He is fulfilling his role when he tells the fabricated story of Abner Vance. We've always had story-tellers in the mountains; they are on display every day in Jonesborough, Tennessee during the season.

In defense of Cousin L.D. Hatfield, I will say that when he introduced the tale of Abner Vance, he made it clear that it was a "story," just as Coleman Hatfield introduced the tale of the bear hunt as a "tale." I am sure that neither of those consummate story-tellers, who took care to warn readers that they were reading a story or a tale, ever dreamed that a "historian" would come along in 2013 and report their yarns as history.

It was after reading this book, written by a kinsman, that I determined that it was not profitable to lend credence to any writer based solely upon kinship or descent from the feudists. It is also the source of my aversion to all books which contain in their title the words *True Story*. L.D. Hatfield did not have the tale of the cow's tail in his book, and for that and the wonderful photo of Uncle Ransom Hatfield standing in front of the Anderson Hatfield home place, I applaud him.

L.D. Hatfield's little book of seventy-five pages, with only the first fifty-four pages about the feud and the remainder about the Matewan Massacre, was reissued by Cosimo Classics in the wake of the Costner 2012 movie.

The Hatfield and McCoy feud was only part of a much larger conflict which featured John Dils, Perry Cline and others in the Pikeville elite versus Devil Anse Hatfield. This conflict had its roots in the Civil War and lasted until Devil Anse surrendered his land and moved away from Tug Valley. The Hatfield and McCoy feud occasionally erupts outside the larger conflict, but it is still very much a part of it.

In order to expand the handful of documentable violent events of the feud era into a book-length story of blood and gore, authors glean everything ever written from the yellow journalists of the 1880s to the current publicity blurbs issued by the various tourism promoters to produce a conflict with dozens of violent episodes. The unpleasant duty to engage the supersizers head-on falls upon this writer.

I am concerned with those instances where something that did not happen, according to any credible source, is presented as fact. I am even more concerned when the movie or book has something happening that is the opposite of what the best evidence says actually happened.

Any attempt to understand the events in Tug Valley during the time of the feud, without understanding what was happening throughout Appalachia at that time, is futile. Trying to explain what happened without knowing what men of power and influence like Dils, Mayo, Nighbert, and Sergeant were doing during the 1880s is like trying to understand the Civil War without considering Abraham Lincoln and Jefferson Davis. If one does not know that Devil Anse Hatfield, in 1887, was sitting on a king's ransom in minerals, with the most powerful forces in the country bearing down upon him, one can never make sense of "the feud."

Most feud writers write off the war, simply because both Ran'l McCoy and Devil Anse Hatfield were Confederates. This is a mistake; while the Civil War was not a cause of "the feud," it affected the thoughts and actions of the men involved in many ways. When the opportunity arose for John Dils to get revenge for all his wartime suffering at the hands of Rebel raiders, while at the same time pressuring Devil Anse to give up his land, he grabbed it and the bloody 1887-8 phase of the feud was on. When Devil Anse was contemplating the fate of the three McCoys who had killed his brother, it was his knowledge that old war-time enmity on the part of the Pikeville elite toward him would not allow justice to be meted out to the McCoys that tipped the scales in favor of executing them himself.

When Altina Waller said, "Tug Valley and Pikeville regions had been at odds since the Civil War; this new 'war' in the guise of a feud could be interpreted as an extension of that struggle...," she was correct. It is vital to note that Professor Waller did not say that the Hatfields and the McCoys had been at odds since the Civil War. The conflict rooted in the War was between the Pikeville elite and the Tug Valley— especially Devil Anse Hatfield.

Devil Anse Hatfield is well known for his story-telling, but he was not alone. In the days before the TV displaced the front porch in summer and the front room in winter almost every family on Blackberry Creek had a story-teller. We never had a TV in the house before I graduated from high school and went away to college, so my information came from reading books and periodicals in the school library, and listening to about half a dozen of the most accomplished story-tellers in the country.

There was a problem with those old story-tellers, though; they would sometimes slip a true story in among their tall tales. They didn't do it very often, but they did it often enough to throw you off balance. The supersizers of the feud story, from the newspaper reporters of 1888 to the writers of new books today, have these tales in their writings as history. The "feud historians" also throw in just enough facts to confuse the reader.

My step-father's father, Pa-Paw George Sullivan, regaled us with front-porch tales that were captivating back in my boyhood days. A natural entertainer, Pa-Paw George was a claw-hammer banjo player and a singer of mountain songs in a high Irish tenor voice. As with most good story-tellers, many of his tall tales grew taller with each retelling. Of course, my siblings, cousins and friends realized by about the age of eight or nine that what Pa-Paw was telling us was a story, more likely to be something he either made up or heard from some other story-teller than it was to be true.

Like most of the story-tellers, Pa-Paw George would work in a true story now and then. He was actually deeply involved in the mine wars, having been armed and shooting, during the Matewan Massacre of 1920. I learned much later, while doing research as a graduate student that most of his tales about the mine wars were actually true. On the other hand, my later research showed that many of his tales relating to the Hatfields (he was married to a Hatfield) and McCoys were made up.

Most of the big city newspaper reporters who visited Tug Valley back in 1888-9 were not as astute as we kids were; most of them ate up those tall tales the Pikeville partisans told them and regurgitated them for the enlightenment of millions of readers.

Tales told by descendants of the feudists are one of the sources of false feud history, and it continues to this day. The magazine for the 2013 Hatfield-McCoy reunion is a case in point:

This publication contains an article about the McCoys accompanied by a photo of the Uriah McCoy home.  The article says that my great-great-grandfather Uriah McCoy's large two story home in the photo is "the home place of Randall McCoy."  Ran'l McCoy lived across the ridge, about a mile as the crow flies, and probably ten miles by today's roads from the house in the photo.

The article further says that the home shown is where Roseanna stayed with her aunt Betty, and where her daughter by Johnse Hatfield was born. This is terribly confusing, because it means that the home of Ran'l McCoy, from which Roseanna was a refugee, was also the home where she took refuge!

The article says that Uriah McCoy was a brother to Ran'l McCoy, when he was actually a first cousin to Ran'l. Uriah was a brother to Sally McCoy, who was Ran'l's wife. Here we see the feud being supersized in 2013, in an official Hatfield-McCoy publication—by a descendant.

An author depending upon newspapers and periodicals for facts could include all this in a book, saying it came from a McCoy descendant, and was published in an official Hatfield-McCoy publication, and he/she would be telling the truth. But none of it is true!

Costner's movie provided a few hours of diversion for the couch potatoes of America, while claiming to teach them a little history. The most outrageous tall tales we see in the books by Alther and King are not in the movie, and for that I commend everyone involved in the movie. They substitute a large number of new inventions, aimed at sustaining a story of a decades-long blood feud between Devil Anse and "Ran'l McCoy, but the net effect is not as damaging to the actual history as are the whoppers in the two books that followed in its wake. The Costner mini-series is great TV drama. I would rank it with *Lonesome Dove* and *Horatio Hornblower* in its genre.

Any action drama with Kevin Costner, Tom Berenger, and Powers Boothe in the cast will be far above average for a twenty-first century movie. Mare Winningham as Sarah (Sally) McCoy gives a stellar performance and gets my best actress award.

Tom Berenger, who plays Jim Vance as a much worse character than the record justifies, and who alone among the players gets much of the language right, is my choice for Best Actor.

Andrew Howard as Bad Frank Phillips was a close runner-up for my best actor laurels. Although many of the things the movie shows Bad Frank doing never happened, or happened much differently, Howard captures the essence of the man superbly.

There were outstanding performances by Jena Malone as Nancy, Sarah Parish, as Levicy Hatfield and Lindsay Pulsipher as Roseanna. The worst bit of casting is Noel Fisher as Ellison "Cottontop" Mounts. Cottontop was over six feet tall and twenty-two years old at the time of the raid on the McCoy home.[14] He was the tallest and strongest man in the gang, but the movie presents him as a slightly built teenager.

This writer is not a movie critic, however, so the opinions expressed above about the performers can be treated with the weight they deserve. More weight can be given to the criticism of the historical content of the movie, as he has studied the history for more than half a century.

The miniseries is the best drama of the century so far, but as history, it stinks. It is inaccurate in the great majority of details. Having decided to present the feud as a decades-long blood feud between Devil Anse Hatfield and Ran'l McCoy, the scriptwriters had no choice but to supersize the sparse record of such a conflict, and they did so with gusto.

The movie's weakness on historical facts is understandable, if you read the feud history as reported by the History Channel itself. In an article that is supposedly describing the feud itself — the history, not the movie — the History Channel says: "Enter Perry Cline, an eager Pikeville attorney who was married to Martha McCoy, the widow of Randall's Brother Asa Harmon."[15] Harmon McCoy's widow, Martha, was Perry Cline's sister. The History Channel has Perry Cline marrying *his own sister*!

Since it is a movie, and will be seen as just a movie by discerning viewers, it does no long-term harm to the actual history. Costner is not traveling around the country telling people that his movie is historical fact. It is not of the same order as a book that claims to be the *"True Story."* When Dean King gives his lectures on "feud history," standing in front of a projection of a fake photograph of Randall McCoy, he is directly attacking historical truth.

1  Crawford, T.C., *American Vendetta*, 9

2  Spears, John, *Mountain Feud*, 4.

3  Spears, 5

4  King, *The Feud,* pp. xii-xiv.

5  King, Dean. *The Feud*, 82-3.

6  Hatfield, *The True Story*, 32.

7  It was the slain man's brother, Daniel Horton, who had a dalliance with Vance's daughter.

8  Alther, *Blood Feud*, 20.

9  King, *The Feud*, 8-9.

10  King, 8.

11  King, 9.

12  King, 18-9.

13  When one of the old front-porch storytellers, like my Pa-Paw George Sullivan began a story with, "This is the true story of....," we kids knew right off that what we were about to hear was a fabricated yarn.

14  Rice, Otis, *The Hatfields and the McCoys*, Lexington. University of Kentucky Press, 1982, 59.

15  https://www.thehistorychannelclub.com/articles/articletype/articleview/articleid/1571/hatfields-and-mccoys-an-american-vendetta

# CHAPTER 4.

# GROWING UP AMONG HATFIELDS AND MCCOYS

I believe everything I heard while growing up for which I have found substantiation from other sources. The rest of it is just folklore, some of it made up for entertainment value, and some of it honestly repeated by people who believed they were telling the truth.

I heard very little about "the feud" at home during my early childhood, except when we drove past the places where Ellison Hatfield was killed and where the three sons of Ran'l McCoy were executed. When it was spoken of in my home or that of my Grandfather McCoy, whose mother was a Hatfield, or that of my Grandmother Dotson, who was born a Hatfield, it was usually referred to as *The Hatfield-McCoy Troubles*. It was never called a feud.

Grandpa Phillip McCoy, a blacksmith by trade, was one of the biggest landowners on Blackberry Creek when I was growing up. He owned several hundred acres in Blue Springs, and the prime land at the forks of Blackberry. He rode a mule across the mountain to his job as a blacksmith for Freeburn Coal Company for more than thirty years, retiring at age sixty on the first day that the United Mine Workers pension plan went into effect, in 1950. Grandpa farmed several acres and kept many head of livestock, while working at his full-time job as a blacksmith. He continued to farm until he had a disabling stroke at age seventy-five.

Phillip McCoy was six feet tall and weighed about one hundred ninety pounds. He was sixty-five the year I spent the summer with him, and it was the talk of the neighborhood that he could carry a one hundred pound sack of feed from Jeff Davis's store to his barn, a distance of about four hundred yards. Now Dean King tells us that Grandpa's father and uncles, and his other relatives of the prior generation were better men than he was--by an order of magnitude! King said that the people in general—not just the outstanding specimens such as Phillip McCoy—"Thought nothing of shouldering a two-bushel sack of corn, weighing112 pounds, for a ten-mile trip to a mill and then turning back again with the milled corn the next day...."[1]

I know I should be proud to be descended from such god-like people, but I have to call BS here. Does King not realize that intelligent readers know that the starting line-up for the Dallas Cowboys could not accomplish such a feat? King grasps every opportunity to make my people *different*—some kind of *other*. Many times he tells a whopper like this, which no sentient reader will believe, for no apparent purpose other than to differentiate his subjects from normal human beings.

My Grandpa McCoy was representative of that eighty percent plus of McCoys who took no part in Ran'l's troubles. They were almost all substantial landholders, who were known for their industry and thrift and for their willingness to help those in need. The "Bad" McCoys were almost all landless men with little or no economic prospects. In fact, all of the men of the McCoy name who killed someone during the "feud" were landless. Sam and Paris, who killed Bill Staton, were orphaned early by the war and grew up landless. Tolbert, the villain of the Election Day, 1882 killing, was a farm laborer, living and working on a neighbor's farm.

Grandpa McCoy never talked about the *troubles*, except for brief remarks such as: "Ran'l's boys shouldn't'a' done Ellison that a' way, but Devil Anse shouldn't 'a burnt that house an' killed them children."[2] That was it; he absolutely refused to elaborate. He would brush off any further query with a negative shake of his head, and change the subject. I spent one entire summer with him, and he never opened up a single time. All of his answers to my questions were single sentences.

When I once asked him if his father was involved in the feud, he said "No, but your Granny's pap was, so maybe you better ask her."

Grandma Ella (Smith) McCoy had no personal knowledge of the actual feud, having been born in 1890, but she was convinced that her father, Curtis Smith, had been murdered by some of the Hatfields, as retaliation for Grandpa Curtis being a member of Frank Phillips' posse.[3]

About twenty-five years after the Phillips raids on the Hatfields, Grandpa Curtis was plowing a field and someone shot him in the head from an ambush position in the bordering forest. There was never a good suspect in the killing of Curtis Smith, and I certainly don't believe that the Hatfields even remembered who he was that long after the events, but some of his family said it might have been the Hatfields who killed him. While it is almost certainly just family folklore, it is more likely to be true than is the tale of seven Hatfields setting up an ambush thirty feet from the road and, being unable to identify Ran'l McCoy from that distance, wounding two non-combatants and killing their horses, as we read in Dean King's "*True Story*" of the feud.

Curtis was recruited for the posse on Peter Creek by Frank Phillips due his reputation for bravery and marksmanship. According to family lore, Curtis Smith made a lot of money during that three month stint in Colonel Dils's posse.

I do not know how much money Dils and company spent paying and equipping the posse, but I would surmise that it was a sizeable sum. After all, only nine of the forty[4] members of the posse were McCoys. A dozen or so were wealthy members of the Pikeville elite, who were probably motivated by a desire to ingratiate themselves with the kingpin of Pikeville business, Colonel John Dils.[5] The rest of them were paid to do it, and they were equipped with the latest armaments.

It became obvious to me as I grew up that most of the old people on Blackberry saw fault on both sides for the feud incidents, and saw no benefit to themselves or their families in talking about it.

After all, given the level of intermarriage, it was almost impossible to criticize anyone without tarnishing the name of a close relative.

I got the impression from some of the oldsters on the McCoy side of the family that they would have loved to blast Devil Anse for the killing of Ran'l's children and the beating of Sally on New Year's, 1888, but were constrained by the fact that the sons of Ol' Ran'l had viciously butchered Ellison Hatfield, and the Phillips posse had illegally invaded West Virginia and kidnapped and murdered members of the Hatfield group.

It is too bad that they didn't have the enlightenment of Mr. King's *True Story*." Had they known that Ellison Hatfield was, in fact, a six foot-six giant who attacked the much smaller Tolbert McCoy with a knife, they would have been free to damn the West Virginia Hatfields to the netherworld.

When I went to Logan in the early 1990s to check on the research of Altina Waller, I found a deed showing that Devil Anse and Levicy Hatfield had sold a tract of land — 239 acres — in 1889, of which the Hatfields were only half owners. The other two owners were great-grandpa Asa McCoy and his wife, Nancy Hatfield McCoy.[6] Grandma Nancy was the daughter of Preacher Anse Hatfield. The land was on Mate Creek, and adjoined the land owned by Ellison Hatfield.

When reading all the sensationalist accounts of a vicious blood feud between the Hatfields and McCoys, the reader is well advised to recall this transaction, which is on record in the courthouse at Logan. My great grandfather, Asa McCoy, a nephew of Sally McCoy and a cousin of Ran'l McCoy, had been a partner of Devil Anse Hatfield during the decade when the so-called feud was raging.

I have a clear memory of being reminded of the troubles as we drove to Matewan, West Virginia. Mom would usually say something as we passed the place where the election of 1882 was held, or passed the spot where the three McCoys were shot.

When we passed the spot on the river where the three boys were killed, my Mother (nee McCoy) often told us that Jim Vance had greased his boots with the brains of Bud McCoy there, after blowing the top of his head off. I heard that so many times that I was actually shocked to learn much later that Jim Vance was not even one of the men indicted for that killing, but it must have been part of the family lore in my branch of the McCoy family, because Mom, who never lied to us, was convinced that it happened.

Mother grew up during a time when most of the feud participants who survived the feud were still alive, and most of the eyewitnesses to the events on Blackberry were alive, and Mom heard all their stories. Yet, when I researched the feud later I learned that a significant part of what Mom knew about the feud was wrong.

The unreliability of descendants' testimony, combined with the paucity of documentary evidence allowed the yellow journalists of the 1880s to have a field day with their feud reporting. It allows modern writers to do the same. A writer in 2013 could write a sizeable book that is ninety percent false, and still have hundreds of footnotes, citing such testimonies. So long as he/she retains the Election Day fight, the killing of the three McCoy boys, the New Year's raid, the killing of Jim Vance, the Battle of Grapevine and the hanging of Ellison Mounts, the author could flesh it out with 200 pages of totally false filler material, most of it supported by footnotes, and no one except the handful of serious feud scholars would be aware of the deception.

I grew up thinking a brain-matter shoe shine must have been a post-murder ritual back in the feud times, because many other oldsters assured me that, when Frank Phillips killed Jim Vance, the other Bud McCoy, son of the murdered Asa Harmon, greased his boots with Uncle Jim's brains. For some inexplicable reason, the brains and shoes stories escaped the attention of almost all of the feud writers, and we are better off for that.

The silence about the feud was broken in 1952, when we were shown the 1949 movie *Roseanna McCoy* at Blackberry Grade School. The feud was all the talk for days on end. To top it off, someone on the school staff procured for the library a copy of Virgil C. Jones' 1948 book, *The Hatfields & the McCoys*, which I immediately checked out and read through the first night.

Of course I started pumping all the old folks for information and taking notes as soon as I read the book. Mom was not much help, knowing only that the McCoys killed a Hatfield at the election; Devil Anse killed the McCoys involved and then burned the McCoy house and killed two more McCoys some years later. And Jim Vance shined his boots with young Bud McCoy's brains.

Grandma Dotson (nee Hatfield) was a little more informative; she said she could only remember the burning of the McCoy home and the killing of Ran'l's two children and the beating of Sally, which happened when she was nine years old. She was also at the burial of Calvin and Alifair. She had been told that Devil Anse also murdered three of Ran'l's sons, but she was only three years old then and did not remember it. She assured me that Devil Anse was a thoroughly evil man, richly deserving of his moniker, Devil Anse.

Then she told me that she had been told that during the Civil War, Devil Anse robbed Grandpa Jordan Dotson and shot Uncle Reuben Dotson, crippling him for life. I filed that away in the folklore file for nearly half a century, until I read the 1985–86 annual edition of *West Virginia History*, sometime around the year 2000.[7]

Genealogies are confusing, but the reader has probably noticed the irony in the story of my ancestors: My four grandparents were named Hatfield, McCoy, Dotson and Smith. None of my Hatfield or McCoy ancestors was ever involved in any violence involving Devil Anse Hatfield or Ran'l McCoy, but several of my Dotson ancestors and my great grandfather Smith were.[8]

My great-great uncle, Ransom Hatfield, who was two years younger than his niece, Grandma Dotson, was the youngest son of Preacher Anse Hatfield. He lived in the old home place of his father, where the events of 1882 took place. He was an old-fashioned, self-read lawyer, who had an eidetic memory and some proclivity for John Barleycorn. I delivered the *Williamson Daily News* at the time, and Uncle Ransom was near the end of my route. I would drop off his paper and then complete the route on my bicycle in seven or eight minutes. By the time I got back to his house, he would have digested the news, and he loved to sit on the front porch and discuss the news with me.

The photo below, courtesy of Ron G Blackburn, a grandson of Ransom Hatfield and a family historian, shows Uncle

Ransom Hatfield in the center, with a neighbor and Ransom's grandson, C.R. Norman. They are standing in front of Preacher Anse Hatfield's home place, where Ransom lived over fifty of his seventy-five years.

Ransom Hatfield Cornnie Norman

As you can see in the photo, Cornie Norman has a bundle of copies of *The Williamson Daily News* under his arm; having just delivered the one Uncle Ransom is holding in his left hand. Notice the intense look on the boy's face as he listens to what his elders are saying. Cornie Norman grew up to be the best teacher I ever had in school. Uncle Ransom was the best teacher I ever had on the front porch. Ransom Hatfield never told me anything about the history of the Valley that turned out to be untrue.

Uncle Jeff Hatfield, Ransom's elder brother, lived with a daughter directly across the creek from the home place, where the 1882 Election Day murders occurred. Jeff was older than Ransom, and remembered the 1882 election, which occurred about the time Ransom was weaned. Uncle Jeff would answer a question, but he was much more reserved than was his lawyer brother.

Both remembered the Hatfields riding by on the night of the house-burning and murders of the two children of Ran'l McCoy, on January 1, 1888. Both had clear memories of the 1889 trials of Wall Hatfield and the others, some of which each attended with their father, Preacher Anse, who was a major witness against the West Virginia Hatfields.

The day after I got the Jones book, I showed it to Uncle Ransom after delivering his paper to him and asked him to tell me about the feud. He told me to wait a minute, and he went inside, returning with a copy of the same book. He opened the front cover and showed me that it was signed by the author. Then he said, "I'm in that book."

I knew he was joshing because I had read the book the night before, and I knew he was not mentioned. He waited a few seconds and then said, "Here it is," pointing to a footnote that read, "These words stuck firmly in the memory of the Reverend Anderson Hatfield."[9]

I had wondered, when I read that footnote, how Jones knew what had "stuck firmly in the memory of Preacher Anse," who had been dead more than twenty-five years at the time Jones did his research. Uncle Ransom said Jones interviewed him, and, after securing Jones' promise not to quote him directly he had told

Jones everything he knew about the subject. The words referred to are the boast of Tolbert McCoy, "I'm Hell on earth," and Ellison Hatfield's rejoinder, "You're a damn shit-hog." Those two and three more statements that he gave me, along with Cottontop Mounts' last words on the scaffold are the only six direct quotations from a feud participant which does not appear in a trial transcript that I could honestly repeat. The others are:

When Ransom's father, Preacher Anse, broke up the early fight between Tolbert McCoy and Anse's Brother, "Bad 'Lias" Hatfield, the preacher told McCoy, "Tolb, election day ain't no day to settle a debt."

When Devil Anse stomped out of the house the day after the wounding of Ellison, he stood on the end of the porch and said, "All friends of *Ellison* Hatfield stand over here." The statement is rendered in every book I have seen it in as "All friends of the Hatfields, line up (or stand) here." That statement, attributed to Devil Anse in virtually every feud book, is silly, once you think about it.

Devil Anse was standing on Preacher Anse's front porch, looking out into a yard where at least two thirds of the men were named Hatfield. The problem was that several of them were Kentucky Republican Unionists, friends of the McCoys and more closely related to Preacher Anse than to Devil Anse. To ask *all Friends of the Hatfields* to separate themselves from a group that is comprised mostly of Hatfields is ludicrous, but that's what the books say.

He said "friends of *Ellison* Hatfield," and that meant something to the men standing there.

The other quote that I am morally certain is correct is what Devil Anse said to Preacher Anse when he visited Devil Anse on Wednesday to try to bring the McCoy boys back to Kentucky. This misquote is not nearly as egregious as the previous one, but it results from conflating two statements from two different men.

Most books say either that Devil Anse was talking to Sally McCoy or to Preacher Anse, but Devil Anse did not talk to Sally McCoy. Most writers say that Devil Anse said, "If Ellison lives, the civil law can have them, but if Ellison dies, they will be killed."

We know what was said to Sally McCoy from her sworn testimony, which I believe to be truthful in every detail. It was Wall Hatfield, not Devil Anse who spoke to Sally, and he told her that if Ellison died, her boys "would be shot full of holes as a sifter bottom."[10]

What Devil Anse said to Preacher Anse was, "If Ellison lives, the Kentucky law can have them" — period. He did not say what would happen if Ellison died, because he knew that by stopping where he did, the preacher would know what he meant to do. Devil Anse was much too smart to make a killing threat to a man whom he knew could testify and be believed by any jury that he might face. So he left it hanging, and stopped short of the threat.

Of course everyone reading this probably knows what my other quote is, and it is: "The Hatfields made me do it." Those are the last words of Ellison Mounts, heard by many hundreds of people, and there is no doubt of their authenticity. In my opinion, those six words deny for all eternity the accusation that Cap Hatfield killed Alifair McCoy. If Cap Hatfield killed Alifair McCoy, as some claim, then that would mean that Cottontop Mounts was innocent. As everyone knows, the last words of an innocent man are "I didn't do it!"

There you have it. After growing up among some who were alive during the feud, and many who knew the feudists in later years, I have only six quotes that you can't read in a court record. So, if you bought this book to learn what color socks Johnse Hatfield wore while courting, or what Devil Anse thought when he was in the woods hunting, or what Frank Phillips said when he shot Jim Vance, or any of the other hundreds of direct quotations you can read in some books, you have wasted your money. I will not claim to know that which no mortal can possibly know.

Ransom Hatfield said that most of the events in the Jones book were things Jones had read in old books and newspapers or else just front-porch tales that various people had related to Jones and Jones had written them as history.

He said that almost everything Jones wrote about what happened after the paw paw murders and before the Frank Phillips raids--with the exception of the killing of Jeff McCoy-- was malarkey. He said that the bloody second phase occurred only because John Dils and Perry Cline and their gang of thieves over in Pikeville decided to take Devil Anse's land and started raiding into West Virginia. I dismissed that as probably just a country lawyer from the backside[11] of Pike County voicing his resentment of the elite who ruled the county, but it leaped out of the folklore file when I read Altina Waller's book, and was reinforced when I read two reported lawsuits.[12]

Uncle Ransom said that Jones read extensively from his notes, and asked him to verify or deny them. He said that they were almost all BS, and he told them so, but most of them showed up in the book anyway. I only have specific memory two of the tales he said he told Jones was spurious — the tale of the cow's tail, and the notorious "hog trial," both of which we will examine in detail later.

About halfway from Ransom's house to the other end of my paper route lived Uncle Elias Monroe Hatfield,[13] son of Constable Floyd Hatfield. He was born in the late 1870's. He lived until the 1960's and was as sharp in the mind as a twenty-year-old when I delivered papers to him in the mid-1950's. After I read the Virgil Jones book, I asked Uncle 'Lias what he knew about the feud. Elias was a former schoolteacher, who had read the Jones book himself. Of course he had also heard his father and uncles, who were at the 1882 election, tell about the killing of Ellison Hatfield, and the lynching of his killers.[14] Elias, himself, remembered the raid on the McCoy home on New Year's Day, 1888, and was at the burial of Calvin and Alifair.

The following is a family photo of Elias Monroe Hatfield on the right, with his father, Floyd Hatfield (not "Hog Floyd),[15] and Uncle Floyd's beautiful second wife, Jenny Hunt Hatfield.

Uncle Ransom sometimes got angry when talking about some of the tall tales in the Jones book, probably because having talked to Jones, he felt betrayed. Uncle 'Lias, on the other hand, would laugh heartily when talking about Jones' tall tales such as the cow's tail tale, or the "ambush of the innocents."

He said that there never was a Hatfield and McCoy feud, and that if he was a McCoy, he'd sue anyone who said there was such a thing as a Hatfield and McCoy feud. I told him that the movie I had recently seen and the Jones book said there was a Hatfield and McCoy feud, and asked him how come he was saying that there wasn't.

Uncle Lias asked me how I would like to have my Grandpa Phillip McCoy in the woods stalking me. I told him that I wouldn't like that at all; Grandpa Phillip could walk silently through dead leaves and hit anything he could see with his .32-20 Winchester. He asked me how many Hatfields were killed by McCoys in the book I had read, and I told him just the one, at the 1882 election. He then asked me how many Hatfields I thought my Grandpa Phillip could kill in a week if he took to the hills and started shooting at Hatfields. I reckoned it would be a passel of them, and told him so. He then asked me how many Hafields I thought that all of grandpa's cousins and uncles could kill in a decade.

He said it was downright ridiculous to claim that those men were in a ten-year feud and never killed a single enemy. He said that if he was a McCoy, he'd sue for slander anyone who said that his whole family was hunting Hatfields for ten years, and was so inept that they only killed one of them.

He said that the McCoys weren't willing to go to war over the three sons of Ran'l, who killed Ellison in broad daylight in front of a hundred witnesses, and therefore there never was a Hatfield and McCoy feud, and that the dearth of dead Hatfields proved it.

Elias said that I should tell everyone who asked me the same thing, and if challenged, I should simply ask: "If there was a Hatfield and McCoy feud, where's all the dead Hatfields?"

For several weeks after that conversation, every time he was outside when I delivered his paper, He'd ask me: "Found any dead Hatfields yet?" I'd usually just shake my head, and he'd laugh so loud I could hear him all the way to Frank Smith's house.

When I told Uncle Ransom what 'Lias had told me, Ransom—himself a lawyer—said he also believed that either a McCoy or a Hatfield could sue Jones and win, but it would be impossible to prove damages. So, unless you could prove actual malice and get punitive damages, Jones would get to keep all the money he had made on the book, even if he lost.[16] He also said that I had no "standing," as my McCoy descent was on the maternal side, and I didn't have the McCoy name which had been libeled. He said that he agreed with Elias that anyone who said that there was a Hatfield McCoy feud, was clearly inferring that dozens of McCoys were hunting Hatfields for many years, and only succeeded in killing one of them, and that accusing an entire family of such gross incompetence was indeed slanderous and probably actionable at law.

At the opposite end of my paper route was Uncle Jeff Davis, who was at the 1882 election where Ellison Hatfield was killed. Uncle Jeff owned and operated a general store. He was a nephew of Joe Davis, who was a friend of Devil Anse and a witness in the trials of 1889. Uncle Jeff remembered the Election Day fight, those trials and the New Year's raid. He was a Democrat and a former Justice of the Peace, who spent time with Cap Hatfield while reading the law. I tarried in his store long enough to have a soda many days, and heard his version of feud events.

Even though the Hatfield brothers, Jeff and Ransom, and Jeff Davis attended the trials, none of the three knew anyone who attended the hanging of Ellison Mounts. That huge crowd at the Mounts hanging obviously included very few people from Blackberry and Peter Creek. Pricy Scott, who grew up on Blackberry Fork of Pond Creek as a neighbor of Ran'l McCoy, was the only person I ever talked to who was at the hanging.

Although Uncle Jeff Davis was a Democrat, whose father and uncles were close friends of Devil Anse, and who had spent considerable time at Cap Hatfield's house while reading the law, his account of the basic facts of the events in August, 1882 and the New Year's raid in 1888 did not differ in any significant detail from that of Uncle Ransom, a Republican whose father testified against the Hatfields at their 1889 trials.

Of course, they all disagreed in almost all particulars with the description of the events presented in Dean King's *"True Story"* of the feud.

---

1 King, *True Story*, 4.
2 It did not occur to me until many years later that he rarely mentioned the killing of the three McCoys who killed Ellison.
3 Waller, Altina, *Feud*, 258.
4 Waller, *Feud*, 255-6.
5 Waller, *Feud*, 187-194.

6 Sold to Cotiga Land Company on July 3, 1989, Deed Book M, p. 136 Logan County Court House.

7 Daniel Cunningham, *The Horrible butcheries of West Virginia*, eds. Johnson and Ludwell in West Virginia History, Volume XLVI, 1985-86. Charleston, State of West Virginia, 1986

8 Curtis Smith, who rode in Frank Phillip's posse, is the only active "feudist" who is my direct ancestor.

9 Virgil C. Jones, *The Hatfields & McCoys* Chapel Hill, University of North Carolina Press, 1948, p. 42.

10 *Plyant Mayhon v. Commonwealth of Kentucky*, Case #19601, KDLA

11 The eastern part of Pike County, which is drained by tributaries of Tug River, and which borders Tug has been known from earliest days as "the backside of the county." That is still the case.

12 Williamson v. Dils, 114 *Kentucky Reports*, p. 962. And *Ellison v Torpin*, 30 *Southeastern Reporter*, 183

13 Elias, who had been widowed, was married to Victoria (Aunt Vic), the widow of my great Uncle, Anderson (Ancie) Hatfield. Uncle Ancie owned the Urias Hotel in Matewan, West Virginia, and was killed during the "Mine Wars."

14 Floyd Hatfield, father of Elias M., was the Constable who arrested the three McCoy boys at the 1882 Election, after they had killed Ellison Hatfield. He was, of course, not "Hog Floyd" as Dean King falsely claims in his *"True Story."*

15 When reading the following chapter, the reader will note that this is obviously the same Floyd Hatfield who is misidentified as "Hog Floyd" in Dean King's book. Even though he is twenty or so years older, his appearance hasn't really changed much.

16 I believe that the "actual malice" in the Dean King book is so patently obvious that he could be stripped of much of the money he has made on his farcical "history." While the McCoys have the same case against King that they had against Jones, the Hatfields have a much better case, because of the terribly damaging lie that King told about Ellison Hatfield starting the Election Day fight with a knife. As I have neither name, although descended from both, I still lack standing. My only chance of recovering anything from King would be for him to sue me for exposing his lies, thus opening up the opportunity for me to counterclaim. I doubt that I could be so lucky, but one can always hope.

# CHAPTER 5.

# THE PICTURE STORY

Novelists writing history are no more careful in their handling of photographs than they are in handling historical records. Dean King's dishonesty — or his complete lack of care in researching and writing — shows up also in his use of photographs. On page 53, there is a photo of my great-great uncle Floyd Hatfield, brother of Preacher Anse and the constable who took the three McCoy boys into custody after they killed Ellison Hatfield on Election Day, 1882. King has it in his chapter on the hog trial, attributed to Dr. Arabel Hatfield and captioned "Hog Floyd Hatfield."

Here is the same photo, from the West Virginia Division of History and Culture:

The caption on the West Virginia site correctly reads: "**Floyd Hatfield, Constable for District 7 of Pike County, made first <u>arrest</u> in famous Hatfield-McCoy <u>feud</u> August 7, 1882, on <u>Blackberry</u> Creek, Pike County, Kentucky.**"[1]

There are dozens of descendants of Constable Floyd Hatfield living within a few miles of the place where the hog trial took place, and they would certainly have been pleased to supply King with the identity of the man in the photo. For the record, my great-great-great-Uncle Floyd Hatfield, was not "Hog" Floyd Hatfield, as King's caption claims. Below is a photo of Uncle Floyd, with his second wife, Jenny Hunt Hatfield. This photo is owned by Floyd's grandson, Jack Hatfield. Anyone can plainly see that this is the same man that King claims to be "Hog Floyd."

Floyd Hatfield and second wife, Jennie

What happens to someone who doesn't know the difference between Constable Floyd Hatfield and "Hog" Floyd Hatfield, and who does not even care enough to ask the descendants when he interviews them? He becomes a recognized feud expert, who is featured on a History Channel documentary.

On page 120, King has a photo of three large male corpses, all of them obviously mature men of large frame, with this caption: "Tolbert, Pharmer and Bud McCoy, laid out for burial at their parents' house."

**Kentucky Historical Society**

King correctly credits the photo to the Kentucky Historical Society. The title of the photograph on the Kentucky Historical Society website is: "Men, possibly the *Hatfield* family, display three of their dead." Of course this title is just as erroneous as King's caption, as there is no case where three Hatfields lay dead at the same time. When I contacted the Society, I was told that their provenance was the word of the auctioneer, from which the photo was bought.

Tolbert McCoy, who is described as a slender man by every person I talked to who saw him alive and by every previous writer, and is described by King himself as both smaller and quicker than Ellison Hatfield, is presented in King's photo as a man similar in size to an NFL lineman.

There were no photographers in Pikeville in 1882. There are no authenticated photographs taken anywhere in the Tug Valley part of Pike County as early as 1882, yet we are expected to believe that someone made a dash from Catlettsburg or Charleston or some other city to Blackberry Fork during the single day between the time the corpses were retrieved and the time they were buried. We are asked to believe this photographer took no other photographs that were worth saving. And, to top it off, we are expected to believe that this photograph, which, had it existed, would have been reported—most likely with an artist's reproduction—on the front page of every big newspaper in the country in 1888, was lost until it was discovered just in time to appear in King's *"True Story."*

The best information I have found on the photo is that it shows three men who were killed in a gun battle between Bad Lewis Hall and some men named Steele, in Perryville West Virginia in May, 1891. Bad Lewis made the participants in our feud look like choir boys. He was known to have killed over a dozen men, and claimed twenty-two victims in his frequent boasting about his badness. One of his sons was killed in the gun battle with the Steeles, and another died with Bad Lewis when a Pike County Constable shot and killed the eighty-three year old Hall and his son, Morgan while they were resisting arrest for bootlegging in 1912.

When Hall reached his belated expiration date in February, 1912, the Big Sandy News said: "LOUIS HALL and his son MORGAN were killed at MILLARD BURKE'S STORE, SHELBY GAP, PIKE COUNTY, by CONSTABLE GEORGE JOHNSON, who had a warrant for MORGAN'S arrest. They resisted and the officer shot both, killing them instantly. The charge was illicit liquor selling. LOUIS HALL was 83 years old and had a bad record. He killed three men named STEEL (sic) on TUG about ten years ago in a fight over whiskey." (Emphasis in original.)

Lewis Hall, who killed a son of General John Hunt Morgan and a dozen other men, is not nearly as famous as Ran'l McCoy, who never killed anyone.[2] The fact that three of Bad Lewis Hall's victims are being used to supersize Ol' Ran'l's feud is more proof that life just isn't fair.

King begins Chapter 9 with a detailed description of the bogus "McCoy brother's photograph." Of the three corpses that are identified as "Hatfields" on the source he cites for his photo, King says: "The three McCoy brothers, who in the midsummer heat had been laid out outside on the porch at Randall and Sally's, were photographed for posterity."[3] Yes, photographed "for posterity," but kept hidden for one hundred thirty years, until discovered just in time to be in the book! Does he really think his readers will believe that Ran'l McCoy had such a photograph and did not show it to Spears, Howell or any of the other reporters who came to his house in 1888?

As in many other places, I am convinced that King knew he was misstating when he said that the three corpses were on Ran'l McCoy's porch. He must know that Ran'l McCoy lived in a log house while the building in the photo has a plank wall. The planks have cracks between that Ran'l could have thrown his cat through, meaning that the building is probably a barn, and not a dwelling at all. The flimsy posts supporting the plank wall also denote an outbuilding and not a dwelling. If Ran'l McCoy's family had lived in a building with walls like the one in the photo, they would have all frozen to death before the Hatfield raiders got there on New Year's Day, 1888.

King knows why the wrists of the corpses are bound, because he says so: He says that it was to "keep them in place,"[4] which is correct. Then he shows a shocking lack of knowledge of the era he writes about, by saying: "Tolbert's and Bud's skulls are held together by fresh white bandages."[5] If King had paid closer attention when he watched Dickens's *A Christmas Carol*, then he would know why those were "fresh white bandages." They are fresh, because, like the bandage worn by the ghost of Jacob Marley; they were placed there posthumously, long after any bleeding had stopped, *to hold their mouths shut!* If King had read the classic Dickens novel, he'd know that when the ghost of Marley took the bandage off, "its lower jaw dropped down upon its breast."

If the skulls needed something to hold them together, the loose parts would have been long-since missing before the corpses reached Ran'l's house, as they were hauled about seven miles over rough ground in a sled to get them home.

On page 22, King has an unattributed photo of a man who appears to be in his late twenties or early thirties, captioned "Randall McCoy." I am sure that there have been several men named Randall McCoy — and the man in that photo may be one of them. It is not, however, a photograph of Randolph McCoy, born 1825, the father of Tolbert, Pharmer and Bud. There are no authenticated pre-Civil War photos of any of the feudists. This also means that the well-dressed young man with a crew-cut on page 37 is not the Asa Harmon McCoy who was shot dead in 1865, even though King labels it as such. There have been men named Asa Harmon in several generations, so it may be one of them, but the old soldier who died in January, 1865, it most certainly is not![6]

Both of those photos feature a clothing style that appeared first in the 1880's. By that time, Asa Harmon had been dead twenty or more years, and Ran'l was in his sixties. Again, King must know these photos are not what he says that they are.

There is a photograph of a man who appears to be in his mid-to-late thirties, on page 26, labeled "Devil Anse Hatfield." No ifs, ands or buts — it's captioned "Devil Anse Hatfield."

Coleman Hatfield has the same photo on page 220 of his book, *Tale of the Devil.* Although Dr. Hatfield called his book a tale and not a history, he is much more careful of facts than is King, the writer of the *"True Story."* Hatfield says that the photo "is believed to be Anderson "Devil Anse" Hatfield, *or a close relative!"* (Italics mine) That author, a grandson of Cap Hatfield and great grandson of Devil Anse, says the photo is either Devil Anse or a close relative. In other words, the Hatfield family thinks the photo is of a kinsman, who could have been Devil Anse, but they can't say for sure. Mr. King says it is Devil Anse, without equivocation.

My personal view on this photo is that it very well could be Devil Anse. Hatfield and Spence say that the man is in his mid-thirties. As this would place it in the mid-1870's, by which time Devil Anse was a prosperous timber man, who visited places like Charleston and Catlettsburg, where photographs were readily available, it could very well be Devil Anse. To say that Devil Anse *may have been* photographed in a nearby city in the mid-1870's is light years from saying that someone definitely took photos of Asa and Ran'l on the backside of Pike County a decade earlier. John Dils was the richest man in Pike County, and lawyer Perry Cline was his protégé. To my knowledge, there are no published photographs of John Dils, who died in 1895, and only one of Perry Cline, taken a couple of years before he died in 1891. The authenticity of the one photograph of Perry Cline is questioned by certain Cline descendants

There is a resemblance in King's photo to Devil Anse in later photos; however, as the nose does not have quite as much hook as the later photos show, I have to side with the great-grandson of Devil Anse, Coleman Hatfield, and say it is probably a Hatfield, and *may be* Devil Anse himself, but no one (except King, apparently) can say for sure.

On page 175, King has an unsourced photo of several men at a structure which may or may not be a moonshine still. The photo is captioned: "A mountain still, purported to belong to the McCoys." King does not say which McCoys are shown, nor does he say who it is that "purports" them to be McCoys. As there is no documented evidence that any of the Tug Valley McCoys were engaged in illegal whiskey-making during the "feud era," this photo is highly suspect. No wonder it is not attributed to anyone in King's book. It is just another example of King's apparent fixation on "moonshine."

I don't know where to start with Lisa Alther's handling of photographs. The only explanation I can think of is that she was in a hurry to get the book out soon in the wake of the hit TV movie.

Alther has the same photo of my Uncle Floyd Hatfield that Dean King has, and she also says it is the Floyd of hog trial fame.[7]

She also has an artist's black and white portrait from the West Virginia State Archives that she presents as if it were an actual photograph of Asa Harmon McCoy, who died in 1865.[8] As it is a black and white portrait, of course the subject has black hair. The hair also has some waves, giving Alther her black, curly haired Asa Harmon, who tried to hide his racial mixture by "slicking down his curls."[9]

**West Virginia Division of Culture and History**

The problem is that the person in the portrait is *not* Asa Harmon McCoy, the West Virginia Archives notwithstanding. The portrait was done by an artist, using a photo of Billy Phillips, father of Frank Phillips. Some Phillips heirs think that the misidentification could have come from someone who was descended from both Billy Phillips and Asa Harmon McCoy being confused as to which grandfather or great grandfather it was. Remember that Billy's son, Frank, married Asa Harmon's daughter, Nancy.

Billy Phillips, a member of Company H of John Dils's 39th Kentucky, died in Confederate captivity.

Alther also has the much-traveled portrait of Frank Phillips (obviously by the same artist who did the above portrait of Frank's father), from the West Virginia Division of Culture and Archives:

Alther identifies this portrait as "a strange undated photo-graph." I am at a loss for words to describe someone who thinks that is *a photograph*. She comments on his "coal black mustache." Of course any mustache in a black and white portrait is "coal black," but she really thinks she is looking at a photograph! She says that Frank, in the "photo," has "a bone or ivory-handled pistol hanging across his abdomen."[10]

What is to be said of someone who thinks that is a photograph of an actual pistol in that portrait? It looks much more like a bone or an ivory tusk than a "bone or ivory-handled *pistol*." We shall see later what a *real* revolver looks like to this "feud expert."

There is a black and white portrait of Colonel John Dils which was obviously done by the same artist who did those of Billy and

Frank Phillips shown here.[11] Both of the cited sources date the portrait from 1876. *A Pictorial History* says that it was done by a Philadelphia artist, while Dils and his wife were in that city, celebrating the nation's Centennial. It seems logical that Dils also arranged for his foster son, Frank Phillips, to have the same artist do portraits from photographs of Frank and his father sometime after the Colonel returned from Philadelphia.

Lisa Alther says of this image, which is labeled a painting from 1876: "A photo of Colonel Dils, taken shortly after the *war* shows a lean and handsome man with dark hair, eyes, and eyebrows." (sic) As she cites the website given below, she must be referring to the 1876 portrait, which is identified on the site as *a painting*, done in 1876. As she obviously knows that she is describing a painting from 1876, her reasons for saying that it is *a photograph, taken shortly after the war*, is a mystery for her readers until they get far enough into her book to see her "mixed race" McCoys.

Her reason for referring to "dark hair, eyes and eyebrows," in describing a black and white portrait must be to convey to her readers that Dils, both of whose parents were born in Germany, was of mixed race, just like her McCoys.

As one of my main purposes for writing this book is to show youngsters how not to do historical research, I hope every reader at least doubts the veracity of any writer who intentionally misrepresents photographs. No matter how may reviewers from big-city newspapers laud a writer as a "historian," or a "feud expert," a portrait is not a photograph and a man who died in 1865 was never photographed wearing clothes from the 1880's.

---

1 http://www.wvculture.org/history/hatfield/htfld032.html
2 The success of the supersizers is evident on the website of the Biography TV channel. Ran'l McCoy, who has never been accused—not even by the supersizers-- of killing anyone in his life, has an entry there. His occupation is given as "murderer."

3  King, Dean, *The Feud*, 119.

4  Ibid.

5  Ibid.  In fact, all three corpses have the jaw-supporting bandages; not just "Tolbert" and "Bud."

6  Both the Randall McCoy and the Asa Harmon McCoy photos in King's book have been commented on by Maureen Taylor, a recognized photographic expert, who dates them in the late 1880's to 1890's. Asa Harmon McCoy was dead about a quarter of a century before that photo was taken, and Ran'l McCoy was at least 60 years old.  http://www.maureentaylor.com/

7  Alther, 42.  Alther got it from the West Virginia Department of Culture and History, as did I.

8  Alther, 5.

9  Alther, 3.

10  Alther, 85.

11  I don't have permission to use the image, but the reader can find it easily enough by doing a Google search for "John Dils," and clicking on "images." The image also appears on page 80 of "Pike County, Kentucky: A Pictorial History, by Ed and Connie Maddox. Donning Company, 1998. Robert Baker has the portrait on his 39th Regiment site at http://www.reocities.com/rmbaker66/jnodils.html

# CHAPTER 6.

# THE PLAYER NO ONE PLAYED IN THE MOVIE

John Dils is not even mentioned in Costner's movie. That is regrettable, but most authors also ignore him. I believe Colonel John Dils to have been the most important man on the Kentucky side of the feud. I said that I *believe* Colonel Dils was the most important man on the Kentucky side; I did not say that I can *prove* that he was. What I will do in this book is provide the basis for my belief, and try to make the case as strongly as I can, given the deep mystery surrounding the man. So deep is the mystery that not a single photograph has ever been published, even though he lived until the time when photography was widespread. You may not be convinced, but I hope you are at least entertained.

**COLONEL JOHN DILS, JR.**

**From Ely's "Big Sandy"**

John Dils was the richest — and, therefore, the most powerful — man in Pike County during the 1880s. The leading Unionist in Pike County, he was a colonel in the Union army, and after he was cashiered for stealing, he became a bushwhacker along the border.

The murky history of John Dils, Jr., begins before he was born in 1818, in Wood County Virginia (Now West Virginia). His father, John Dils, Sr., was a neighbor of Prince Blennerhassett of Aaron Burr fame. When the Burr Conspiracy fell apart, and Blennerhassett went bankrupt, Dils wound up with much of Blennerhassett's former wealth, including the celebrated continental slave tutor, Ransom, who guided the education of the young John Dils, Jr.[1]

Dils came to Piketon, Kentucky (now Pikeville) in 1842. He quickly married the daughter of the richest man in the county, General William Ratliff, and went into the riverboat and mercantile businesses. Dils's business thrived, and he soon became the leading figure in Pike County. In the late 1840s, he established a large tannery near Pikeville, which thrived on the labor of his slaves and low-wage colored freed men.

Dils raised a company, of which he was elected Captain, for service in the Mexican War, but was never deployed. A Colonel in the Union Army during the Civil War, he was discharged for thievery in December, 1863.

Dils was the biggest buyer of land in Pike County during the post-Civil War period until his death in 1895 and was the foster father of both Perry Cline and Frank Phillips. I believe it was Dils's lifelong hatred of Confederate guerillas/bushwhackers, combined with his desire for the five thousand acres Devil Anse had wrested from Perry Cline, which led to the revival of the feud in 1887 which became the bloodiest part of the entire affair.

The record shows that John Dils bought one hundred fifteen tracts of land by way of land warrants from Pike County, Kentucky between 1865 and 1882.[2] He probably bought at least that much more land from private parties during that period, making him easily the biggest player in gathering up the riches of Pike County for big Eastern money. Anyone who doubts that John Dils was involved in acquiring Pike County land in a big way needs only to read the case of Williamson vs. Dils.[3]

In this case, decided in 1896, we see that Dils had bought thirty thousand acres along Peter Creek and the Tug River. Dils bought that land from the county for twelve and one-half cents per acre in 1872; fifteen years before the big push against Devil Anse began. The land was across the river from the old Cline home place, where Devil Anse lived from 1872-88, and just up-river from the five thousand acres that Anse took from Perry Cline.

After the railroad was built in West Virginia, Dils, knowing the value of his land on the wrong side of the river would not increase greatly in value until bridges were built across the river and spur track laid up the Kentucky creeks, sold the land. He did not sell all his interest at once. The last third interest was sold in 1892, to Wallace J. Williamson, the man for whom Williamson, West Virginia was named.

Williamson was himself a smooth operator, having become very wealthy buying and flipping land and mineral rights, but he was out of his league with John Dils. The sale contract called for one-third interest in approximately eighteen thousand acres, at a price of two dollars an acre. Land that Dils had bought in the 1870s for twelve and one-half cents per acre was now worth six dollars per acre. You can build a lot of mansions on a few deals like that.

The land had never been surveyed, so the exact acreage contained in the boundaries was not known. As part of the contract, Dils got Williamson to agree to have the land surveyed, at Williamson's expense, and the final deal would be two dollars per acre for a one-third interest in whatever acreage the survey found. Williamson had six months to get the survey done, and if he didn't get the survey, he had to pay Dils for eighteen thousand acres.

When Williamson sent a surveying crew to the property, he got a jolt. There were several families claiming ownership that had been living on the land for a generation or more. For readers who are not familiar with the places we are talking about, let me assure you that there is no better way to get yourself shot dead than to go onto someone's land on Peter Creek and tell the man in residence that he doesn't own what his Pappy left him. It wouldn't work today, and it certainly didn't work in 1892. People with venerable old Peter Creek names like Blankenship, Dotson and Hurley, created a very hostile work environment for Williamson's surveyors, by firing at them from the timber with their Winchesters.

When the first surveying crew beat a hasty retreat, Williamson sent in another crew, with the same result. The word had gotten around; Williamson couldn't get any more surveyors to accept duty in a combat zone, so he was faced with paying Dils thirty-six thousand dollars, a veritable fortune in 1892, for a one-third interest in eighteen thousand acres when, absent a survey, there might not be half that much.

Then Williamson did something that was usually a very stupid mistake; he sued John Dils to get his two thousand dollars earnest money deposit back — in Pikeville!  Suing John Dils in Pikeville, Kentucky in 1892 was generally equivalent to suing Adolf Hitler in Berlin in 1938, and the result was what you would expect.  Dils countersued, demanding specific performance of the contract. The court, owned of course by Colonel Dils, ordered Williamson to cough up the thirty-six grand.  Williamson, having the wherewithal to fight Dils, then took the case away from Dils's cronies in Pikeville, by appealing the decision.

The Court of Appeals reversed Dils's hometown judge and ordered Dils to refund the earnest money deposit to Williamson. The Appeals Court's language shows that they had Colonel Dils's number, as the opinion said that Dils had known before the contract was signed that Williamson could never successfully complete a survey, because Dils knew that any survey crew would meet armed resistance.  It just goes to show that you never know what will happen when one big fish tries to swallow another big fish; especially when a school of minnows is swimming in the same waters with Winchester rifles.

I don't know what finally happened to the land — Dils died in 1895 — but I hope some Blankenship and Hurley heirs are enjoying peaceful possession of it today.

Dils's land deals come up again in the case of Parsons v Dils.[4]

This case arose out of the actions of Dils's heirs in cutting timber from one thousand twenty-five acres in Pike County, beginning in 1902, seven years after Dils's death.  Eight hundred twenty-five acres of the land were in five tracts, which had been acquired from the Jailer of Pike County.  An auction sale was scheduled, but, in some unexplained fashion, the land was sold before the auction, and ended up in the name of John Dils. This shows the importance of controlling county offices to an operator like John Dils, and why it was important to him to have his foster son, Perry Cline, in the position of Deputy Jailer.

Again, as in the Williamson case, the Pike Circuit Court unsurprisingly decided for the Dils heirs. Parsons appealed, and the court of appeals reversed the Pike Court. It is obvious that Dils never reached the level that John C.C. Mayo attained, as Dils frequently won in his wholly-owned Pike Court, only to be reversed by the State Court of Appeals. Mayo owned them all.

The Dils heirs then brought the case back up, claiming new evidence of their ownership by adverse possession. Of course, the Dils heirs won again in the Pike Court, and this time, the Court of Appeals, faced with a matter of the lower court's fact-finding rather than a matter of law, affirmed the decision. It seems that when the little guy took on John Dils or his heirs, he lost even when he won.

The court doesn't say how the jailer came to own the land. Maybe it was bought by the county for a work farm; we don't know. All we know is that it ended up in the name of John Dils, and he didn't even have to bid at an auction.

One historian wrote that Dils flooded the courts with postwar lawsuits against the Rebel raiders who repeatedly robbed his various businesses during the war: "While he succeeded in getting judgments, it became nearly impossible to collect restitution... he secured numerous government contracts to carry the mail throughout Pike County...and between Louisa and Piketon."[5]

As the disgraced Colonel Dils was on the winning side of the war, reconstruction in Pike County meant mainly the reconstruction of the fortune of John Dils. The power of Colonel Dils is evident in the fact that several former Confederates supported him in the lawsuits Dils filed after the war.[6] It is ironic that Dils made money after the war by carrying the mail over the very same Louisa-to-Pikeville route that he used government transport to haul his merchandise over during the war, and for which he was dishonorably discharged.

If you visit Pikeville today, you will see and hear much about the great Colonel Dils. The tourism folks will point out the various mansions he built for himself and his children. You might even stay in one, which is a bed and breakfast, called *The Historic Mansion.*[7]

**1. Pikeville B&B, once owned by a Dils daughter.**

What you will not be told by the tourism folks is how the colonel came to be separated from the regiment he raised and wound up leading an irregular band of guerilla raiders for the last third of the war.

Special Order #548, issued December 10, 1863, and signed by Secretary of War Stanton, dishonorably discharged the Colonel. The Special Order says: "By direction of the President, Colonel John Dils, 39th Mounted Infantry, is hereby dishonorably dismissed from the service of the United States for selling captured property; and using the proceeds for his own use, using government transportation for private purposes, improper treatment of a Non-Commissioned Officer (NCO) while the NCO was in the discharge of his duty, and incompetetancy (sic")."[8]

In addition to his thievery, Dils also kept a paramour named Carolyn Rose in his headquarters tent, whenever he was in the field and away from home. The secretary had that evidence before him, but, knowing what went on virtually every night at the headquarters of General Joe Hooker, I guess the secretary thought it politic to leave Dils's extramarital sex life out of his list of charges.[9]

After being cashiered as a thief, Dils organized a Home Guard, composed of a core of deserters from the 39th and various and sundry local ne'er-do-wells, and continued to raid, rob, and pillage for the duration of the war. A little thing like a dishonorable discharge ordered by the president himself was no hindrance to a man of John Dils's audacity.

Strangely enough, the only places we find Dils connected directly to the feud are in things written by his friends and admirers. The advertising flyer for the bed and breakfast in Pikeville, which is one of the houses Dils built for one of his daughters, says, "He built a successful riverboat trade, then became a colonel in the Civil War. Later he was part of a group formed to legally quiet the Hatfield & McCoy Feud."[10] Note the word *legally*.

The Pikeville, Kentucky, website, has a page for the Garfield Community Center, which says, "The Garfield Annex Building, named in honor of President Garfield, is a large structure that was owned by Colonel John Dils, Jr.... He was a prominent businessman who was said to be admired or hated, depending on who you asked. It is believed that some banks were targeted for robbery because of Dils accounts. It is also believed that *he was heavily involved in the later stages of the Hatfield-McCoy Feud*."[11]

(Italics mine)

**2. Pikeville Community Center, once owned by Dils**

The website of Dils's 39th Kentucky Mounted Infantry has this: "After his dismissal from the 39th, it is believed that the Colonel continued serving the Union as a partisan leader or bushwhacker. In early November of 1864, he was captured by Bill Smith and his band of cavalry. Since Dils survived the war, it is assumed that he was able to bargain for his freedom a second time. I wonder what he had to do to secure his liberty. *He also had some sort of involvement with the Hatfield-McCoy feud.* The information about Colonel Dils is very sparse. He is a very enigmatic individual. There are two very common views of him in his native Pike County, KY: he was either a great hero or the worst sort of scoundrel."[12] (Italics mine)

It has always puzzled me that people who are admirers of John Dils always refer to his involvement in the Hatfield and McCoy feud, but most of the feud writers seem to be unaware of it. John Dils signed one of Ellison Mounts' confessions. This definitely shows more than a passing interest in the feud on the part of the Colonel.

Note also that the City of Pikeville's website does not only say that Dils was involved in the latter stages of the feud, he was *"heavily involved!"*

While there is no known photograph of Dils's residence, which was razed in the 1940's, there is a drawing in the Ely book, on page 46.

**Residence of Colonel John Dils, Jr., Piketon, Ky**

The larger conflict between Dils and Devil Anse was ongoing during the years when there was no conflict between Anse and any of the McCoys. In 1873, Devil Anse made a deal with John Smith, a merchant at the mouth of Pond Creek, whereby Smith would allow Anse and his crew to obtain supplies from Smith's store and Anse would pay him back with a certain amount of timber to be delivered the next year. Anse delivered on time, but found that Smith had over-charged him by several thousand dollars, so he sued the merchant, who then counter-claimed against Anse. This suit, which continued for more than three years, brought Anse to the brink of bankruptcy.

John Smith, whose store was on the Tug River at the mouth of Pond Creek, 25 miles from Pikeville, had a partner. That partner was John Dils, of Pikeville. Devil Anse was just one of many Tug Valley men that Dils and his partner sued during the 1870s and 1880s. It was almost always a suit for collection of money claimed due to the merchants from the Tug Valley folks.[13]

Dils's dealings with the Tug Valley residents were, in most cases, just a continuation of the war by other means. Dils did not break Anse in the lawsuit, but he never gave up trying until Anse surrendered his five thousand acres in 1888.

---

1  Pikeville Historic Mansion, Bed and Breakfast.
http://www.pikevillehistoricmansion.com/OurHistory.html
2  Waller, Feud, 281, n.5.
3  Williamson v Dils, Kentucky Reporter, Vol 114, 962.
4  *Parsons v. Dils, 189 Southwestern Reporter, 1158.*
5  "McKnight, Brian D. *Contested borderland: The Civil War in Appalachian Kentucky and Virginia*". Lexington, Ky, 2012. 231-232.
6  Weaver, Jeffrey, *Bushwhacker's Paradise*, 104.
7  http://www.pikevillehistoricmansion.com/
8  http://files.usgwarchives.net/ky/pike/bios/dils.txt    http://www.reocities.com/rmbaker66/jnodils.html
9  Weaver, Jeffrey C., *Bushwhacker's Paradise*, 103.
10  http://www.pikevillehistoricmansion.com/OurHistory.html#OurHistory
11  http://visitpikevillc.com/garfield-community-center/
12  http://www.reocities.com/rmbaker66/jnodils.html
13  Waller, 45-49, is a good recap of the entire proceedings, and is the basis for most of what I say about the Smith case.

## Hatfield-McCoy Timeline

**1740-1760:** Most of the Hatfields, McCoys and associated families came to America.

**1795-1825:** Most of the families came to Tug Valley.

**1861:** Devil Anse a border raider. Colonel John Dils arrested by Confederates and sent to Libby prison in Richmond, Virginia—paroled after two months.

**1862:** Devil Anse joins Confederate Virginia State Line, elected 1st Lieutenant.  Colonel Dils organizes the 39th Kentucky Mounted Infantry Regiment. Dils's 39th defeated at Wireman's Shoals and Bull Mountain by VSL cavalry, including Devil Anse Hatfield.

**1863:** Dils raids Logan County, VSL raids Pike County. Ran'l McCoy captured in July. VSL disbanded and Devil Anse joins 45th Battalion, elected 1st Lieutenant of cavalry. Colonel Dils discharged by order of President Lincoln for thievery and incompetence.

**1864:** Devil Anse deserts regular army and forms guerilla band, raiding in border area and riding with Rebel Bill Smith's raiders, robs stores belonging to Dils and other Pike County merchants, capturing and ransoming Colonel Dils. Dils forms Unionist raider group, raiding border area, including burning the town of Wise, Virginia.

**1865:** Asa Harmon McCoy killed by Devil Anse's raiders. War ends.

**1868:** Devil Anse enters upon five thousand acres of Grapevine Creek land owned by Perry Cline. Cline chooses Dils as legal guardian.

1868-1890: John Dils buys hundreds of tracts of Pike County land, including thirty thousand acres directly across Tug River from land owned by Devil Anse.

1871: Devil Anse trades Perry Cline land on Kentucky side for the far more valuable Cline home place on West Virginia side.

1872: Devil Anse files suit against Perry Cline, claiming the five thousand acres on Grapevine is his. Cline moves to Pikeville.

1873: Pond Creek store owned by John Dils and a partner sues Devil Anse, putting Anse in danger of bankruptcy.

1874: Perry Cline elected Sheriff of Pike County, at age 25, after only two years in residence.

1877: Perry Cline, faced with the possibility of an adverse judgment in Logan County court, settles suit with Devil Anse by signing over all he inherited from his father on Grapevine Creek.

1878: Ran'l McCoy charges Floyd Hatfield, a cousin of both Devil Anse and Preacher Anse of stealing a hog. Trial held in Preacher Anse's court, where jury decides in favor of Floyd Hatfield. Ran'l McCoy upset, but Devil Anse not involved in the case.

1880: In West Virginia, Sam and Paris McCoy, Ran'l's nephews, kill Bill Staton, who testified for Floyd Hatfield in the hog trial. Paris McCoy found not guilty in Staton killing by a Hatfield-controlled court in West Virginia, on grounds of self-defense.

Johnse Hatfield takes Roseanna McCoy home with him from the election on Blackberry Creek. Roseanna returns home after a few weeks, pregnant and still a McCoy.

Roseanna's brother, Tolbert, accompanied by his younger brother, Bud, arrests Johnse on a charge of carrying a concealed weapon. Devil Anse, informed by Roseanna, intercepts party on way to Pikeville and forces release of Johnse.

**1881:** Johnse Hatfield marries Nancy McCoy, daughter of slain Union soldier, Asa Harmon McCoy.

**1882:** In Hatfield controlled court in West Virginia, Sam McCoy found not guilty in killing Bill Staton, on grounds of "self defense."

Ellison Hatfield killed by three McCoy sons of Ran'l, Tolbert, Pharmer and Bud. The three killers of Ellison are executed by Devil Anse and company. Devil Anse and nineteen supporters indicted for the murders in Pike County.

**1883-1885:** Ran'l McCoy complains to everyone, including Pike County officials, about the lynching of his three sons. Nothing else feud-related happened, except in the supersized feud stories

**1886:** Cap Hatfield and Tom Wallace visit home of Bill Daniels, father of Wallace's estranged wife, Victoria. Situation turns ugly and one or more of the Daniels womenfolk are assaulted.

Jeff McCoy, son of Asa Harmon McCoy and sister of Mary Daniels, who was mother of Wallace's wife, Victoria, attempts revenge on Wallace, shooting into the home of Cap Hatfield, where Wallace is hiding.

Cap Hatfield arrests Jeff McCoy and then shoots him dead as Jeff exits Tug River on the Kentucky side. Devil Anse writes conciliatory letter to Perry Cline, disavowing Cap's shooting of Jeff McCoy, Cline's nephew.

**1887:** Devil Anse writes strongly worded letter to Perry Cline, cautioning against an invasion of Logan County, telling him to "back off, or else."

Kentucky governor, under pressure from Dils and his Pikeville cohort, who want Devil Anse's land, issues extradition requests for Hatfields in the execution of the three McCoys in 1882, and publishes larger rewards for their capture. Governor appoints Bad Frank Phillips, son of a Union soldier who died in a POW camp and also a foster son of Colonel John Dils to "receive" the Hatfields. Phillips leads posse made up of three fourths Pikeville area men unconnected to Ran'l McCoy on illegal invasions of West Virginia, where he kidnaps several Hatfield associates and murders two.

1888: Pressured by the Phillips raids, on New Year's Day, a squad led by Jim Vance and Cap Hatfield burn the home of Ran'l McCoy. Two more of Ran'l McCoy's children, Calvin and Alifair, are killed, and his wife Sally maimed.

Jim Vance murdered in West Virginia by Frank Phillips. Devil Anse capitulates, but deprives Dils and company of his land, by selling it to J.D. Sergeant, of Logan. Devil Anse moves out of Tug Valley to Island Creek, near Logan.

Bounty hunters enter the picture chasing Hatfields for reward money. West Virginia governor backs Hatfields taking case all the way to the Supreme Court in an effort to free the kidnapped Hatfields. Kentucky wins case and Hatfield gang ordered to stand trial.

1889: Hatfield gang members tried. Ellison Mounts, sentenced to hang, others get life in prison. 1890: Ellison Mounts hanged in Pikeville.

# CHAPTER 7.

# IN THE BEGINNING

The movie gives us nothing of the pre-Civil War history of Tug Valley. Early books have little or nothing about the Valley before 1865. The books by Lisa Alther and Dean King, which followed the Costner movie, have some comments about the antebellum period, but are generally so erroneous that they are less than useful. King starts Chapter 1 off with the statement that at the time of the Civil War there were "no churches in the area."[1] After claiming four years of intensive research, King doesn't even know that there were enough Primitive Baptist Churches in the area to organize the Mates Creek Association of churches in 1849.[2]

The progenitors of the feudists came to Tug Valley around the turn of the nineteenth century. A few of the founding stock arrived in the 1790s, and the remainder came during the first two decades of the nineteenth century.

Most of the families who settled the Tug and Guyandotte Valleys originated in the border areas of Scotland and England. About a third of the families originated in Germany, with names such as Dils (Diltz), Cline (Klein) and Hager.

Some were the border ruffians, or the reivers of the borderlands. They moved from one side of the border to the other, recognizing no government, either English or Scottish. If the Scots had the upper hand at a given time, they'd live in Scotland and raid into England. When the English were riding high, they'd live in England and raid into Scotland.

Hatfield is an English name. There are actually three different towns in England today named Hatfield. That being said, it has not been proven that the Hatfields of Tug Valley are of English origin. McCoy is Scottish. Many of the founding families of Tug Valley were among the people who moved to Northern Ireland in the seventeenth century. They are referred to in this country as the Scots-Irish.

Other strains were introduced over the years. Captain William Francis, a significant character in this story, was the son of a Native American mother, who was brought to the Valley from South Carolina by her husband. I know of no one in the Valley who exhibited any ill-will toward the Francis family on that account. It certainly did not hamper his effort in recruiting his Peter Creek neighbors into his Home Guard Company, as about seventy-five of them rallied to his side.

The people of Tug valley were no more racially tolerant of Blacks than was Abraham Lincoln, who said in the debates with Douglas in 1858 that he had no intention of making citizens or voters of Negroes, or allowing them to inter-marry with White people.

Racism, as it applied to White and Negro relations, was a factor in major events in the area as we shall see and cannot be glossed over in a serious study of history. Of course, they didn't call it "racism" back then, as the word was not invented until the 1930s.

After England established control over Scotland, the Reivers had no choice but to seek ways to make a living that did not involve raiding across the border. Beginning with King James I (the Bible guy), thousands of border residents were encouraged — many not so gently — to move to Northern Ireland, to establish a Protestant presence in Catholic Ireland. The Hatfields and McCoys weren't interested in spreading the Gospel; they continued to be herdsmen and small farmers who converted a good part of their grain into distilled spirits.

Never really happy in Ireland, they began to leave for the colonies. Some came early in the eighteenth century, but the great migration was in the two decades surrounding the year 1750. Several extended family groups of them — Hatfields, McCoys,

Smiths, Scotts, and most of the other old Blackberry Creek names — boarded ships for the New World. Some entered the port of Philadelphia and headed straight for the hill country of central Pennsylvania, where they could continue the old ways.

We don't know how many of the progenitors of Tug Valley families entered either port, but we do know that the grandfather of Perry Cline lived in Pennsylvania before coming to Tug Valley, because he was there when he joined the revolutionary army. The Mounts family was also in Pennsylvania at that time.[3] The Cline progenitor had emigrated from the Palatinate about the same time as the great influx from Northern Ireland.

Most landed at Baltimore and Norfolk, and then migrated to the western part of Virginia. Why did they come to the wild, uninhabited Tug Valley? Why did they come at that particular time?

The primary motivation for the move across the mountains to Tug Valley was to find open land, the rich lowland area of Virginia having been appropriated by their English predecessors. A secondary motivation came from the federal government. In 1791, Congress passed (and Washington signed) a tax on whiskey. This brought forth the first active resistance to an edict of the new government. The farmers, many of whom made whiskey on their farms, considered the whiskey tax worse than the excises that had been levied by King George, and they did not pay it. They considered it a treasonous act by a government they had fought to establish.

We were all taught in our American history classes that the Whiskey Rebellion was confined to four counties in western Pennsylvania, but we were misinformed. No one in the frontier areas of any state paid the tax.[4] Resistance was virtually universal in the hinterlands.

The violent resistance came in western Pennsylvania only because that was the only place in the back country where an attempt was made to collect the tax. Interestingly enough, the man Alexander Hamilton commissioned to oversee the collection of the tax just happened to be the biggest whiskey distiller in Pennsylvania. Why, one might ask, would a distiller want to enforce a tax on his own product? It was because the tax was a *regressive* tax, hitting the smaller distillers hardest. Big distillers could pay a one-time, up-front fee, and then produce all the whiskey they could run through their stills; whereas the little guys, who could not afford the flat fee, had to pay a percentage of their production. That was enough to render them uncompetitive with the large producers.

The uprising in Pennsylvania continued for more than two years and included the burning of courthouses and the tarring and feathering of collectors. The rebellion was suppressed only after President Washington himself set out at the head of a thirteen-thousand-man militia, marching toward the rebellious area. When the farmers heard this, they gave up the fight.

For those readers who think that such shenanigans started about the time of Lyndon Johnson, let me point out that the biggest whiskey distiller in the entire United States at the time Washington left office was none other than George Washington himself! Old George's whiskey business thrived so greatly after his tax took hold on the little guys that, during his second term, he expanded his operation by building the biggest whiskey distillery in the new world at Mount Vernon, comprising five large copper stills and over fifty mash barrels. Before he left office, he was producing over ten thousand gallons of rye whiskey a year, yielding him a profit that exceeded the annual salary of a US senator for the first hundred years of the nation.[5]

It is surprising how few people know about Washington's whiskey making, as USA Today reported it on April 15, 2009, saying, "George Washington boasted many honorifics in his life, but owning the country's largest and most successful whiskey distillery in the late 1700s is perhaps one of the least known accomplishments of the first president."

As the man said way back in Ecclesiastes, "There's nothing new under the sun."

Although most of the early Tug Valley residents did not make whiskey, some of them set up stills which they did not shut down even after the government reinstated the tax during the civil war.

Johnse Hatfield was a moonshiner as shown in the movie, but so was his father. Devil Anse was charged multiple times with running illegal corn likker.[6]

In 1889, the enforcers nabbed Devil Anse. They did not arrest him and take him to jail, probably because they thought they would not make it back to Charleston alive. They simply gave Anse a date to appear in federal Court in Charleston, and then went on their way.

Anse's lawyer made a deal with the US attorney: Anse would appear for trial, but only if the government would guarantee him that no other warrants of any kind would be served on him during his visit to the capital and that he and his men could appear armed. The government agreed to Anse's conditions, and he appeared in federal court, along with several armed relatives and employees, where he was promptly found not guilty!

During his stay in Charleston, Anse gave a lengthy interview to a newspaper reporter, in which he assured the newspaper's readers that he had no knowledge of any of the crimes that the Commonwealth of Kentucky had charged against him.

The case was a setup arranged by the bounty hunter Dan Cunningham, using a local enemy of Anse named Dave Stratton. Cunningham hoped to take Anse when he came to Charleston, but the judge nixed the plan by agreeing with Anse's terms.

After Anse was found not guilty, the judge ordered everyone to stay in the courtroom until he released them. Anse told the judge he only needed enough time to get across the river, and into the timber. The judge held the bounty hunters in court long enough for Anse to get into the timber, and then he announced that they were free to go and take Devil Anse in the timber, if they could.[7]

Life in Tug Valley in the antebellum years was not idyllic, but it was not really a hard life. It was, above all, *peaceful* in the Valley before the Civil War. Each family had enough land, usually between two hundred and five hundred acres, to sustain themselves as subsistence farmers, with some cash income from ginseng, tobacco, liquor, and timber. But the generation that went to war, Devil Anse and Ran'l McCoy's generation, was sowing the seeds of future trouble and turmoil — *in their bedrooms!*

The thirteen and 16 child families of Anse and Ran'l were not uncommon in the Tug Valley at that time. As the children of the war veterans matured, there just wasn't enough land to give each child enough to sustain a family. It would hit home in the decades following the war.

Ran'l McCoy and Devil Anse each owned about three hundred acres, until Anse got the Grapevine land from Perry Cline. As of the war's end it was impossible for either to bequeath enough land to all his sons to allow them to be successful subsistence farmers. After the war, Anse took steps to rectify his situation, by entering the timber business, while all of Ran'l's grown sons were still listed as farm laborers or share-croppers in the 1880 census.

The families in the Valley were caught between pincers; on one side were the large families, and on the other side the land was being gobbled up in huge chunks, by speculators like Dils, Mayo, Williamson, Sergeant, and Nighbert.

After the big boys had got their thousands of acres, there were not enough hundred-acre tracts left for the large families raised by the generation that fought the Civil War. This shortage of land for the Civil War generation to pass on to their sons yielded a large number of landless men, who, with little prospect for self-betterment, too often ended up among the men known colloquially as *bad men*, who drank too much and were given to rowdiness. Of the seven Tug Valley McCoys who rode with Frank Phillips in 1887-8, five were landless.[8]

The men of Tug Valley continued to raise their crops and tend their free-ranging hogs from their appearance in the Valley until the outbreak of the war. The Civil War changed everything, and that is where Costner's movie begins.

1  King, Dean. The Feud, 15.
2  See: http://www.matescreek.com/
3  Cline, Cecil, *The Clines and Associated Families*, 51.
4  Murray N. Rothbard, *"The Free Market, September, 1994.*
5  http://dc.about.com/od/museumsinnorthernva/a/GWGristmill.htm  A good source on the Whiskey Rebellion is a book by that name, written by Professor Thomas Slaughter.
6  Waller, 267, n. 24.
7  Hatfield and Spence, *Tale of the Devil*, 186–87.
8  Waller, *Feud*, 255.

## The War on the Map

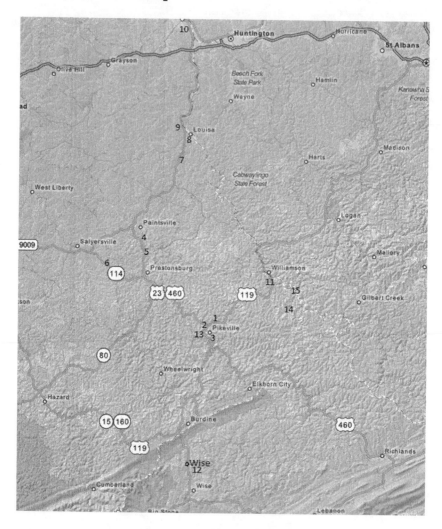

## Legend:

1. **Dils's tannery robbed, April, 1864.**
2. **Dils's store robbed, October, 1862**
3. **Dils's arrested, October 1861**
4. **Dils's 39th Regiment defeated, Wireman's Shoals, December, 1862**

5. Dils defeated and wounded, Bull Mountain, December, 1862

6. Union General Garfield wins major battle at Middle Creek, January, 1862

7. Rebel Bill Smith's raiders, including Devil Anse Hatfield, raid peach orchard, robbing stores and sinking boats, November, 1864. Dils captured and ransomed.

8. Devil Anse indicted for interfering with election, November, 1864.

9. Union headquarters, where members of the 39th Regiment opened fire on the 109th Colored Infantry, August, 1864. Mass desertions of Pike County soldiers followed.

10. Catlettsburg, the terminal for logs rafted downriver by Tug Valley loggers.

11. Battle of Pond Creek, July, 1863. Ran'l McCoy captured.

12. Dils sacks and burns most of town of Wise, August, 1864.

13. Dils dishonorably discharged from Union army, December, 1863.

14. Devil Anse and his guerilla group terrorize Unionists on Peter Creek, robbing and killing several Unionists, 1864-65.

15. Dils raids Mate Creek, robbing and burning homes of Devil Anse and his commander, John Buchanan, July, 1863.

# CHAPTER 8.

# THE FEUDISTS AT WAR

It is hard to overestimate the depth of the enmity that arose in Tug Valley during the Civil War and continued throughout the lifetimes of many of the men involved. The war along the Tug was extremely bloody and very personal.

General James Garfield wrote that his purpose as Union Commander in the Big Sandy Valley was "to weed out from the war here the infernal devil that has made this valley a home of fiends, and converted this war into a black hole in which to murder any man...from envy, lust or revenge..."[1]

One of Garfield's staff officers wrote: "Men who for years were neighbors now hunt each other." Captain Charles Henry continued to say that the war in the Valley would not end when the big war ended, saying, "They reduce the war to too horrid an individuality to say quits and be good friends."[2] Both these letters were written early in 1862, when the bloodletting along the border had just begun.

The Costner movie opens with Devil Anse and Ran'l at war in a fierce battle at Devil's Backbone, West Virginia. There was no such battle in West Virginia. There was a battle at a place called the Devil's Backbone, but it was in Arkansas, a state neither of them ever visited.

There was a place some writers have called The Devil's Backbone in West Virginia, a few miles from Devil Anse's home. It was a craggy rock formation at the top of the ridge, where Anse and his kinsmen were said to have taken refuge when the bounty hunters were scouring the area for them in 1888-9. There have been some stories saying that Devil Anse once took a position there and single-handedly held off an entire company of Federals. Some say he killed them all. That never happened.

I recently saw a photo on the Internet, purported to have been taken recently, showing The Devil's Backbone of feud fame. If the location I was given for the Devil's Backbone years ago was correct, it is gone. Just as it says in the John Prine song, "Mr. Peabody's coal train done hauled it away," it was the victim of a mountaintop removal strip-mining project some years ago. Of course, the Devil's Backbone may not have been where I was told it was. It could have been somewhere else, or it could never have existed at all. The one thing we can be sure of is that it was not blown to smithereens by a posse in an effort to dislodge Cap Hatfield in 1897, as related in Dean King's book.[3]

The next action in the movie is at Droop Mountain, where there *was* a battle, in November 1863. Devil Anse could have been at Droop Mountain, where a Union victory ended effective Confederate resistance in West Virginia. If Anse came home when his father and brother Elias deserted in October, he wasn't at Droop Mountain, either. The official record shows him AWOL as of February 1, 1864, so he might have been in the fight at Droop Mountain. Costner's problem with his Droop Mountain segment is that Ran'l couldn't possibly have been there, as he was in Camp Douglas prison as a POW at the time. Ran'l was taken prisoner by the Federals in July 1863, spending time in Camp Chase, Ohio and Camp Douglas, Illinois before being paroled in July 1865.

Many feud writers say that Ran'l never served in the Confederate army. Lisa Alther makes that claim at least three times in her New York Times best-seller on the feud, saying in one place, "...of course no evidence exists to prove that Ran'l was in prison — or even in anyone's army, confederate or Union."[4]

Alther gives a source for her claim that Ran'l was never a member of any Confederate unit. She cites Phillip Hatfield's *The other Feud*, p. 72.[5] Page 72 in *The Other Feud* is a blank page!

*Dean King* says that the Prisoner records at Camps Chase and Douglas refer to a Randolph McCoy from Pike County, Kentucky, but says they may refer to some other person by that name. Of course he says nothing about who this other Confederate Randolph McCoy might have been.

3. POW Slip with penciled notation. This slip is from the National Archives, NARA M347 Unfiled Papers and Slips Belonging in Confederate Compiled Service Records — cat#2133276.

We have little solid information about Ran'l's war activities. Some say he was with Devil Anse when Anse killed Captain Bill Francis, and that is possible. We can be pretty sure that he was involved in the Battle of Pond Creek, in July 6, 1863, because that involved the 45th Battalion, of which Ran'l and Anse were members, and the record shows that Ran'l was captured in Pike County at that time. The notation on the POW slip shows that he, like Devil Anse, was a member of the VSL before joining the 45th Battalion. Costner's writers at least got it right about Ran'l being in the Confederate army and a prisoner of war.

Ran'l McCoy was thirty-seven years old when he was captured by the Union army in July 1863. I know that sounds old to a modern, but the father of Devil Anse, Ephraim "Big Eph" Hatfield joined the VSL at the same day his sons joined in the summer of 1863, and he was a seasoned gent of fifty-one winters at the time.[6]

Ephraim went into the 45th Virginia along with his sons when the VSL was disbanded in the spring of 1863, but he didn't stay long. He and his son Elias were listed as AWOL from October 5, 1863.[7] The Hatfield patriarch was not nearly seven feet tall, as legend has him; he was measured by the army at an even six feet.

The VSL and, later, the 45th Virginia had a legitimate giant they could parade Goliath-style before the enemy. First Lieutenant Martin Van Buren "Baby" Bates, from Letcher County, Kentucky,[8] was over seven feet tall and weighed over four hundred pounds. The army listed him at various heights, ranging from six feet ten inches to seven feet four inches tall. After the war, Bates joined the circus and married a Canadian lass who stood a few inches taller than Bates. They are still listed in the Guinness Book of World Records as the tallest married couple in history. Guinness has "Baby" at seven feet two-and-a-half inches and Anna at seven feet five-and-a-half inches tall.[9] Lieutenant Bates was discharged in July 1864, because they couldn't find a horse that could carry him.[10]

Kevin Costner could have made a more exciting and interesting film if he had shown what really happened in the border area where the two feudists served. Nowhere, not even in Kansas or Missouri, was the war any bloodier than it was along the Tug River.

A soldier in action at Gettysburg on July 3, 1863, was about as safe as one on furlough on Peter Creek in Pike County.

From the website:

After the Battle of Gettysburg 37,574 rifles left lying on the battlefield were collected.

- 24,000 were still loaded
- 6,000 had one round in the barrel
- 12,000 had two rounds in the barrel
- 6,000 had three to ten rounds in the barrel[11]

I always wondered how *any* of Pickett's men made it across a mile of open ground, all the way to the stone wall on Cemetery Hill and now I know. Most of the guys up there on the ridge weren't even shooting! Of course, those who were shooting were doing it ineffectively, as the Union army only issued twenty cartridges a year per soldier for target practice.

A store clerk from Philadelphia or a factory hand from Massachusetts does not become a sharpshooter on twenty practice shots; so for most Union soldiers, it was a matter of schooling on the job. In this school, tens of thousands of them received failing grades from their Southern tutors.

It was different among the bushwhackers of Tug Valley. If Anse Hatfield or Harmon McCoy raised his rifle, anyone looking at the wrong end of it was in a world of trouble. The woods along Tug River were infested with men from both sides, prowling every day, and they meant business. When one of those bushwhackers, whether a Unionist or a rebel, fired at someone, the victim was usually either dead or seriously wounded. Men who hunt squirrels with a .22 rifle are deadly with a rifled .58 caliber musket at the short distances encountered in the narrow valleys along the Tug.

If you believe, as I do, that Devil Anse's reputation as a killer of his enemies was largely earned, then what does that say about Anse's character? What kind of man shoots Asa Harmon McCoy dead, just because he wore the enemy uniform?

The answer is that Anse was the same kind of man as those who were fighting against him. On September 9, 1862, the pro-Union *Louisville Journal* said, in an article on the Unionist Pike County

Home Guards, "Home Guards are said to have sworn vengeance against the rebel sympathizers and have determined to shoot them wherever they are found."[12]

Note that Anse's enemies didn't say they were going to shoot rebel *soldiers* wherever they found them — they were going to shoot *sympathizers*, wherever they were found.

Speaking of the early days of the War, in 1861, King says of the mountaineers: "The men who lived in these mountains had learned to fight from the Indians and had honed their craft of wilderness warfare—defending, tracking, ambushing, killing..."[13] King says that, even though he knows full well that no Tug Valley man of fighting age in 1861 had ever laid eyes on an Indian warrior,[14] much less taken fighting lessons from one. Neither does King explain how the men of the Valley had "honed their craft of killing," when at the time of which he speaks, there had not been a single known case of murder since they came to the Valley. Of course King knows better, but he has a "story" to tell, and he lays his foundation early in the book.

The fact is that the bloodletting was initiated by the Unionists from outside the Valley,[15] and then the mountaineers responded in kind.

I don't consider Anse to have been as low on the scale of morality as were many of his enemies. The governor of Kentucky gave orders to the Union military in Kentucky to take five confederate *sympathizers* from the local population for every Union soldier killed in the area by guerillas.[16]

Lincoln himself ordered General Burbridge to arrest all "*aiders* and *abettors* of rebellion, regardless of age or sex."[17] Notice that Lincoln did not restrict his order to combatants but included *sympathizers* of all ages, male or female. This is the same Lincoln who ordered the hanging of thirty-eight Sioux Indians in one day, after five-minute military trials, without benefit of counsel.

On July 5, 1864, Lincoln declared martial law and suspended the right of habeas corpus throughout the state of Kentucky. Pursuant to Lincoln's orders, General Burbridge issued an order that four rebel prisoners would be shot for every Union soldier killed by guerillas. Rebel *sympathizers* within a five-mile radius of any guerilla action would be banished from their homes, and their property would be seized.[18]

Burbridge's subordinates vigorously carried out his orders. General Eleazer Paine, one of Burbridge's commanders, hanged over two hundred guerillas.[19]

The bushwhacking began very early in the war and was not a one-sided issue; the Union side was as guilty as the Confederate side. An Ohio newspaper carried a story in November 1861 that quoted an Ohio soldier as saying, "...the Kentucky Union men are the worst set of soldiers, in the way of destroying secession property, we have in the army; they are controlled by the worst passions; and they all swear they take no prisoners — meaning they kill all which chance offers."[20]

On July 16, 1864: Gen. Burbridge issued Gen order #69, saying that whenever a Union citizen is murdered, four guerillas will be taken from prison and shot to death at a convenient place near the site where the Unionist was killed.[21]

On August 7, Burbidge issued Gen order 240, which gave the army power to seize property or shoot suspected rebels, without charge or trial.[22]

On August 23, Confederates captured sixteen Negro Union soldiers in Carroll County and executed them all.[23]

While the Confederates were killing Negro soldiers in other parts of Kentucky, Union soldiers were killing their own Negro soldiers in Louisa. John Britton Wells, III, wrote that when the 109th colored Infantry marched into the Federal camp at Louisa, "Insults filled the air and were soon followed by a devastating volley of fire, which ripped into the ranks of the black troops. The Unionist mountaineers of the 39th Kentucky had fired on the black troops of the 109th Colored Infantry..... When the smoke had finally cleared and the officers had their men under control, fifteen of the new recruits from the 109th lay dead and "unknown numbers" lay wounded on both sides."

Wells mentions that Rebel Bill Smith was able to recruit an entire battalion from deserters from the Union Army following the

Battle of Louisa... a significant minority felt so strongly about the idea of fighting to gain emancipation for the blacks that they chose to change their allegiance: between 130 and 150 deserted from a total strength of at least 600 to 800 in the wake of this tragedy."[24]

Among those deserters were several Pike County Unionists, who figured in the story of Devil Anse's war exploits, including Asbury and Fleming Hurley, and Jacob Cline.

War-time racial friction pops up again when, on October, 17, Confederate General Lyon captured eight officers and twenty soldiers of the 13th US colored artillery. The Federals took Gen. Lyon's wife captive and traded her to him for the 28 Negroes.[25]

On Feb 4, 1865: The Loyal League of Louisville approved Burbridge's actions, and suggested to him that he should confiscate the money and property of any suspected rebel sympathizers. General Burbridge approved the League's plan, and, on Feb 16, ordered Col. Dils — who had been dishonorably discharged just 14 months earlier — to implement it as soon as possible.[26]

It was too bad for Dils that the war ended so soon after this order was promulgated. If he had been allowed a few months of operating under that order, he would have owned a lot more of the Valley than he actually owned.

On April 24, 1865, in Louisville, the Fifth and Sixth Brigades of the US Colored Cavalry presented Gen. Burbridge with a set of silver spurs, a sword and a belt, in appreciation of his fine service to the cause.[27]

Compared to the men he was fighting against in the Civil War, Devil Anse comes out looking pretty good. If General Stephen Burbridge can be a hero, who is to say that Devil Anse can't be a hero, too?

It would have made great TV if the History Channel had shown it the way it was during the Civil War along the Tug River. Colonel John Dils raiding in Logan County and burning the homes of Captain John Buchanan and Lieutenant Anse Hatfield, with Buchanan's Company riding up to catch them in the act and pursue them across the river to engage in battle on Pond Creek, where Ran'l is captured, would have brought things together very nicely.

Devil Anse came out of the war with a reputation. He was reckoned to be a man not to be crossed. He must have done something notable to gain that reputation, but there is nothing in any official record about him doing anything other than joining the VSL in the summer of 1862 and then company B of the 45th Battalion a year later. He joined both as a private, and in both cases he was made a first lieutenant within a month. Sometime around the end of 1863, he deserted.[28] There are fourteen or fifteen months at each end of the war that are blank, as far as official records go.

While there is no reason to doubt Devil Anse's post war claims that he served from the beginning of the war, there is no documentary proof of such service until he joined the VSL in the spring of 1862. Anse was elected 1st Lieutenant of his company soon after joining the VSL, and it is not reasonable to believe that the men would have elevated someone to that rank had he not been in the fight with them.

Official records do not show Devil Anse's uncle, Jim Vance, on any roster, either, but he admitted under oath in the post-war case of Hatfield vs. Mullens that he had stolen Richard Hatfield's horses in 1862, while acting under orders from Colonel Witcher.[29] If Anse's Uncle Jim was serving under Witcher during the first year of the war, it is reasonable to conclude that Anse was with him. It is certainly not reasonable to say he was inactive during the first year and was elected 1st Lieutenant of his company by men who had been in arms from the beginning. His election to that position had to be a result of his actions against the enemy and not just his reputation as a hunter in Logan County.

We know that Anse joined the VSL in 1862 and the 45th Battalion in 1863, because there is documentary evidence proving such service. No one asks and answers the question, "Why did Anse join the Virginia State Line in 1862?" To answer this question properly, one must know what the VSL actually was.

The Virginia State Line was created by the Virginia Legislature in order to rehabilitate John B. Floyd after the disaster at Fort Donelson. Floyd, who was singlehandedly responsible for the Confederacy's ability to prosecute the war in 1861, by sending large amounts of military supplies to Southern forts while serving as Secretary of War under Buchanan, was also the strongest political leader in Western Virginia.

In the Fort Donelson debacle, Floyd and his division were able to escape and General Nathan B. Forrest's men fought their way out, but the remainder of the Confederates were taken prisoner and sent to camps in the North. Unable to accept the fact that ten Confederates could not really whip a hundred yanks, the Southern populace demanded someone's scalp after the Fort Donelson disaster and the scapegoat was General John B. Floyd.

The same Confederate population could not even entertain the thought that the result of the Fort Donelson affair could have been due to the brilliance of the Yankee commander, but it was. General Ulysses Grant has never been given much credit as a strategist and tactician, simply because the strategy of the Union during the last year of the war, when Grant was Commander in Chief, was continual engagement with Lee's Army, until attrition destroyed the Confederacy's ability to continue. An examination of Grant's campaigns in the West, before he came to Virginia, shows that Grant was as good a commander as the South had — with a couple of exceptions, of course.

The citizens of the western part of Virginia raised such a protest when Floyd was relieved of command that the State Legislature had no choice but to give him some kind of command. The Virginia State Line was the bone thrown to the old statesman and General.

The VSL was, by law, to be men not subject to the conscription law. Its stated purpose was to defend the western border area of Virginia. Floyd paid little attention to the part of the law restricting him to old men and boys, not subject to the draft, enrolling at least two thousand men who were just as fit, and just as subject to the draft law as was the twenty-three-year-old Anse Hatfield. Devil Anse, whom I am convinced had been engaged in guerilla activities from the beginning, found a natural home in the VSL. The VSL was created to defend the border area, which was the only thing Anse was ever interested in. Devil Anse, who owned

no slaves, never cared a whit for the government in Richmond —
Confederate or state.

While some have noted that the VSL violated the law by enrolling the healthy young Devil Anse, I know of no writer who has
mentioned the obvious fact that, by joining the VSL, Devil Anse
was, under the law, a *draft-dodger*!

The VSL was extended the advantage of a Partisan Ranger service, which meant that "...all property taken from the enemy will
be equally distributed among those capturing it."[30]  This was the
old British navy's prize money system on steroids!  A man could
fight and become wealthy at the same time, and Devil Anse surely
appreciated that.

On the back end of the war, we have hard evidence of Anse's
participation.  On November 5, 1864, when Dils's store was robbed,
along with the stores belonging to his fellow Pike Countians and
officers in the 39th Kentucky, the Sowards brothers, and Dils was
captured, Devil Anse and his brother Wall were charged with
horse theft in Lawrence county court.[31] Anse had taken the horse
of a Union Captain during the fight.

The Sowards brothers, officers in Dils's 39th Regiment and large
merchants in the Valley, filed a post-war lawsuit against several
Confederates for the merchandise taken from their Peach Orchard
stores during this raid, and Devil Anse was one of he named
defendants.[32]

When the same group of raiders disrupted the election in
Louisa three days later, the name of Anderson Hatfield topped the
list of indicted rebels.[33]  Devil Anse and some thirty of his rebel
comrades insisted upon being allowed to vote at the Louisa polling place.  They cast a unanimous vote for Abe Lincoln, telling the
precinct workers that they knew that they could whip Lincoln, but
they weren't so sure they could prevail against Lincoln's opponent,
George B. McClellan.[34]  Of course, the votes of the rebel marauders were not counted in the election results, but it was the kind of
prank Devil Anse would have participated in, and possibly even
thought up to begin with.

That Rebel Bill's son was married to Devil Anse's sister only strengthens the case that Anse rode with Rebel Bill.

The clincher for me is Rebel Bill Smith's letter to Kentucky governor Buckner, written in October, 1889, wherein he offered to help capture Devil Anse and bring him to Kentucky. In that letter, Smith said that Anse was an officer under him during the last year of the War.[35]

It is not surprising that Devil Anse Hatfield's name is not on any roster of any guerilla band, since the Union army was hanging every guerilla they captured. Less than two months before the November raids, Burbridge had ordered two men shot at Louisa. The two were *suspected* guerillas.[36] The two were charged with no specific crime; mere suspicion that one was a guerilla was enough for Burbridge to have someone shot. This shooting of two men on suspicion only of guerilla activity surely sent a message to the local bushwhackers, including Devil Anse Hatfield.

Soon after the outbreak of the Civil War, confederate forces occupied Pikeville. John Dils, himself a slave owner, was stridently pro-Union. In October, 1861, the Confederate commander, Col. Williams, ordered Dils's arrest.[37]

Dils was released from Libby Prison in December, 1861. We don't know precisely why Confederate Colonel Williams ordered the arrest of Dils. Since he was a slaveholder, he was not someone the Confederates would naturally perceive to be an enemy. What he did to attract attention is anyone's guess. It could have been that he was profiteering on his dealings with the occupying army, or that he was just too vocal in his praise for Abe Lincoln.

That Dils had to give his parole — a promise never to take up arms against the Confederacy — in order to gain a release after only two months in prison is a given. That it was a problem for him is shown by the fact that, while he said nothing to explain his dishonorable discharge in the blurb he wrote for William Ely's *The Big Sandy Valley*, he spent several sentences on his discussions with President Lincoln about whether or not he had a disability as a result of a parole given to obtain his release from Libby Prison. Dils denies that he gave his parole, but that is not credible, given the practice of both sides to require such as a condition of release.[38]

What Dils needed to know from Lincoln was whether or not the government would support him in raising and commanding a regiment knowing that he had given his word not to fight against the Confederacy. Honest Abe clearly saw Dils's oath as no disability, and pledged his full support, after which Dils came home and raised his regiment.

Since the victors always write the history in any war, most books about the Civil War, even the best ones by legitimate historians, contain some pro-Union slant. Virtually no one knows that three months after Dils was arrested, the Federals, under Col James A. Garfield, arrested Pike County Judge William Cecil, and County Clerk, Dr. John Emmert. These two elected officials did not fare as well in the hands of the Federals as did Dils in Rebel hands. They were both shot while in captivity.[39]

The man who shot the Judge and the Clerk was Thomas Jefferson Sowards, who was not a soldier at the time. How he got access to the unarmed prisoners is anyone's guess. A few months later, this murderer became a Captain in John Dils's 39th Kentucky, commanding Company C. He was one of the merchant brothers who sued Devil Anse after the war for robbing their store. Captain T.J. Sowards' son, James, was one of the wealthy men of the Pikeville elite who rode with Frank Phillips posse in 1887-8.[40]

The men Devil Anse was killing during the war were not his moral superiors at all.

Two months after the Judge and clerk were murdered in his custody, Garfield, the preacher and future President wrote a letter to his wife in which he complained that the Confederate prisoners in Camp Chase prison in his own state of Ohio were being treated too gently. Garfield told his wife that "the dead of his brigade would be crying from their graves for vengeance."[41] He made speeches while occupying Pikeville calling for the mountaineers to eschew seeking revenge.

Dils moved his family out of Pikeville in 1862, after Virginia State Line troops raided his store and tannery, for fear that raiders, which probably included Devil Anse, would harm them. Dils himself said in the autobiographical article he wrote for William Ely's book that he had to move his family out of the Valley for their safety during the war.[42] "I had to flee the country for my life," wrote Dils.[43]

His hatred of Confederates was well founded: they arrested him and imprisoned him for a couple of months in Libby Prison early in the war.[44] They raided his store in Pikeville in 1862.[45] They defeated him at Wireman's Shoals[46] and wounded him at Bull Mountain that same year.[47] In 1863, they cleaned out his warehouse in Louisa and robbed his tannery on Johns Creek.[48] In 1864, Bill Smith's guerillas, with whom Devil Anse was riding, robbed his Peach Orchard store and captured him, forcing him to pay a ransom for his release.[49]

Robert Baker, historian of the 39th Regiment, says of Dils's capture in November, 1864: "In early November of 1864, he was captured by Bill Smith and his band of cavalry. Since Dils survived the war, it is assumed that he was able to bargain for his freedom a second time. I wonder what he had to do to secure his liberty."[50] We know that Devil Anse Hatfield was on that raid because he was charged with interfering with the election in Louisa, and stealing horses during that raid by Smith's raiders. It is highly likely that Devil Anse, as an officer under Rebel Bill, pocketed a share of the ransom that Dils paid to secure his freedom.

Osborne and Weaver sum it up with: "When filing his pension years later, Dils cited the injury received at Bull's Gap as his primary disability. *The Virginia State Line had literally become the lifelong antagonist of the merchant-soldier.*"[51](Italics mine)

Devil Anse Hatfield was a cavalry officer in the VSL, and was, therefore, *a lifelong antagonist of Colonel John Dils.*

The battle of Wireman's Shoals, on December 4, 1862 has some interesting details. Col. Dils sent Lieutenant Levi Hampton, with 200 men, to Catlettsburg to escort a convoy of supply boats up the river to Pikeville. Colonel Cranor, the Union commander in that area, feared an attack on the convoy and sent a detachment to ride with the 39th to Peach Orchard, where Dils was to send another detachment to replace them.

When they got to Peach Orchard the reinforcements from Col Dils were not there, and Lieutenant Hampton decided to bivouac there until he got help, because he had intelligence that a large force of Virginia State Line cavalry was nearby. Dils sent Hampton word that he was under no danger of attack, and ordered him to come on up the river.[52] Had Lieutenant Hampton only known why Dils was in such a sweat to get those boats up the river, he might have refused the order; but he continued up river with his mixed cargo of military supplies and Dils store merchandise, paying with his life.

The boats made only a few miles before eight hundred VSL cavalry, which included Lieutenant Anse Hatfield, hit them at Wireman's Shoals, completely routing the Federals and capturing all the supplies on the boats.[53] According to the Federals, the take included 500 rifles, 300 uniforms, 7,000 rounds of ammunition, 500 overcoats, 500 pairs of pants, 500 pairs of underwear, 500 hats, 800 pairs of shoes, 3,000 pairs of socks, a tent, and two push-boats.[54]

There was a lot more than military supplies aboard those boats, though. There were large quantities of merchandise meant for John Dils's warehouse, thus explaining his urgency in ordering Lieutenant Hampton to ignore the threat of attack and bring the goods on upriver.[55]

This episode was part of President Lincoln's evidence against Dils that caused him to order Dils dishonorably discharged the following year. One of the charges set forth in the order from Secretary of War Stanton dismissing Dils was misuse of army transportation for personal profit.

Some men died in that war to free other men, some to keep them enslaved; some died to save the Union, some to break it; Lieutenant Levi Hampton, of the 39th Mounted Infantry, died to stock the shelves in John Dils's store.

Phillip Hatfield writes that there were two coal barges in the convoy, which means that was John Dils's first involvement in the coal business.

When Dils heard about the disaster at Wireman's Shoals, he took the remainder of his command and hurried downriver, meeting the VSL near Prestonsburg at Bull Mountain the following day. This battle was also a disaster for Dils and the 39th, with Dils himself being unhorsed and seriously wounded.[56] The horse Dils rode into battle at Bull Mountain had never been exposed to gunfire. The first volley spooked the untrained animal, and Dils was immediately unseated. With his foot still in the stirrup, he was dragged a considerable distance down the hill side. First reported dead, he survived, but the effects of his injuries lasted for the remainder of his life.[57]

The battles at Wireman's Shoals and Bull Mountain decimated Dils's regiment, to the point where he had to re-muster and reorganize it.[58] On their return trip to Virginia from the victories at Wireman's Shoals and Bull Mountain, the VSL picked up several prisoners, including Asa Harmon McCoy.[59] [60]

After Dils was booted out of Mr. Lincoln's army in December, 1863,[61] his guerilla activities covered Pike County as well as neighboring counties in West Virginia and Virginia. He burned much of the town of Wise, Virginia, then called Gladeville, including the courthouse, in 1864. "The last skirmish took place in Gladeville between October 23rd and October 25th, 1864. Colonel Dils was in command of the Union force. There was no command of Confederate forces in the village at that time; only a few members of the Militia stood in defense of the attack. These were quickly overcome.

"The invaders destroyed a cannon belonging to the Home Guard and a store of ammunition. They burned the courthouse and the homes of Bill Davis, J.W. Vermillion, Tom Bohannon and others."[62]

The only difference between Dils's raids in 1864 and those in 1863, like the one during which he burned the homes of John Buchanan and Anse Hatfield, was that in the former he had the official backing of the Federal government. He was always a raider, a robber and bushwhacker — just like Anse Hatfield. The main difference between the two men during the war was that while both robbed and killed, Anse lacked Dils's proclivity to burn buildings, both public and private.

According to the website of the 39th Kentucky, "After his dismissal from the 39th, it is believed that the Colonel continued serving the Union as a partisan leader or bushwhacker. In this capacity he may have been joined by such desperate men as Alf Killen and Joel Long." Compared to these two worthies Devil Anse's guerilla associates were choirboys.[63]

Luther Addington gives us a story of Killen's activities from a witness: "Tandy was brought home a corpse. Some of the Union Home Guards had passed Uncle Tandy's house and had stolen a horse. Uncle Tandy followed them and was killed. They knew Uncle Tandy was a Rebel sympathizer...Alf Killen was Captain of that Home Guard...Alf Killen and his Home Guard were met later by a Rebel force in Floyd County, KY, and during a skirmish, Alf was killed."[64]

One may wonder what a Wise County, Virginia Home Guard was doing in Floyd County, Kentucky, but that was the way those groups operated, on both sides of the conflict. They went wherever the pickings were the easiest. Killen actually operated mostly in Pike County, Kentucky.[65]

The cross-border raiding, while trying to the ordinary citizens, was lucrative for the men who led the opposing forces. Uncle, Ransom Hatfield, told me that John Dils went into the war wealthy, and came out rich, while Devil Anse went into the war poor and came out wealthy.

To do that, Dils had to steal a trainload of stuff, because he was robbed several times by rebel guerillas, which included Devil Anse.

---

1 Pritchard, *The Devil at Large*, 56.
2 Ibid.
3 King, *The Feud*, 318-321
4 Alther, Lisa, *Blood Feud*, 35.
5 Alther, 242, n. 43.
6 Pritchard, *The Devil at Large*, 59.
7 Osborne and Weaver, *The Virginia State Rangers*, 200.
8 Bates was an uncle of Devil John Wright, about whom more later.

9  http://www.guinnessworldrecords.com/records-10000/tallest-married-couple/

10  Osborne and Weaver, *Virginia State Rangers*, 148.

11  http://www.gettysburg.stonesentinels.com/Gettysburg_Facts/Gettysburg_Facts.php

12  Pritchard, *The Devil at Large*, 59.

13  King, 23.

14  King, himself says that the Indians were gone from the Valley by 1824.

15  The earliest case of war-time murder that I have found was the murder of the Pike County Judge and County Clerk, while in the custody of Garfield's troops.

16  Daniel E. Sutherland, *A Savage Conflict: the Decisive Role of Guerillas in the American Civil War* (Chapel Hill: University of North Carolina, 2009), 220.

17  Sutherland, *Savage Conflict*, 222.

18  Sutherland, *Savage Conflict*, 222.

19  Sutherland, *Savage Conflict*, 223.

20  Preston, *The Civil War in the Big Sandy Valley*, 50.

21  Beach, 177.

22  Beach, 183-184.

23  Beach, 187.

24  *The Rebel Yell: The Eastern Kentucky Brigade Newsletter, March, 1996.*

25  Beach, 196-197.

26  Beach, 217-219

27  Beach, 224.

28  The official record says he deserted before February 1, 1864, but both his father and brother were listed as AWOL from October 5, 1863, and I believe he went at the same time.  Osborne and Weaver 200–01.

29  *Hatfield vs Mullens, Pike County Circuit Court Case number 2175*, Kentucky Department for Libraries and Archives.

30  Jeffrey C. Weaver, *45th Battalion Virginia Infantry Smith's and Count's Battalions of Partisan Rangers* (Place: Publisher, Year), 4.

31  Pritchard, 71.

32  Preston, John, *The Civil War in the Big Sandy Valley*, 508.

33  Ibid.

34  Pritchard, *The Devil at Large*, 71.

35  Pritchard, *The Devil at Large*, 68.

36  Beach, Damian, *Civil War Battles*, 191.

37  Ely, Wm. 52-53. Preston, 33.

38  Ely, William, *The Big Sandy Valley*, 53.

39  Preston, 91.

40  Waller, *Feud*, 256.

41  Preston, 104

42  Ely, William. *The Big Sandy Valley: A History of the People from the Earliest Settlement to the Present time*, 47.

43  Ely, William, 54.

44  Preston, John David, *The Civil War in the Big Sandy Valley of Kentucky,* 33.

45  John David Preston, *The Civil War in the Big Sandy Valley of Kentucky* 120.

46  Preston, *Civil War,* 140–42.

47  Preston, *Civil War,* 142–43.

48  Preston, *Civil War,* 171–72.

49  http://www.reocities.com/rmbaker66/jnodils.html

50  Robert M. Baker, http://www.reocities.com/rmbaker66/jnodils.html

51  Osborne and Weaver, 89-90.

52  Preston, 140.

53  Pritchard, *The Devil at Large,* 62.

54  Preston, 142.

55  http://www.reocities.com/rmbaker66/index.html

56  Preston, 142, 143.

57  Ibid.

58  Preston, 144-145.

59  Pritchard, 62.

60  http://hiramjustus.hubpages.com/hub/39th-Kentucky-Mounted-Infantry-US-Volunteers

61  Preston, 437.

62  Addington, Luther F. *"The Story of Wise County, Virginia,* 108-109.

63  http://www.reocities.com/rmbaker66/index.html

64  Addington, 110.

65  See the website of the Kentucky Partisan Rangers http://geocitiessites.com/Pentagon/Fort/2754/Alf_Killen.html )

# CHAPTER 9.

# DAN CUNNINGHAM ON ANSE AT WAR

The testimony of a sworn enemy of Devil Anse, Dan Cunningham, though obviously exaggerated to Anse's detriment, is helpful in understanding the reputation Devil Anse gained during the war.

Cunningham — feudist, detective, bounty hunter, coal company gun thug and sometime deputy U.S. marshal — operating with only one or two associates, was responsible for bringing in four of the most notorious Hatfield feudists

Largely ignored in previous books, the mass murderer of coal miners at Stanaford, West Virginia in 1903 is presented in heroic terms in Dean King's book. In fact, Cunningham can be properly characterized as *the* hero of the book. King said in a CBS television interview: "I was surprised and happy to discover a fascinating hero in the story, a U.S. deputy marshal named Dan Cunningham, who arrested McCoys and Hatfields."

The plain words of King's book make Cunningham a questionable choice as a hero. "In 1902, while serving warrants and arresting violators of the injunction against union organizing in the New River coal fields, he was involved in several spectacular gun battles with striking miners, including the battle of Stanaford. While six union sympathizers were killed in that battle, Cunningham remained impervious to the whizzing bullets."[1]

The Stanaford Massacre, which King includes as one of Cunningham's "spectacular gun battles," involved a posse of more than seventy men, including some thirty of the Baldwin-Felts gunmen, under Cunningham's leadership, riding into Stanaford, West Virginia in the pre-dawn hours of February 25, 1903, and opening fire on the miners while they were asleep in bed. It hardly fits the description of a spectacular gun battle, as the only bullets whizzing in Cunningham's vicinity were those leaving the barrel of his own gun, as he fired into the homes of the sleeping miners.

The Baldwin-Felts gun thugs, who murdered miners from Ludlow, Colorado[2] to Paint Creek, West Virginia[3] and many points in between, stand as the premier murderers of working Americans throughout history. King says that by 1902 — the year before the Stanaford massacre — Cunningham was already on the Baldwin payroll, although still a deputy U.S. marshal.[4]

Cunningham was an equal opportunity murderer, as the Stanaford home of an African-American miner, G.W. Jackson, with Jackson, his wife and four children, plus eight other miners asleep inside was fired upon, resulting in three fatalities and several wounded. The murderer of the Jacksons castigated Devil Anse for allegedly joining the Ku Klux Klan after the war.

Cunningham and his cohort were exonerated in the Stanaford Massacre by Federal Judge Keller; the miners they slaughtered were in violation of an injunction the judge had issued against their strike.[5] Only in West Virginia, during the time of coal company enforcer, Dan Cunningham, was violating an injunction ever a capital offense.

Dan Cunningham was an important figure in the last bloody phase of the feud, but he was hardly what enlightened persons would call a hero. King obviously knows the facts about Stanaford, but he calls the massacre a battle and lionizes the murderer of the sleeping Jackson family as a hero.

When I saw a recent press report showing King being received in Matewan, West Virginia as an honored guest, I cringed. There were people in that crowd whose ancestors had been evicted from their homes, beaten or killed by Baldwin's men, and they were lauding a man who considers Baldwin a moral icon, and one of his close associates a hero.

The grandfathers of today's Matewan citizens partially got even on May 19, 1920, when Dan Cunningham's nephew, C.B. Cunningham, was one of the Baldwin gun thugs killed in the Matewan Massacre.

Jean Thomas, who is wrong on a great majority of her "facts" about the feud,[6] mistakenly says it was Dan Cunningham, and not C.B. Cunningham, who was among the Baldwin-Felts thugs riddled with bullets that day in Matewan. Regrettable as it is, she was mistaken. Old Dan lived another twenty years after the Matewan Massacre.

As we look at some of the horrible charges Cunningham lays on Devil Anse, it is well to note that Cunningham, himself was no stranger to feuding and murder.

At the same time the Hatfield-McCoy trouble was occurring in Pike County, there was a feud ongoing in West Virginia, known as the Roane-Jackson County feud. The underlying cause of the conflict in Cunningham's home county of Roane in 1887 was the same as it was in Pike County that same year: Eastern finance capital was taking up land, by hook or by crook. Dan Cunningham's brother, Nathan, was also a deputy US marshal. At the same time, Nathan was on the payroll of the Bruen Land Co., a New York firm of land and mineral speculators, which had bought up old Virginia land grants on some two hundred thousand acres of West Virginia.

While forcibly evicting residents from their homes on the land claimed by the New York syndicate, Dan's brother, Nathan Cunningham was shot and killed by a farmer who was defending his homestead (shades of C.B. Cunningham evicting miners in Matewan many years later). Just as Devil Anse reacted to the killing of his brother, Ellison, Dan Cunningham made haste to go to Roane County and avenge his brother, Nathan. He killed the man he thought had killed his brother, and was indicted for murder. With the support of his powerful backers, Cunningham was found not guilty, which freed him to go to Logan and hunt Hatfields.

Let's see what this life-long enemy had to say about Devil Anse during the war, as reported in *Volume 16 of West Virginia History*, which was the annual issue for 1985-86. The article, spanning eighteen pages, beginning on page 25, is from a hand-written manuscript of the 1890s and is edited by Ludwell H. Johnson, III.

The article is entitled, *The Horrible Butcheries of West Virginia, Dan Cunningham on the Hatfield-McCoy Feud.* If the reader senses a little irony in a man who had shed as much blood as Cunningham, referring to what happened in Pike County in the 1880s, as "horrible butcheries," well, join the club.

The West Virginia History article is from a manuscript given to the uncle of the editor, Ludwell Johnson, along with this picture:

**West Virginia Archives and History**

Editor Johnson says that Cunningham's reminiscences, while in error in places where he relies on second hand information, are generally in accord with *recognized experts*, such as Jones and Rice.[7] Johnson says that Cunningham is very accurate in his description of the raid on the McCoy home and that his description of the captures of Mounts and Messer are the best.[8]

I say that Cunningham's testimony is what it is, and should be weighed the way I think everything else connected with the feud should be weighed: Does it fit the character of the people involved, and does it make sense in the context of the times, while not conflicting with the known facts?

I personally credit some of it, especially the part about Devil Anse—or men under his command— raiding my great-grandfather, Ransom Dotson's farm and shooting Uncle Reuben Dotson and Uncle Mose Coleman, because that is part of my own family's oral history.

One more caveat: Cunningham begins his manuscript with the title, *A True Story of the Hatfield and McCoy Feud*. The first reaction any discerning reader should have to the title *A True Story* is to exercise great caution in accepting anything the writer says that is not supported by external evidence.

Eleven pages of the article are devoted to Cunningham's hopelessly garbled version of the feud events, every one of which, of course, shows the Hatfields to be the worst of villains, and their adversaries to be men of the highest character. Of course Cunningham's version of the feud climaxes with his heroic capture of the three desperados, Gillespie, Mounts and Messer.

The part of Cunningham's paper that interests me comes last, where, in three and a half pages, he gives what he calls: *Ans* (sic) *Hatfield War History*." All of it is second hand, of course, as Cunningham was a personal witness to none of it, but, if he follows the same method he used with the feud, then there is some relationship between what he says and what actually happened, albeit slight at times. The fact that Cunningham is exaggerating is obvious as he, like Dean King, claims to know what someone said when there were no witnesses, as when Old Dan tells us what Devil Anse said to my Uncle Reuben Dotson after shooting him.

Cunningham starts Anse's war history with the story of Negro Mose, saying: "Jacob Cline of Logan County raised a negro named Mose, and said to be one of the best negroes that lived.....Capt Ans (sic) Hatfield in company with Riley Sanson entered Mose's house without any provocation and shot him dead on the floor."[9]

Altina Waller,[10] Cecil Cline and James Pritchard[11] tell us there was quite a bit more to the killing of Negro Mose than we get from

Cunningham. Mose, who belonged to Perry Cline and his brother Jacob, spent most of his time with their older brother, Peter, who was a member of the Union Home guards. Mose fought alongside his master in many engagements against the Confederates of the VSL and the guerilla units. Cline family history says he fought vigorously against the rebels.[12]

In 1870, Riley Sanson was tried for the war-time murder of Negro Mose. Devil Anse testified in the trial that Negro Mose was in arms against the Confederates, and was seen "waylaying the roads to kill rebels as they passed."[13]

We see here that Perry Cline's trouble with Devil Anse predates the entry of Devil Anse onto Cline's land in 1868. Devil Anse — or an associate acting with/for Anse — had killed a slave that was worth as much as a mountain farm, and Perry Cline was one-half owner of the slave.

Anse also testified that a Union soldier named Enoch Cassidy had told him that Mose had offered him twenty-five dollars to kill Devil Anse.[14] Anse testified that he informed his commanding officer of the threat from Mose and that the Colonel ordered Mose killed forthwith. Therefore, Anse argued, the killing of Mose was a war-time act, carried out under orders. As the threat was against Anse personally, and the order to kill Mose given to Anse, it is quite possible that Cunningham is correct in crediting Anse with the kill. Of course, Sanson was found not guilty, but the most interesting part of Anse's testimony concerns the purported conversation with Enoch Cassidy. That places Devil Anse present at the capture of Asa Harmon McCoy.

Enoch Cassidy was a member of Colonel John Dils's 39th Kentucky. He was one of some twenty-five Unionists, including Asa Harmon McCoy, captured during early December, 1862 by VSL cavalry, led by Colonel John Clarkson. This is important because the only time Cassidy could possibly have told Devil Anse about the threat from Negro Mose would have been at the time that he was captured. This would show that Devil Anse was, indeed, riding with Clarkson's VSL cavalry in December, 1862, and was there when Asa Harmon McCoy was captured.[15]

Families were divided in both the War and in the feud. Riley Sanson, who rode with Devil Anse's raiders, was married to Sarah (Sally) Cline, a first cousin to Perry Cline. Shortly after he was freed by the court, Sanson moved his family to Minnesota.[16]

Sarah's sister, Hannah, was married to A J. Francis, a member of Colonel Dils's 39th Kentucky,[17] and a brother to Captain Bill Francis, whom Devil Anse killed during the war.[18]

Anse's next exploit in Old Dan's story appears nowhere else in the literature and is unknown in any family oral history. I consider it one example of many spurious stories circulated about Anse, enhancing his well-earned reputation as a war-time bushwhacker. Dan says: "Ans' next victim was John Poss. This occurred near the mouth of Grapevine Creek in Logan County. Mr. Poss was walking along the road and Hatfield lay in ambush and shot him as he came along."[19]

It doesn't make sense that Anse would have a killing enmity for a man who is not listed on any Union roster and carried a name unknown in the Valley. The surname, Poss, never appears in the Census for the Valley, or in any history that I know of, and, therefore, the whole thing was probably made up by Cunningham. It is surely not the only concocted tale of Anse's war exploits, which helped to build the reputation he carried out of the conflict.

Cunningham then tells of the killing of Charley Mounts: "Mounts was a Union man at home. Ans sliped(sic) up on him and shot him dead, the ball passing through his heart."[20] Note that Cunningham admits that Mounts was "a Union man." He was, indeed, a former Home Guard and a member of Dils's 39th Kentucky, and was the nearest neighbor of Asa Harmon McCoy.

So, this man, who was in arms on the Union side, sworn to "kill rebel sympathizers wherever they were found," was killed by Devil Anse, and it is presented as a clear-cut case of murder. Cunningham says: "Mounts was making sorghum molasses and his head went into the furnace of fire. No one was present except two of his children, and they succeeded in getting him out of the fire."[21] The story would have had to come from one of Mounts' children, since Cunningham says they were the only witnesses, but Cunningham doesn't tell us which child was his source, or how old the child was. He simply says that Anse compounded his crime by killing the poor innocent man in front of his children!

Then Cunningham tells the story of two more Union soldiers, "brutally murdered" by Anse Hatfield. "In the third year of the war Ashby Hurley and his son 16 years of age, and Union soldiers came home on a furlow(sic)." Cunningham says the Hurleys learned that Anse and his gang were after them, so they abandoned their home and hid in a cave. The bear hunter from Logan County found them, and coaxed them out of their cave by promising to treat them as prisoners of war. Then, says Dan, "they were taken to a large flat rock and tied side by side. Ans went back about 30 paces, fixed a rest, laid his gun on those logs and shot the two soldiers to death, the boy begging Hatfield for the privilege to see his mother before he was killed."[22]

Note the similarity between this scene and the murder of the three McCoy boys two decades later. They are bound before they are shot, with the teenager begging for mercy.

Cunningham leaves out the part about Devil Anse and his raiders stealing a cow from the Hurleys and butchering it. Cecil Cline says that the Hurleys followed the rebel raiders and shot into the group as they sat around a fire eating the slain Hurley beef, killing one of Anse's men.[23] Cunningham has the Hurleys home on a furlough, when, in fact they had deserted when the 109th Colored Infantry showed up at headquarters in Louisa.[24]

One might say that Cunningham's version is probably true, because it fits Anse's character, or it could be that Cunningham, being aware of the story of the 1882 murders when he wrote this a decade later, copied the modus operandi. The Hurleys were definitely killed by confederate raiders during the war, with Devil Anse almost surely the leader. Knowing the likely result for anyone shooting one of Devil Anse's men, I believe it happened in the firefight by the barbeque.

Anse's next victim is John Sanson. Sanson was one of Anse's pals, Cunningham says, but, because Anse believed Sanson might also be a friend of the recently deceased Hurleys, he "went deliberately into his house and shot him down."[25]

Cunningham then introduces a second villain, Wall Hatfield, into his narrative: "Sanson called for water. Ans gave it to him and raised him up and combed his hair; then *Wall Hatfield shot his brains out* before his wife and children."[26] I have to raise the caution flag here. If Anse shot the man inside his house, the wound from such a distance would probably have been fatal. We are being told that a man who went back thirty paces to shoot the Hurleys dead only wounded their friend, Sanson at a distance of a few feet.

If Devil Anse went into his house and shot him, and he lived long enough to ask for water, Devil Anse would probably have immediately delivered the coup de grace. Giving the man water and combing his hair just doesn't fit the character of Devil Anse. Neither does shooting the man's brains out fit the character of Wall Hatfield.

Cunningham says that Sanson "lived at the mouth of Pounding Mill Branch, in Kentucky,"[27] making him another Unionist neighbor of Asa Harmon McCoy.

In his recounting of the shooting of Captain Bill Francis, Cunningham really outdoes himself. Without even mentioning the fact that Francis was head of one of the biggest and most destructive gangs of Union Home Guard guerillas, he says: "Bill France (sic), a citizen of pinke (Pike) County Kentucky was at home."[28] Captain Francis, in Old Dan's tale, was not the leader of several scores of marauders who raided rebel homes and businesses and were pledged to shoot rebel sympathizers wherever they were found; he was just a citizen of Pike County enjoying the peace of his home.

It is impossible to know where Cunningham got his "facts" for many of his stories about Devil Anse, but I am pretty sure I know the source of his version of the shooting of Bill Francis. A comparison of two versions is in order: Cunningham says: "A stone fense (sic) was just in front of the door a dense thicket of willows extending up to the fense. Ans Hatfield and Randolph McCoy sliped (sic) behind his fense, there (sic) deliberations was to each one shoot, but on seeing the poor fellow at home and unconscious of his approaching end, McCoy refused shoot. (sic) France steped (sic) to his door, his wife began to fasten a neck tie to his neck, when all at once a sharp crack of a rifle fired. France fell dead at the feet of his wife."[29]

Remember that Cunningham wrote the foregoing in 1892. On October 21, 1888, four years before Cunningham's writing, the following, written by the yellow journalist, John Spears, appeared on page 8 of the New York Sun: "Old Randolph McCoy and Bad Anse before the feud began, killed a man when out together. His name was Bill France, and he lived on Peter Creek. France was standing in his cabin door and his wife was tying his neck tie previous to his going to an election. Bad Anse and Old Rand'l came along behind a stone fence and shot him as he stood unsuspicious of danger. But one bullet struck him. It spattered his life blood in the face of his wife as she stood before him. Both Bad Anse and Old Rand'l have always claimed the credit of firing the fatal shot. France was killed because he was going to oppose the candidate favored by the murderers. No arrests were ever made." Here we see Spears painting both Ran'l McCoy and Devil Anse Hatfield as cold-blooded murderers of a man who was simply going about his business as a good citizen, with no mention of the fact that it was a war time event.

As that particular version of the event is found only in the Sun and in Cunningham's tale, I think it is safe to conclude that the latter version is drawn from the former. This means we have a man who actively participated in the feud and claimed personal knowledge of Anse's activities giving testimony gleaned from a tale told by a reporter in a newspaper hundreds of miles from the area. Note also that Cunningham inserted a few words into the Spears account that drew a sharp distinction between the murderous Devil Anse and the compassionate Ran'l McCoy.

In Pritchard's article,[30] Devil Anse was ordered by his regimental commander to take out Captain Francis following a raid by Francis' unit upon the home of Mose Christian (Cline), wherein Cline was gravely wounded and his farm stripped bare.

Devil Anse, accompanied by Ran'l McCoy scouted the area around Captain Francis' home on Peter Creek, and learned that the general habitually walked out on his back porch to relieve his bladder upon arising each morning. Anse secreted himself in the woods, and, while "General France" was answering nature's call, "shot him right between the galluses." [31] [32]

Applying my rule of looking at whether a claim fits the character of the person involved, the Pritchard version wins over the Cunningham version. When Devil Anse scouted and learned the habits of his target, he was applying the methods of the mountain hunter. Anse had, no doubt, scouted the territory of many a big buck in the fall, learning where all his rubs and scrapes were located. There is no better time to take a big buck than when he is urinating in his scrape to signal his presence to passing does during the rut. The similarity between the urinating buck and urinating Union officer is striking, to say the least.

There is no doubt that Anse shot Bill Francis. No one, on either side, denies it. I am almost as sure that the captain was taking a leak off his back porch when it happened.

Spears says that Anse and Randal went after "France," and Anse shot him down in cold blood, simply because France supported a candidate in an election that the two feudists opposed. Presenting the leader of a company of raiding, robbing and murdering Home Guards as a peaceful, innocent citizen is representative of the work of the yellow journalist, John Spears. And Spears didn't even know the man's name.

As Cunningham continues his story, we see that Asa Harmon McCoy is literally surrounded by Unionist neighbors and in-laws, which flies in the face of the commonly held view of feud writers that Harmon was some kind of outcast because he served the Union cause. Cunningham's version of the killing of Asa Harmon is not far from the accepted version. He says that no one would even help Harmon's wife drag his body home. Then he names the names of nineteen of Harmon's neighbors, all within a five mile radius, and all of whom were robbed by Devil Anse.[33]

When we read that list of homes pillaged by Devil Anse, we could wonder if there was anyone within five miles of Asa Harmon McCoy who was not a Unionist! Cunningham's list of men whose homes were invaded and robbed includes several familiar names, like Bill France, A.H. McCoy, Trigg Cline, and my great-great- grandfather, Jordan Dotson (which Cunningham misspells as "Datson" several times).[34]

On the same page, Cunningham says: "Ans shot Reuben Datson (should be Dotson). He found Mr. Datson gathering paw paws on Peter Creek in Kentucky. He deliberately shot him down. The ball passed through his abdomen. Ans went to Datson and striped (sic) him of his pants saw the wound, and remarked to Datson 'dam you that will do you.'"[35]

Other than the correct spelling of his name, Cunningham knew a lot more about Uncle Reuben than my granny knew. He even knew what Anse said to him after he shot and disrobed him. Reuben Dotson was shot by Rebel raiders under Devil Anse Hatfield, but I think it more likely that it was in a skirmish, as Uncle Ruben was a member of Bill Francis' Union Home Guard company, and later in Colonel Dils's 39th Mounted Infantry.[36]

Elijah, George W., John and the unfortunate Reuben were all brothers of my great- great-grandfather, Ransom Dotson and all were first members of Francis' Home Guards, and then later of Colonel Dils's 39th Regiment.[37] In Cunningham's story, Uncle Reuben was not alone, because "About the same time Datson was attacked Ans Hatfield shot Moses Coleman (another of my great-great-uncles) in like manner to Datson. Coleman is still living (Reuben died in 1886) but dieing (sic) every day from the effects of the wound received of Hatfield."[38]

Cunningham concludes his scourging of Devil Anse by saying: "The above is horrible to reflect over, but it is true. Innocent children, women and men have filled untimely graves at the curel (sic) hands of the gangs named."[39] This is from a man who killed more men than Johnse Hatfield's whiskey, including the six innocent coal miners gunned down in their homes in Stanaford in 1903.

I include Cunningham's writing because he was an important participant in the latter part of the feud, capturing four of the most wanted of the Hatfields. Even though the writing has been available for over twenty-five years, Dean King was the first to mention it in a book on the feud, however slightly. I salute James Pritchard, a legitimate historian and archivist, for writing about it in depth in his short article in *"Virginia at War, 1863."*

More importantly, it gives the reader an idea of how Devil Anse's reputation was gained and embellished during the war producing a man whose very presence caused many to tremble. This was the man who took the three McCoy boys from the Kentucky authorities, without even brandishing a weapon. He succeeded based only on the reputation he had acquired, regardless of how much of it had been genuinely earned.

When we see that Anse had such a reputation near the close of the war, you realize that he must have been much more active than the official records show. Cunningham, who said that Anse raided at least nineteen houses and killed at least six men during the war, might have been understating the case.[40]

As most of the atrocities Cunningham attributes to Anse are supported by other evidence, his post-war reputation appears to have been earned. Of course Cunningham exaggerates and twists the facts to show Anse in the worst light possible, but the deeds are mostly real.

Contrary to the way Kevin Costner portrayed him, Devil Anse was not in the timber business during the last year and a half of the war; instead, he was terrorizing Unionists all over the Valley, especially those on Peter Creek. He might have cut down a few trees, but he probably cut down just as many Unionists.

---

1 King, Dean, *The Feud*, 341-2.
2 See *"The Great Coalfield War*, by Senator George McGovern and Leonard Guttridge, University of Colorado Press, 1996.

3 Corbin, David A., *The West Virginia Mine Wars: An Anthology*, Charleston, Appalachian Editions, 1990.

4 King, Dean, *The Feud*, 390, n3.

5 http://www.wvencyclopedia.org/articles/547

6 Thomas, Jean, "*Romeo and Juliet*," in *Big Sandy*, Henry Holt and Company, 1940. King cites her several times.

7 Note the reference to Virgil Jones as a "feud expert." Jones, a reporter and not a historian, wrote his 1948 book, *without giving the source of any on the tales* he included.

8 Cunningham, Dan, *The Horrible Butcheries of West Virginia*, in *West Virginia History, Volume XLVI, 1985-86*, editor's note, 26.

9 Pritchard, *The Devil at Large*, 40.

10 Waller, 89.

11 Pritchard, 63.

12 Pritchard, 62-3.

13 Pritchard, 63.

14 Waller, *Feud*, 89.

15 Pritchard, 62.

16 Cline, Cecil and Harry Dale, *The Clines and Allied families of the Tug River Region*, 67.

17 The nature of the border war is illustrated by these two sisters, who lived near each other, knowing that their husband's might be meeting in a fight to the death at any time.

18 Ibid.

19 Pritchard, 40.

20 Cunningham, Dan. *West Virginia History, Volume XLVI, 1985-86*, 40.

21 Ibid.

22 Ibid.

23 Pritchard, 70.

24 Pritchard, 69.

25 Cunningham, 40.

26 Ibid.

27 Cunningham, 40.

28 Cunningham, 41.

29 Ibid. (Cunningham's words are unedited for spelling and grammar, except in the places noted)

30 Pritchard, 65.

31 Hatfield and Spence, 80-82.

32 Pritchard, 65.

33 Cunningham, 42.

34 Ibid.

335  Ibid. Here we see Dean King's Hero, Cunningham, engaging in one of King's favorite ploys — telling his readers that he knows what someone did or said in the woods where there were no witnesses.

36  Preston, 438.

37  Preston, 437-438.

38  Cunningham, 42.

39  Cunningham, 42-43.

40  Cunningham, Dan, 42.

# CHAPTER 10.

# THE MISUNDERSTOOD CASE OF ASA HARMON MCCOY

Everyone seems to be perennially searching for the "Real Fighting McCoys." The feud industry has become so desperate that it is mounting a serious effort to make the hapless Ran'l McCoy a fearless feud leader, posthumously. They are obviously unaware that the real fighting McCoys have been there all along, but they just haven't figured it out yet. The real fighting McCoys were Asa Harmon McCoy and his sons.[1]

When a gang of Rebel bushwhackers under the leadership of Devil Anse Hatfield killed Asa Harmon McCoy on January 7, 1865, it was not the result of a chance encounter. The Rebels were looking for him, but most feud writers don't asks why they were looking for him, much less give an answer.

There must have been a reason for the Rebels to be looking for Asa Harmon McCoy. There were several dozen other former Union soldiers on Peter Creek, who had deserted in August, 1864, when the 109th Colored Regiment showed up at Union headquarters in Louisa. The obvious answer is that they were looking for Asa Harmon McCoy because they either had a grudge against him and/or they feared him. I think it was the latter.

Asa Harmon McCoy was a man of action. He, along with Bill Francis and Cline's slave, Mose, staged a raid into West Virginia that robbed and shot Mose (Christian) Cline. Devil Anse, a close friend of Mose Cline, is said to have vowed to kill every man involved in that raid, and Anse or his men did kill Francis and Negro Mose. Coleman Hatfield said that the Hatfields feared that Asa Harmon would try to kill Anse to avenge his friend and leader, Bill Francis.[2]

Asa Harmon was shot through the chest during a skirmish less than a week after joining the Home Guard and was captured by VSL cavalry, including Devil Anse Hatfield, in late 1862. After his release in the spring of 1863, he travelled to Ashland to enlist in the 45th Infantry. A thirty-five-year-old man who has been nearly fatally shot through the chest, and who has enjoyed the hospitality of a Confederate POW camp, who then travels a hundred miles to enlist for more fighting, is not your ordinary man. The Army measured Asa Harmon McCoy at nearly six feet three inches, and he was obviously every inch a fighter. He passed the same height and fighting genes to his sons.

In 1954 or '55, I found an old *Life Magazine* from May, 1944 in the Belfry High School Library. That issue had an extensive article, complete with some rare pictures, about "the feud." There was a photo of the mouth of Grapevine Creek, accompanied by text which said that, on that spot, Lark McCoy and some of his friends ambushed a company of forty Hatfields and killed fourteen of them. I didn't believe that, because that was more casualties than Virgil Jones had in his entire book. I had heard some of my McCoy relatives talk about *Bad* Lark McCoy, but I had never heard any story of him killing fourteen men in one day. When Lark McCoy — who died three years before I was born — was spoken of by my close relatives, it was usually in hushed tones; as if they were worried that Lark might be listening. He was still feared, even in the grave.

I asked Uncle Ransom Hatfield about the *Life* article when I took his newspaper to him that evening, and he said it was hokum. He said that Lark McCoy was the most feared of all the McCoys and that he had killed several men, but that there was no such action as that which was reported in Life magazine. I have heard from many McCoys, including some of Lark's direct descendants that Lark McCoy said that he lived every day for decades with the desire to kill the men who killed his father.[3] I have also heard of long sessions on his knees late in his life, seeking forgiveness for the murders he had done. While he never killed any of the Hatfields, I am sure that former rebel bushwhackers were among his victims.

When I told Grandpa McCoy about the *Life* article, he, too, said it was bogus. When I asked him to tell me about Lark McCoy, Grandpa said, "Nobody messed with Lark McCoy." Bear in mind that this was the same man who told me, "Nobody paid Ran'l no mind."

Is it any wonder that once Frank Phillips took command and had behind him, for the first time, Jim McCoy and the sons of Asa Harmon McCoy, the Tug Valley quickly became too hot for Devil Anse? That Phillips had a couple of dozen Pikeville merchants and loafers in his posse was irrelevant to Devil Anse, but Frank Phillips, along with the four fighting McCoys at the head of that posse was a different matter.

Frank Phillips, a large landholder, might have been a psychopath, because the most common attribute of the "bad men" of that era in Pike County was lack of land ownership.

The father of Sam and Paris McCoy was a farm laborer who died while the boys were very young, leaving them to fend for themselves.

Asa Harmon was a man of some substance, but only two of his sons, Jake (100 acres) and Lark (150 acres) were land owners. The sons of Ran'l who were of age at the time were all farm laborers or share-croppers.[4]

Five of the seven Tug Valley McCoys who rode with the Pikeville posse in 1887 were landless in a society that valued land ownership above all. In the Tug Valley in the late 19th century, land ownership was of such paramount importance that young men without land were outcasts from the get-go, and they comprised almost the entire cohort of bad and dangerous men.

The fighting, feuding McCoys were there all the time; they just wouldn't rally to Ran'l McCoy, who had fought on the side of the men who had murdered their father. The attitude of Asa Harmon's sons toward Ran'l is understandable, as their mother wrote on her application for a veteran's pension: "killed by rebels."[5] She did not say "killed by Hatfields." With Frank Phillips, like them the son of a Union soldier who died for the cause in command, these real fighting McCoys were present and accounted for during the feud's second phase.

The movie shows the killing of Asa Harmon McCoy as a simple murder by Jim Vance. In *The Tale of the Devil*, the Hatfield writers say that it was a two-man job, involving Jim Vance and one Jim Wheeler Wilson, who appears nowhere else in feud literature. As is usually the case, the Hatfield writers assign the actual killing to the non-Hatfield, Wilson.[6]

Most writers say that Harmon was killed by a group known as the Logan Wildcats, which they say was a guerilla unit led by Devil Anse Hatfield. In reality, the Logan Wildcats was a militia company formed in Logan County before the war. When the war broke out, the Wildcats became Company D of the 36th Virginia infantry and remained there for the duration of the war.[7][8] Although the compiled service records do not show Anse as a member, Coleman Hatfield says he was, and that he fought with the 36th in the first year of the war, including at the debacle of Fort Donelson. As the military records of the Confederacy are lacking in many respects, this could be true, but I doubt it. There is no documentary evidence of any unit known as the Logan Wildcats operating in Tug Valley at any time.

The movie version of Harmon's killing is not credible, simply because Rebel partisans from West Virginia did not go on one-man raids across the river into Kentucky. The Hatfield version appears to be just another effort to shift blame from the family.

Because the Costner movie did not address the war as it really was in the Valley, it became necessary to set up a spurious motive for the killing of Harmon McCoy. Some script writer should have been unemployed when he brought the idea forward that Jim Vance went gunning for Harmon McCoy because Harmon accused him of illicit relations with his canine companion.

Did you see that dog in the movie? No animal resembling that dog was ever seen in Tug Valley before World War II, unless it had a Yankee tourist on the other end of its leash. Surely they could have found at least one genuine hound still alive in the world, somewhere, to cast in that part.

Had such an accusation actually been made by Harmon, it is understandable that Jim Vance would have been furious enough to commit murder. Not only was the dog in the movie ugly as sin, it was obviously a male, as its name was *Mr.* Howls.

I seriously doubt that such a tryst between Uncle Jim and his dog ever took place. I am dead sure that it didn't happen with an animal that looked like the one in the movie. No true southern West Virginian would even waste his table scraps on such a specimen as we see in the film. To insinuate that a mountain man was in love with any breed of dog *other* than a blue tick, redbone, black-and-tan, or walker hound is preposterous!

Most writers have the same trouble handling the killing of Asa Harmon McCoy. Unable to connect Harmon's death with the early feud violence, they don't properly consider the facts that the only man killed between 1882 and 1887 was Jeff McCoy, Asa Harmon's son, and that, of the McCoys who rode into West Virginia with Frank Phillips during the last few violent weeks of the feud, three were sons of Asa Harmon McCoy.

Other than Ran'l's sons, all the non-Pikeville area members of the Phillips posse were from Peter Creek, where Harmon lived. So, we have three sons of Asa Harmon McCoy, several of his Peter Creek neighbors, who had shown no loyalty to Ran'l previously, plus Frank Phillips, the soon-to-be husband of Asa Harmon's daughter, making up the lion's share of the McCoy contingent in the Pikeville posse. Once you look at the big picture, who can say that the death of Harmon McCoy did not motivate some of the participants in the second phase of the conflict?

When Asa Harmon McCoy was wounded in the chest in a skirmish near Sandy River,"[9] G. Elliot Hatfield repeats a claim that I heard from many people that Devil Anse was the shooter. No official record exists of Devil being in arms at that time; however, as it is unlikely that Anse was idle the first year of the war, and records for militia and guerilla units are so sparse, he could have been there, firing that near-fatal shot.[10]

The VSL cavalry captured Harmon on Peter Creek, as they were returning to Virginia after routing Colonel Dils at Wireman's Shoals and Bull Mountain. Devil Anse, a first lieutenant of cavalry in the VSL, was undoubtedly part of Clarkson's unit. Harmon was held prisoner until April, 1863. He was still suffering from his chest wound and was discharged in May, 1863.

In October 1863, Asa Harmon went to Ashland and joined the 45th Kentucky Mounted Infantry. In May of 1864, he suffered a broken leg in a wagon accident, but he was back in action less than two months later.[11] As his enlistment was for twelve months, he was discharged on Christmas Eve, 1864, at Catlettsburg and began his fateful trip home.[12]

**4. Asa Harmon McCoy, muster-in slip**

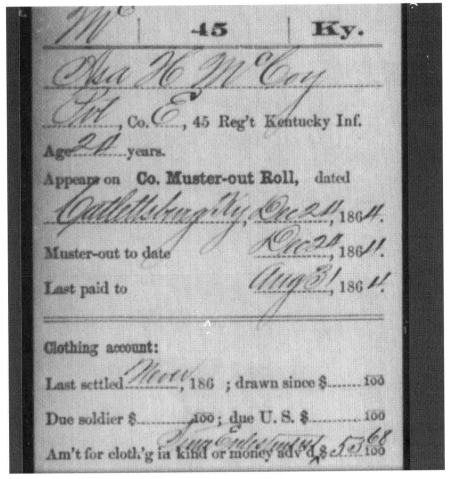

**5. Asa Harmon McCoy discharge slip**

Dean King's treatment of the service of Asa Harmon McCoy is atrocious. He says that Harmon "joined the Thirty-Ninth's Company H,"[13] when the record seen here above clearly shows that he joined the 45th Kentucky Infantry. Asa Harmon McCoy was never a member of the 39th Kentucky Mounted Infantry. King proves that this was not a mere misstatement by saying, "On the day before Christmas, Harmon McCoy...was honorably discharged from the Thirty-Ninth Kentucky Mounted Infantry."[14]

In order to have the date right, King must have seen the discharge slip reproduced above, but he still claims Harmon was in Dils's 39th Kentucky Infantry.

On January 7, 1865, a complement of Devil Anse's raiders, which may or may not have included Devil Anse, followed the tracks of Harmon's Negro slave, Pete, to the cave where Harmon was hiding, and killed him. Costner has Harmon hiding out in a still house—not a cave. If he had been in a shack like the one they showed, with large gaps between the boards, he would have been frozen stiff long before the Hatfields found him on January 7.

Accounts differ as to who pulled the trigger on Asa Harmon, but most writers, including Truda McCoy, say that it was a gang, led by Jim Vance.[15]

It could have been Anse, as Cunningham claimed, because it fits his pattern. As a returning Union soldier, especially one who had violated his parole and took up arms again after being released, Harmon would have been fair game in Anse's mind. Another reason that I lean toward Anse as the shooter is the lack of any evidence that Jim Vance ever killed anyone. When I have to choose between two possible suspects, one of whom was said to have "killed more men in Pike County during the war than consumption," and a man who never killed anyone else, I tend to believe it was the former.

Truda McCoy says the McCoys did not react to Harmon's slaying because they considered it an act of war.[16] With all the back and forth raiding along the Tug during the war, this is probably closer to the truth than any other explanation given for the lack of retaliation by the McCoys. With Pike County Home Guards pledged to kill rebel sympathizers wherever found, the killing of a returning soldier would not be much of a stretch. Harmon's widow, in her post-war petition for veteran's benefits, said that Asa Harmon was "killed by rebels,"[17] which shows that she considered his death a war incident.

There were two Union Home Guard companies in the Peter Creek Area, one under Captain Uriah Runyon and one under Captain William Francis (sometimes referred to as General Bill

France). While these two companies were active almost exclusively in the backside of Pike County, mostly on Peter Creek, and in the nearby section of Logan County, West Virginia, they were attached to, and appear on, the roster of the 167th West Virginia Militia.[18]

In the list of Pike County Union soldiers in *The Civil War in the Big Sandy Valley* there are the names of more than seventy-five Peter Creek area residents on the rolls of these two Union companies.[19]

None of the thirteen Pike County Hatfields who served the Union was in Harmon's 45th infantry company. Three of them, who were Peter Creek residents in the 1860 census, were in Captain Francis's company. The other ten were in Colonel Dils's 39th Kentucky.

There are nine Pike County McCoys on Union rosters[20] and four on Confederate rosters.[21]

The roster of Company H of Dils's 39th Kentucky, raised in Pike County, bears the name of dozens of Tug Valley men. Company E was raised entirely in Pike County.

The list of Pike county Confederates spans eleven pages in Preston's book, whereas that of the County's Union soldiers is thirty-eight pages long. The claim that Harmon was considered a traitor by most of his neighbors is not tenable.

## Lisa Alther, Feud Expert

The reader can decide whether the following quotation comes from a non-fiction history or a novel:

"It was January 9, 1865, *night would soon fall*, and Harmon *McCoy's mouth was parched.* His water jug lay empty, but *he felt too weak* to drag himself to the cave's edge to collect some snow. The *sweat dampening his black hair* made it even *curlier than usual.* His wife, Patty, *loved his curls*, but *he always tried to slick them down.* She also liked him clean shaven, which made him about the only man she knew who didn't have a beard or at least a mustache. Those curls and bare cheeks *made him look younger than his thirty seven years.* So, to command respect when serving with his Union regiment, the 45th Kentucky Mounted Infantry, he let his beard grow out. He would be with his regiment still but for his leg."[22] (The italics are mine, and show words that indeed 'read like a novel')

Since the writer claims to know how Harmon felt and what Patty loved and what she knew, it is obviously from a fictional novel, right? Wrong! It is from the best-selling non-fiction history of the Hatfield and McCoy Feud by the Wall Street Journal's "Expert on the Feud," Lisa Alther. Note that this "historian" is not even aware that Asa Harmon's enlistment had ended, saying that "he would be with his regiment still but for his leg."

The reader may wonder why Alther makes so much of Harmon's black, curly hair, and her assertion that he "always tried to slick them down." Well, when you read the rest of her book (if you must) you will see that she really did have a reason. You see, according to Alther, the Hatfields and McCoys were not, as everyone previously thought--about as pure a strain of British people as ever existed, but are, instead, actually a mixed race people.

Alther says: "Recent genetic and genealogical research has established that some early settlers in the southern Appalachians were racially mixed."[23] As most people know that any area in America as large as Southern Appalachia contains some racially mixed people, one wonders why she mentions it. But one soon finds out, as she continues; "Ranel McCoy's forebears are believed to have been Lowland Scots, perhaps mixed with Highland Celts. Lowland Scots were themselves a mixture.....including Africa."[24]

If Ranel had African blood, so did his brother Harmon, and it was only natural that Harmon, a slave-owning White man, tried to hide it by "slicking down his curls."

The military records give a physical description for a majority of the men who served in the Civil War. Of the nine McCoys from Pike County who served in the Union army, five are described in the records. All five have fair skin four have blue eyes and one had gray eyes. Four of the McCoys had light or fair hair. The one who had dark hair had blue eyes. Not one had either dark skin or dark eyes.[25]

So intent is Alther upon making the Hatfields and McCoys mixed-race people that she claims that "Johnse was said to have a dark complexion."[26] Alther is referring to the same Johnse Hatfield who was presented, in her own words earlier as: "Johnse, for his part, was a fair-haired, ruddy-cheeked, blue eyed eighteen-year-old rake."[27] Alther's early description agrees with two writers who knew the man personally. Truda McCoy said "he was a good-looking sandy-haired young man."[28] G. Elliott Hatfield said, "He was ruddy-faced, ham-handed and sandy-haired, with a pair of insinuating blue eyes.[29] The descriptions of Truda McCoy and G. Elliott Hatfield agree with the descriptions I heard from several people who knew Johnse in the flesh. But that doesn't keep Alther from darkening him in her chapter on the mixed race Hatfields and McCoys.

I don't know why this novelist went off on this particular tangent, but, as it appears in the same chapter where she endorses the discredited von Hippel Thesis, I presume that it is an attempt to assert that Tug Valley people were hyper-violent, because people of mixed race are more prone to violence. If so, she fails, because the record shows that the descendants of Captain William Francis, the only man of proven mixed-race who figures in the story, have been peaceable people since the Civil War. Bill Francis's mother was a Native American.

The part of Truda McCoy's book that reads most like a novel is the first chapter, which describes the death of Asa Harmon McCoy. Alther's first chapter is also on Asa Harmon.

Truda McCoy, who did not claim to be writing a history, used her imagination to tell the story of Harmon McCoy's death the way she envisioned it. Since no one knows the details, McCoy does no violence to historical fact by telling the story the way she imagines it might have happened. Knowing what it represents, this chapter is actually the best part of McCoy's book. Although one can get a real feel for the event in January, 1965 by reading McCoy's chapter, no serious scholar would mistake it for real history.

It is a far different thing for a later writer to use it as if it was real history, but that is what Lisa Alther did, in a near-verbatim regurgitation of McCoy's first chapter. Alther said Truda McCoy's book read like a novel, and that is true of most books by descendants. Of course, Alther's 2012 book, *Blood Feud*, reads even more like a novel than does the one by Truda McCoy. In fact, in her fictional chapter on Asa Harmon, she follows Truda McCoy so closely that one has to look at the title to know which book one is reading

Here are two examples among many sentences that are so similar that it is hard to distinguish Alther from McCoy:

TM: Pete and Patty started toward the cave. "*They had not gone far after they reached the woods, until other tracks joined the tracks that Pete had made* on his previous journey to the cave."[30]

LA: "*they reached a junction at which new boot prints emerged from the woods to join Pete's tracks* up the hill toward the cave."[31]

TM: Then, "*Halfway to the cave, they found Harmon lying across a snow covered log. The snow around him was red with his blood.*"[32]

LA: Alongside the trail, *just below the cave, they spotted a fallen oak tree. Across its trunk sprawled Harmon McCoy. The snow on the ground around him was stained scarlet.*"[33]

Alther takes McCoy's harmless fiction and transforms it into "history," without even giving McCoy credit for her words. Knowing what it represents, this chapter is actually the worst part of Alther's book.

Alther admits that many of the slave-holders in Pike County,[34] such as Harmon McCoy and John Dils, who fought in Mr. Lincoln's War, were on the Federal side; then she proceeds to make them liberals. She says that although John Dils was a slave-owner, he was an abolitionist. Alther says of the slave-holding Dils: "He hired many free blacks to work in his tannery, and allowed 130 of them to be buried in his family cemetery."[35]

The historical marker placed at the Dils cemetery by the state of Kentucky has the same malarkey, saying that Dils was "opposed to slavery." That's like saying Bad 'Lias Hatfield was a drunk, but he was a prohibitionist. Dils is lauded for hiring free Blacks to work in his tannery during the pre-war era. Dils's supporters ignore the fact that it was much cheaper to hire a free Black to work in his tannery than to use slaves. After all, a free Black could be discarded if he became sick or injured, while a slave would have to be cared for until he died.

Free Blacks worked in Dils's tannery because they would work cheaply, and most White men — even the poor Whites — avoided working in such a stinking place.

After telling her readers what a great guy the disgraced, dishonorably discharged Dils was, Alther never mentions the fact that he was dishonorably discharged by order of Lincoln for thievery. Instead, she makes the false claim that the reason for the disbanding of the VSl was that General Floyd was charged with dishonesty. For this spurious claim, she cites Phillip Hatfield's The Other Feud, p. 42.[36] Page 42 of The Other Feud mentions neither the VSL nor General Floyd.

The last part of Alther's sentence is a whopper. Dils bought the land where the cemetery is in 1870, and lived another twenty-five years, dying in 1895. The University of Kentucky website gives the following figures for the black population of Pike County in 1870:

1870 U.S. Federal Census
- 64 Blacks
- 32 Mulattoes
- At least 7 U.S. Colored Troops listed Pike County as their birth location.

So, of the ninety-six Blacks and Mulattoes in Pike County in 1870, one hundred thirty died and were buried in John Dils's cemetery. I guess the remainder migrated north. If Dils buried one hundred thirty Blacks in his cemetery, then the mortality rate among the county's Black population during that twenty-five year period was more than one hundred percent. Tannery work must have been an extremely dangerous and debilitating occupation.

Alther makes the silly claim that Harmon McCoy told his slave, Pete, that the Emancipation Proclamation had set him free, and he could leave at his pleasure. "When Lincoln had emancipated the slaves — over a year ago now — many had headed north to escape the wrath of their owners, who had supported the Union in the belief that they would be able to keep the slaves they already had, or would at least be compensated for their loss. But Pete and

Chloe had wanted to stay *even after Harmon had told them they were free to leave.*"[37]

Alther doesn't tell us how the illiterate plantation slaves learned about the Proclamation at the time it was issued. After all, none of the plantations had CNN or MSNBC.

While she says that Asa Harmon told Pete and Chloe that they were free as a result of the Proclamation, I am sure that no slave owner anywhere told his slaves that they were freed by Lincoln's Proclamation. In fact, the Proclamation did not free a single slave, including Harmon McCoy's Pete and Chloe.

When she says that the slave owners who fought for the Union thought they would be able to keep their slaves, she is correct. After all, they knew what Lincoln said in his 1861 inaugural. He told them in very clear language that he had "Neither the power nor the inclination" to free the slaves.

After the Proclamation took effect on January 1, 1863, the Union army told the slaves in any conquered part of the ten states Lincoln enumerated that they were free. Of course they generally did that even before the Proclamation. The Proclamation applied only where the Federal government had no power to enforce it. Furthermore, since Kentucky remained in the union, it was not one of the States in rebellion, listed by Lincoln in the Proclamation; therefore, the proclamation *did not apply* to the slaves owned by John Dils, Perry Cline, Harmon McCoy, or any of the other slave-holding Pike County Unionists.

Pete and Chloe were part of Asa Harmon McCoy's estate when Harmon died in January, 1865. They were freed at the same time John Dils's and Ulysses Grant's slaves were freed — at the passage of the post-war 13th Amendment.

It is noteworthy that John Dils and several of his officers in the 39th Kentucky (US) were slaveholders, while Devil Anse Hatfield and his Rebel raiders owned nary a human being.

In the same Inaugural Address where Lincoln assured southern slave-holders that he had "neither the power or the inclination" to free their slaves," he told them exactly what would lead him to invade their states: "The power confided to me will be used to hold, occupy, and possess the property and places belonging to the Government and to collect the duties and imposts; but beyond what may be necessary for these objects, there will be no invasion, no using of force against or among the people anywhere."

Fort Sumter was neither a slave jail nor a terminus of the Trans-Atlantic slave trade. It was one of the properties and places belonging to the government, and its purpose in Charleston Harbor was to ensure the government's ability to collect the duties and imposts. When that place came under Rebel attack, Lincoln's war was on, and loyal slave owners, from Harmon McCoy to John Dils to Ulysses Grant, enlisted in the Cause.

After reading a few pages of Alther's book, and getting her general drift, I fully expected to run into the discredited Von Hippel-Lindau thesis, and, sure enough, she comes out with it, saying that a Vanderbilt doctor had "published research indicating that some contemporary McCoys suffer from a disease called Von Hippel-Lindau disease (VHL)." Of course she doesn't cite this published research, giving us only an article from the Associated Press.[38]

She says nothing about whether or not the incidence of VHL is higher among McCoys than among other people—Hatfields, for example. What she says is that three quarters of the McCoys *the doctor had tested*, who had VHL, presented with tumors on their adrenal glands.[39] Even worse, Alther says that one of the McCoy kids had ADHD,[40] as if it is really surprising to find a McCoy child with a diagnosis that is shared by 10.5 million other children, according to Northwestern University.[41]

When I first heard about the Vanderbilt doctor a few years ago, I wondered how many McCoys he had tested, but I could never find the number. Then Barry McCoy published his *The Story of the McCoys* in 2012, and I got the answer. Mr. McCoy went directly to the source and had a twenty-minute interview with the Vanderbilt Endocrinologist. The doctor had treated a grand total of ONE McCoy family![42]

Of course Dean King includes the Von Hippel-Lindau thesis in his "True Story." After stating that certain families were predisposed to violence, [43] King says of the McCoys: "*the family* suffers from a rare

hereditary condition now known as von Hippel-Lindau disease....
which can 'trigger warrior, or fight-or-flight reactions.'"[44] (Italics
mine)

Notice how King supersizes even Alther's exaggeration. While
Alther says "*some* contemporary McCoys" have the malady, King
says "*the family.*" In King's version, we *all* have it. According to
King, one doesn't have to have an adrenal tumor in order to be
dangerous—possessing the McCoy gene is enough! As a McCoy
descendant, I am just as likely to physically assault him as to pil-
lory him in writing.

So, based upon a doctor's study of one modern McCoy family,
are we supposed to believe that it was a tumor on their adrenal
glands—or, in King's version, just being a McCoy—and not a combination of anger, envy, frustration and moonshine that caused the
three McCoy brothers to stab and shoot Ellison Hatfield in 1882?
Of course VHL is no help at all in explaining the behavior of Cap
Hatfield and Frank Phillips, neither of whom were McCoys, and
thus presumably free of tumors on their adrenal glands.

I can explain the two cases where McCoys attacked people
quite easily; there is no mystery requiring an adrenal tumor to
solve. Sam and Paris McCoy killed Bill Staton in a gunfight that
a Hatfield court found to have been instigated by Staton. Tolbert
McCoy and his brothers killed Ellison Hatfield in a drunken brawl
on Election Day.

It becomes almost comical to see so many supposedly smart
people trying to figure out why the Hatfields and the McCoys were
so violent back in the 1880s. During a decade when dozens of
feuds, involving much higher body counts were underway,[45] Wyatt
Earp and Doc Holliday were wiping out the Clanton Clan at the OK
Corral, John Wesley Hardin was killing several men a year and Billy
the Kid was back-shooting a dozen or so, we are supposed to get all
upset about a dozen people being killed during the same decade in
Tug Valley.

A dozen dead are twelve too many, but we are applying 21st
century metrics to a 19th century phenomenon, and it just doesn't
work. New York bankers and Boston professors didn't tame a

continent. It was men like Cap, Elias and Troy Hatfield, and like Tolbert, Jeff and Bud McCoy.

Remember also that the late 19th century was a time when violence was common all across the American landscape, from the gangs of New York to the gunslingers of the frontier west. In 1882 when Devil Anse lynched the three McCoy boys who had killed his brother, according to the Tuskegee Institute, there were one hundred thirteen lynchings in the United States, with sixty-four of the guests of honor being white.[46] The three McCoys constituted less than five percent of the white men lynched that year, but no one knows anything about the other sixty-one.

The New York writer who wrote the most scabrous articles about the people of Tug Valley, T.C. Crawford, admitted that there was no inordinate tendency to murder among the people of the Valley, saying: "While there may be no more murders committed in proportion to the population than in more civilized states, it is a fact that the murders committed are by men in a different rank in life."[47] So, our murder rate is no worse than the rate in New York, but we are people of "a different rank," so it's OK to write scandalous lies about us in your newspapers. Right, Mr. Crawford?

The "feudists" were just men of their time, but to some city-bred reporters and novelists they were terrible. When you boil it all down, I think the real complaint those types have against men like Devil Anse Hatfield and Asa Harmon McCoy is the simple fact that *they were men*!

---

1 This writer has no personal prejudice, being the same relation to both Ran'l and Asa Harmon McCoy, and not a direct descendant of either.

2 Hatfield, *Tale of the Devil*, 84-5.

3 There is no evidence of any ill-will over the death of Asa Harmon McCoy between any of the two families other than that of the sons of Asa Harmon. There were several marriages and land transactions between the families in the

post-war period. My great grandfather, Asa McCoy married his Hatfield bride in 1875. Thomas McCoy, a cousin of Asa Harmon, signed the marriage certificate of Ellison Hatfield, only eight months after Harmon's killing.

4  Waller, The Feud, 255.

5  McCoy, The *McCoys*, 221, n.1.

6  Hatfield and Spence, *Tale of the Devil*, 84–86.

7  Hatfield and Spence, 63.

8  G. T. Swain, *History of Logan County, West Virginia* , 198.

9  Pritchard, *The Devil at Large*, 58.

10  G. Elliott Hatfield, *The Hatfields* 192.

11  Pritchard, 74.

12  Pritchard, *The Devil at Large*, 72.

13  King, *The Feud*, 32.

14  King, 36.

15  McCoy, *McCoys*, 7–10.

16  McCoy, *McCoys*, 11.

17  McCoy, *The McCoys*, 221, n.1.

18  See the roster of Pike County Union soldiers in John D. Preston's *The Civil War in the Big Sandy Valley of Kentucky*, 428–65.

19  *Ibid*.

20  Preston, *The Civil War in the Big Sandy Valley,* 448–49

21  Preston, *The Civil War in the Big Sandy Valley,* 304.

22  Alther, 3.

23  Alther, 174

24  Alther, 176.

25  Preston, 448-9. As I have never seen a McCoy with "black, curly hair," I wonder how Alther knew this about Asa Harmon.  After all, there are no authenticated photographs of the man.

26  Alther, 176.

27  Alther, 54.

28  McCoy, 26

29  Hatfield, G. Elliott, The *Hatfields*, 54.

30  McCoy, 9.

31  Alther, 9.

32  McCoy, 10.

33  Alther, 9.

34  Preston, John D., *Civil War in the Big Sandy Valley*, p. 252. Slave-holders in the Valley were evenly split between those who served in the Union army and those who wore the gray of the Confederacy. The Pike County division was about the same.

35  Alther, 31.

36  Alther, 243, n. 13.

37  Alther, 4.

38  Alther, 183.

39  In fact, adrenal gland tumors are not the most common presentation. Clear cell kidney cancer is the most frequently occurring tumor, occurring three times in my generation of McCoys. While they have not been tested for VHL, I can attest to the fact that neither of them has ever killed anyone, or even done anyone great bodily harm.

40  Ibid.

41  http://www.northwestern.edu/newscenter/stories/2012/03/adhd-diagnosis-pediatrics.html

42  McCoy, Barry, "*The Story of the McCoys*," 190.

43  King, 139.

44  King, 140.

45  The feudists, Devil John Wright and Bad Lewis Hall each killed more people than died in Tug Valley during the entire "feud era."

46  http://law2.umkc.edu/faculty/projects/ftrials/shipp/lynchingyear.html

47  Crawford, *Vendetta*, 7-8.

# CHAPTER 11.

# AFTER THE WAR IS OVER

The Costner film shows Devil Anse in the timbering business before the war ended. We are led to believe that Devil Anse deserted from the regular army and was done with fighting. Nothing could be further from the truth, as we have seen.

I was shocked at the size of the tree the Hatfields were cutting in the movie. One would think from the size of that specimen that Devil Anse's only customers were manufacturers of toothpicks and match sticks. Surely they could have found at least one tree of saw-log size somewhere in Bulgaria for that scene. The trees Anse actually cut in the virgin forests of West Virginia were, with the exception of poplar, usually more than three feet in diameter, with some of them more than ten feet at the butt end. Poplar trees, some approaching two hundred feet with a forty-foot log before the first limbs, were taken at smaller diameters, down to about two feet.

In the movie, Anse comes home to a wife who can't wait to get him into the boudoir, in a house that would have been considered a mansion in Tug Valley in those days, but he lived in a two-room log cabin. The only houses like the one shown for Anse in the movie were those envisioned by Preacher Anse's congregation when he was preaching about the New Jerusalem.

Anse is interrupted in his sapling harvest by a visit from Patty McCoy, wife of Asa Harmon. Patty is great with child, a condition that is somewhat disturbing, considering Harmon had been away for a year — but there were such things as furloughs. How else can we explain Ran'l having children born in 1862 and 1863, unless the men got occasional furloughs? Of course, Bud being born in 1864 might be a problem, if his birthday was any later than April, as Ol' Ran'l was sent north to a Yankee POW camp in early July 1863.

Then they show Ran'l having a letter from Sally read to him by a fellow prisoner— but Ran'l could read and write. It was Anse who was illiterate, but I guess Costner felt that was beneath a character he played. The letter mentions the killing of Harmon, so it must have been written in 1865. The caption in the movie says "Camp Chase Prison," but Ran'l was transferred from Camp Chase in Ohio to Camp Douglas in Illinois in 1863.

Then we have Ran'l coming home from up north by way of Anse's timbering operation, which is highly unlikely, if my maps are correct. The mental condition of Ran'l at the time of his homecoming is pretty close to what someone would look like after spending two winters at Camp Douglas, although in the movie Ran'l had about 40 pounds too much meat on his bones for a man fresh out of Camp Douglas. The wild look in Ran'l's eyes is about what one would expect in a man who had been in that hellhole of a prison as long as he had been there.

Ran'l comes home to a wife who apparently is not at all pleased at his reappearance, and to a tiny shack that looks like a real dump in comparison to Devil Anse's McMansion. In reality, Ran'l lived in a double log house with a covered walkway, or "dogtrot," connecting the two parts. Ran'l's house in 1865 was more than twice the size of Anse's.

Ran'l's fragile mental condition is further shattered when Sally tells him that after having ten of his children, she is through with such doings. Sally tells her husband, no doubt exceedingly anxious after two years in prison, that she will "do my duty as your wife" if he insists, but she demands that he "spill your seed outside of me."

If the History Channel writers had read Lisa Alther's book, Sally wouldn't have had to tell Ran'l that because Ms. Alther assures us that contraception was readily available. All the trouble that swept through the mountains — not just the Tug Valley — following the war, which resulted from too many people and not enough land, would have been prevented if only those hillbillies had been given access to Lisa Alther's book. They would have learned about readily available contraception in the hills. The old joke, "He's screwed hisseff outta a place at the table," which was often thrown at a man after about eight or nine children, would have been passé.

Of course, the fact that it was a federal crime under the 1873 Comstock Act to sell any contraceptive at that time seems to have eluded Alther, the "feud expert."[1] In her chapter entitled *The Corsica of America*, Alther says: "If only the feudists had spent as much money and effort on acquiring contraception (which was, in fact, available in other regions of the United States at this time) as they did on acquiring guns, ammunition and moonshine, a different scenario might have evolved.

I must admit that the scenario would have been quite different if someone had sold condoms to the feudists. When Devil Anse went to federal court in 1889 on a moonshining charge, he faced the standard year-and-a-day if convicted. Had he been peddling condoms, however, he would have faced up to five years in the pokey and a two thousand dollar fine plus court costs.

The Comstock Act became law in 1870. That law read, in part: "...whoever shall sell...or shall offer to sell, or to lend, or to give away... any drug or medicine, or any article whatever, for the prevention of conception, or for causing unlawful abortion, or shall advertise the same for sale... shall be imprisoned at hard labor in the penitentiary for not less than six months nor more than five years for each offense, or fined not less than one hundred dollars nor more than two thousand dollars, with costs of court."[2]

Whether this declared expert is ignorant of history or simply chose to condemn several generations of Appalachians while knowing her statement was untrue, I know not. The Comstock Law remained in full force against contraceptives until 1936.[3] The 1936 decision applied only to married couples. The right to contraception for unmarried persons was not recognized until 1972.[4]

Lisa Alther, whose previous novels dealt a lot with sex, has much more sex in her fictional "history" than any other feud writer.

Everyone knows sex sells in 21st century America-- and the kinkier the better. Alther mentions at least three times that Ran'l McCoy's cousin, Pleasant, was accused of copulating with a cow.[5] When describing the widely publicized photo of Ellison Hatfield in his Civil War uniform with his revolver in front of him, she says he is "fondling his pistol."[6]

We learn more about the mind of the novelist who penned this screed when she says she was driving through the Cumberlands and saw a billboard advertising an indoor firing range. Alther says: "At the top stood a large cutout of a pistol, pointed upward at an angle. The barrel resembled *an erect phallus*, the trigger guard outlining a *testicle*."[7] Now we know why she thinks Ellison Hatfield was 'fondling' his pistol in his Civil War photo. To some people everything is about sex, and those folks write a lot of books — and buy a lot of books.

The movie introduces Perry Cline as a lawyer before 1870, but at least ninety percent of everything in the movie about Cline is just not true. He was not a lawyer who introduced himself to Devil Anse as a lawyer in the late 1860s or early 1870s, as we see in the movie, and he was not a cousin of Ran'l McCoy, as he says in the movie. He did not become a lawyer until 1884. Furthermore, Perry Cline didn't have to introduce himself to Devil Anse as a mature man and a lawyer because he had been Anse's neighbor from the day of his birth until Anse ran him off when he was about twenty-two years old.

If the movie had showed what really happened, it would have made a better drama. Where the movie has Anse telling Jim Vance that he would take the profit from his ten acres of timber and buy twenty more, and so forth, they could have had him tell Vance that he was going to solve his shortage of timber acreage once and for all by moving onto Perry Cline's five thousand acres. That is, of course, is what actually occurred.

Perry Cline's pursuit of Roseanna McCoy, which lasts for the entire movie, is one of the grossest distortions in the movie. Perry Cline had married over a decade prior to Roseanna's fling with Johnse, and he stayed married to the same woman until his death in 1891. He had several children and, so far as we know a peaceful domestic life.

The references in the movie to blood kinship between Ran'l and Perry Cline are spurious. Perry Cline's relationship to the McCoys was through his sister Patty's marriage to Asa Harmon McCoy, Ran'l's brother. This made him the uncle of Sam, Jeff, Lark, and Bud McCoy, sons of the slain Asa Harmon.

The movie scene with Devil Anse and Ran'l together at church was very unlikely to have happened. For it to have happened at a church in town, where the singing was as shown in the movie, is practically impossible. If the two had ever been together in a church, it would probably have been for a funeral, at which Preacher Anse Hatfield would most likely have been the preacher, and the singing would have featured the preacher "lining out" the song, with the congregation then singing the words after the preacher gave them out, line by line.

The insertion of the wounding of Cap Hatfield's eye in this section of the movie is also misleading. Cap's eye problem was not the result of a logging accident. Cap ruined the eye by placing a blasting cap on an anvil and striking it with a hammer — a Darwin Award type of stunt that has been performed at least once in each generation in that area, from the time the blasting cap was invented until today.

---

1 The first blurb in the *Wall Street Journal's* review of Alther's book on Amazon reads: "Alther is an expert on the subject of the feud." *Wall Street Journal* (http://www.amazon.com/Blood-Feud-Hatfields-McCoys-Vengeance/dp/0762782250/ref=sr_1_1?s=books&ie=UTF8&qid=1366569556&sr=1-1&keywords=blood+feud)

2  17 US Statutes 598.

3  United States v One Package of Japanese Pessaries, 86 F.2d 737 (2d Cir. 1936).

4  Eisenstadt v Baird, 405 US 438, 1972.

5  Alther, Lisa, *Blood Feud*, 36, 46, 121.

6  Alther, 49.

7  Alther, 229.

# CHAPTER 12.

# IT WAS ALL ABOUT A PIG—OR A PRETTY GIRL

## The Pig:

Many writers say the feud started with the court case wherein Ran'l McCoy accused Floyd Hatfield, a cousin of Devil Anse, of stealing a hog. As of 1878, when the hog trial occurred, there had been absolutely no trouble between Ran'l McCoy and Devil Anse Hatfield. Floyd Hatfield was one of dozens of cousins of Devil Anse Hatfield.

Although the loss of the hog probably caused Ran'l to grouse about it at the dinner table, it is an extreme stretch to base his enmity toward Devil Anse on something so trivial. Many writers talk about how important hogs were to mountaineers of that time, but, folks, we're talking about *one* hog here. Ran'l McCoy, a man of some substance, owning three hundred acres of land, was hardly broken by the loss of a single hog.

The TV movie showed Ran'l charging Floyd Hatfield with stealing a hog, and that was accurate. Virtually every other detail about the hog trial in the movie is factually incorrect. Costner has the trial taking place in West Virginia, in the court of Magistrate Wall Hatfield, when it was, in fact, held in Kentucky at the Blackberry Creek home of Preacher Anderson Hatfield.

The hog case is more properly categorized as an intra-McCoy incident. The star witness, Bill Staton, was the son of a cousin to both Ran'l and Sally McCoy, and the deciding vote on the jury was cast by Ran'l's cousin, Selkirk McCoy. Coleman Hatfield, in *The Tale of the Devil*, says that Anse considered it just that — an intra-McCoy squabble—[1]and I agree.

The hog trial turned on the testimony of Bill Staton, who swore that he had seen Floyd Hatfield mark the hog in question. Selkirk McCoy said he based his "not guilty" vote on Staton's testimony, and Ran'l lost the case. Staton was not married to a Hatfield, as Ran'l claims in the movie, but two of his sisters were married to Floyd and Ellison Hatfield.

Many writers strongly suggest that the outcome of the hog trial represented a miscarriage of justice. Most people I talk to believe that Floyd Hatfield stole Ran'l's pig and got away with it because Bill Staton lied to favor his Hatfield employer and Selkirk McCoy, who worked for Devil Anse, "voted his paycheck." I submit that it is at least as likely that Ran'l brought a spurious charge against Floyd, simply because he resented Floyd — at that time a Kentucky neighbor of the McCoys — working for Devil Anse on his timber-cutting job.

As we know that Ran'l's cousin, Pleasant McCoy, swore that Ran'l had lied about him copulating with a cow, it is no great stretch to believe that he might have falsely accused Floyd Hatfield of stealing a hog. I do not know if justice was done in the hog trial, but neither does anyone else.

Giving due weight to the influence of the employment of Staton and Selkirk McCoy on Devil Anse's timber crew on the outcome of the hog trial contravenes Dean King's claim that economics had nothing to do with the feud. To writers like Alther and King, the feud was a senseless blood feud, but he also includes Bill Staton among his "feud fatalities." Bill Staton was a blood relative to the McCoys who shot him, so how does the *blood feud* thesis explain that killing? Of course a "blood feud" doesn't explain it, but to scholars, who have studied the real history, it is not difficult to make the proper connection — Bill Staton and Selkirk McCoy worked on

Devil Anse's timber crew. So we have two incidents that King and Alther say were part of a blood feud, in which the antagonist of the McCoys was an employee of Devil Anse, but who were more closely related by blood to the McCoys than to Anse.

Much has been made of the jury's composition — six each of Hatfields and McCoys. Every feud writer says that there were six McCoys and six Hatfields on the jury, but they are all wrong! Under Kentucky law, in courts inferior to the circuit court, the jury has *six*—not *twelve*—members.[2] Uncle Ransom said that Virgil Jones asked him if he could name the twelve jurors in the hog trial, and he told Jones that there were only six men on the jury. He said he told Jones, who had just had a tour of the house the he ought to know that there was no way to seat a twelve man jury, a judge, the parties and witnesses in that front room—to say nothing of the alleged spectators. He said that he told Jones that he—Ransom--was a lawyer, and damn sure knew that much about Kentucky law, having tried scores of cases in JP court. He said that when he read the book and saw the twelve-man jury in it, he swore he'd never talk to another writer.[3]

I don't fault most writers for this, because it is so universally believed that one would not normally expect a writer following Jones to research it. I do , however, hold Dean King derelict, but only because he writes as if he knows more about the trial than anyone who ever lived, including my Uncle Ransom who grew up and lived his life in the house where the trial was held.

King even claims to know what his mythical *twelve* jurors said to each other during their deliberations, having several direct quotations from the jurors, enclosed within quotation marks in his description of the proceedings. The other writers merely repeat the old tale, without embellishment, so they did not seriously violate the trust of their readers. But a man who claims to know what was said in the jury room must be held to a higher standard. If he claims to know what they said, then he should at least know how many said it and how many heard it.

It's too bad that Uncle Ransom Hatfield died before Dean King was born, as I am sure that he wondered all his life what had been said in his house by the deliberating jurors. Thanks to Mr. King, we now all know details that a man who lived in the house where the trial took place never knew.

King even says that the jurors agreed among themselves that a majority vote would carry the issue—as if a jury possessed such a power. It took four votes to decide a civil case in a justice of the peace court, and four votes were cast for Floyd Hatfield.

King changes the identity of the star witness, making the aged William Staton, Sr. the man who testified for Floyd. I can see no reason for this, other than possibly the simple desire to contradict Altina Waller on a point that is not amenable to documentary proof. Waller makes the valid *economic* connection between Bill Staton, Jr. and Floyd Hatfield—they worked together. By substituting the seventy-year-old Bill, Sr. King removes economics from the equation and moves this little argument into the realm of his "blood feud."

For what it is worth, the witness was Bill Staton, Jr., who was killed two years later in a fight with Sam and Paris McCoy..

King also claims to know who attended the trial, although he obviously does not. There were normally a dozen or so loiterers present when Preacher Anse held court, and the crowd for the hog trial was no more than a few persons larger than normal. People of that time and place did not abandon their chores and hang around Preacher Anse's place unless they had a material interest in what was transpiring. King says; "both sides showed up in force."[4]

The clear implication from the phrase, "both sides," is that there was some kind of "feud" underway in 1878, and that an argument over a hog caused large numbers of kinsmen from both sides to turn out. King has numbers of people from ten different families in Preacher Anse's front yard, heavily armed. Unfortunately for Mr. King, he is once again up against the Census. He names several names, all of them in the plural, meaning several of each name were present. As the Census shows no one named Gates, Sowards or Stuart on Blackberry or nearby in the backside of Pike County, are we to believe that a large number of people traveled a day or more to find out who got the hog? Or are we to conclude that Mr. King knows no more about the number of spectators than he knows about the number of jurors.

The jury was, as all the writers say, evenly divided between Hatfields and McCoys. Most feud writers say this jury composition was to make sure that Devil Anse would not think that his cousin was railroaded, should Ran'l win. This is an error, resulting from the false idea that there was an ongoing blood feud at that time, with Hatfields on one side and McCoys on the other. The reality of the situation was that the Hatfields on the jury were as closely related to some McCoys as they were to Devil Anse Hatfield. They were, however, all very closely related to Preacher Anse Hatfield, and that was why the preacher balanced the jury.

Preacher Anse maintained his standing among all the families by being careful not to show partiality. He had a problem in that his Hatfield relatives were so numerous on Blackberry Creek that it was difficult to empanel a jury that did not have an outright majority of Kentucky Hatfields, much closer related to Preacher Anse than to Devil Anse. In fact, that would be the case in most randomly picked juries. The foreman of the jury in the hog trial was preacher Anse's brother, Elexious (Leck).[5] So, to protect his own reputation for fairness, he went the extra mile and found enough McCoys to balance the jury.

Having three Kentucky Hatfields, who were no closer to Devil Anse than were a hundred or more people in the valley by the same name, and who were mostly Republicans, supporters, parishioners, and close relatives of Preacher Anse, would do nothing to reassure Devil Anse, if he had an interest in the case. On the other hand, having three McCoys to balance his three Hatfield relatives would insulate Preacher Anse against any future claims of bias by the McCoys, should Ran'l lose.

Preacher Anse had far more to lose in the hog trial than did Devil Anse because the justice of the peace/preacher needed the votes of the McCoys, and many of them were his parishioners. The jury composition was to protect the preacher, not to placate the Devil.

If Ran'l McCoy had gone gunning for Floyd after the jury decided for Floyd and against Ran'l, then that would have fit the classic feud scenario. Mark Twain said in "Huckleberry Finn" about the feud Huck ran into that there was a lawsuit and one side won, after which the losing party *naturally* killed the victor. Had that happened between Ran'l McCoy and Floyd Hatfield, then it could be seen as part of a feud, but that did not happen.[6]

Despite the movie showing Devil Anse at the trial, he was actually miles away. Devil Anse's attitude toward the hog trial was no doubt total unconcern. If Devil Anse reacted to every loss by a cousin of something as inconsequential as a pig, he would have been involved in several feuds simultaneously.

Ran'l McCoy said in 1888, "I used to be on very friendly terms with the Hatfields before and after the war. We never had any trouble till six years ago."[7] This statement, recorded by Charles Howell, who wrote very friendly articles about the McCoys, gives the lie to every claim that there was a feud ongoing between the two families ten years prior, at the time of the hog trial and the killing of Bill Staton and the trial of Sam and Paris McCoy for the killing of Staton.

The movie connects the killing of Bill Staton in June 1880 with the hog trial, as he was the key witness for Floyd Hatfield. The actual killing of Staton is another incident with which the movie takes great liberties. The scene has Staton menacing the two armed McCoys with a knife, but not even a drunk Bill Staton would try to take down the armed Sam and Paris McCoy with a knife.

By connecting Staton's killing to the hog trial, many seem to think it is then connected to the feud, even though the hog trial had nothing to do with Devil Anse Hatfield, and Ran'l himself later said that his relations with the Hatfields remained friendly afterwards. The movie, like most of the books, goes to great lengths to connect every act of violence over a twenty-five-year period to the feud because a feud, by definition, requires a long, continuous period of inter-family violence.

The movie shows Devil Anse leading a posse that captured the McCoy brothers after they killed Staton. In fact, Anse had no part in the capture of either Sam or Paris. Paris was arrested about a month after the incident, but Sam eluded capture for nearly two years. Both were set free by a West Virginia court on the grounds of self-defense. Again, the movie has Perry Cline acting as a lawyer in court at the trial of Sam and Paris, several years before he got a law license.

The movie intimates that the "not guilty" verdict was a gesture of peace on the part of the Hatfields to lessen the strain between the families, but this just does not hold water, for two reasons: First, according to both Devil Anse and Ran'l, there was no strain between the families of sufficient magnitude to justify overlooking a murder in order to lessen it at that time. Secondly, the McCoys were in court only because Ellison Hatfield, Staton's brother-in-law, had pressed the charge and wanted very much to see the killers of his brother-in-law and work mate punished. It is not credible that Anse overruled his brother, Ellison, and ordered the killers set free. Devil Anse was always a *blood for blood* man, who believed that unprovoked killing had to be answered in kind. Had Devil Anse believed that Bill Staton, an employee of Anse's timber business, had been murdered, he was more likely to have killed Sam and Paris himself than to arrange their deliverance.

Here again, we see that the men of Tug Valley were not lawless men, with no respect for the law. Ellison Hatfield pressed the charges against the McCoys, but accepted the verdict when it came. Ellison remained a friend to the accused, according to Sam McCoy, himself. Ellison Hatfield, called a "splendid Man" in Truda McCoy's book, was probably a closer friend to Sam McCoy than were Ran'l's sons. Sam McCoy said in his memoirs, "If I ever had a friend in the world Ellison Hatfield was. In fact all of them were good to me."[8] The McCoy who said the foregoing killed one of his own cousins, and Dean King says the slain man was a fatality of the "Hatfield and McCoy feud." Who's kidding whom?

For Staton's death to be part of the feud, Sam and Paris must have had so much enmity toward Staton, simply because of his testimony in the hog trial involving their uncle, that they would kill him. If that were the case, then how does one explain the fact that after three of Ran'l's sons, cousins to Sam and Paris, were slaughtered on the riverbank, neither Sam nor Paris tried to get revenge? Surely the slaying of three of their kinsmen should have aroused more hatred in Sam and Paris than the swearing of a lie over a hog, but it did not. It didn't simply because there was no feud between the Hatfields and McCoys at that time.

The killing of Bill Staton was the result of an altercation in the woods where there were no witnesses to contradict the claim of the two McCoys that Staton's killing was an act of self defense on their part. That Paris McCoy was wounded in the fight gave weight to their uncontradicted claim. The Hatfield-controlled West Virginia court had no legitimate choice other than to exonerate them.

Dean King's description of the killing of Bill Staton is a glaring example of *supersizing*. The incident happened in an isolated section of forest land, with no witnesses other than the three men involved—Sam and Paris McCoy and the unfortunate loser, Bill Staton. The lack of eyewitness testimony does not hamper our "deflator of legends" as he proceeds to "restore accurate historical detail" to the fight in the woods.

King fills three pages with meticulous detail of the fight, describing the confrontation just as if he had been standing within arm's length of the combatants, saying: "Hiding behind a bush, Staton raised his gun, propped it in the vee of the limbs, shut an eye, squinted down the barrel, and took a bead..."

Claiming to know details that no one could possibly know is about as prevalent in his writing as is the gross exaggeration of numbers. Does King think any sentient reader will actually believe that King knows how Bill Staton braced his rifle and that he "shut an eye and squinted down the barrel?"

King says that Staton filled his lungs until they were swollen with "honeysuckle and deep forest scent," as he "stilled his body for shooting." Not only does King know what people said and thought in the woods; he even knows what they smelled!

King obviously does not know that a shooter does not fill his lungs to still himself for a shot — he actually does the opposite.

Continuing his detailed description of a fight to which there were no witnesses, King says that Staton shot Paris and "Staton's rifle slug pierced him (Paris) through the hip." This was not a "flesh wound" as you see in so many westerns; it hit so much bone that it knocked him down. I know that in normal circumstance, a man hit through the hip so solidly by a high-powered rifle bullet that it knocks him down will not take another step for several months, but not when Dean King is calling the "play-by-play."

With such a crippling, and often fatal wound, you might expect him just to lay on the ground moaning until the EMT's arrived, but Paris "bounded to his feet" and shot Staton through the chest! Staton's wound was no simple "flesh wound" either. It was "spurting blood!"

Now I know you would expect that a man shot through the chest with a high-powered rifle, with the bullet placed so that the wound "spurted blood," would immediately resort to prayer, or at least a verse or two of "O, Come, Angel Band," but Staton shook it off in King's tale.

Both men, one shot through the hip and the other through the chest, discarded their rifles and went at it, man-to-man.

King's narration continues: "When they collided, they fought like cornered animals...punching, clawing and biting. Staton clenched his cousin's (a McCoy) cheek in his teeth and slashed his face with *dirt-rimmed fingernails*. Blood spewed everywhere. Staton would have had Paris licked if it had not been for Sam."

Sam closed the deal by blowing Staton's brains out at point-blank range.[9] This gives us the unprecedented case of a man who has just been shot through the chest with a high-powered rifle proceeding to win a fist fight. I am just as proud as punch to be related to such superior specimens of manhood!

We now know the basis for Sam McCoy's successful plea of self defense. No jury would ever convict a man for shooting someone who was clawing the defendant's brother's face with *dirty fingernails*.

Of course the confrontation between Devil Anse and Ran'l, shown in the movie at the conclusion of the trial of Sam and Paris, like all the other face-to-face encounters between the two that appear in the movie — with the one exception of when Devil Anse took Ran'l's three sons from Kentucky custody on August 8, 1882 — never happened. But the moviemakers, like most of the authors, know the definition of a feud, and they supply the necessary elements to create a long, continuous conflict.

Ran'l likely had some concern about how his nephews would fare in a West Virginia court, but he would have been pleased at the actual outcome, not spurred to more hatred of Devil Anse. His own words to Charles Howell eight years later give the lie to such a contention. Ran'l considered his relations with the Hatfields friendly at the time of that trial. We know that because he said so.[10]

Devil Anse might have been displeased at the verdicts in the killing of his employee, Staton, and Ellison probably resented his brother-in-law's killers being exonerated, but their acceptance of the verdict proves that they were generally law-abiding men, who respected the courts. It is a real stretch to say that either Anse or Ellison hated Sam and Paris' *uncle* as a result of the verdict, especially when Sam McCoy, himself, said that Ellison Hatfield was as good a friend as he ever had.

In spite of all the foregoing evidence to the contrary, almost every feud book connects the hog trial and the Staton killing to the feud. Some say that the McCoys were not satisfied by the acquittals of Sam and Paris and bore a feuding hatred toward the Hatfields simply because they were charged in the first place.[11] Of course to do this the writers must ignore the documented fact that eight McCoys, including three of Sarah's brother Allen's children and her daughter, Josephine, were witnesses *against* Paris.[12]

As usual, Dean King's "True Story" goes far beyond all others in this. King makes the trials of Sam and Paris McCoy not only part of the feud; he has them both on the same day, featuring the largest gathering of armed Hatfields and McCoys ever recorded!

King says:"More than a hundred armed McCoys showed up in Logan Courthouse on the day that Sam and Paris were brought to trial. Hatfields were everywhere, too."[13] Hatfields were everywhere, but we're not told how many were there. As the Hatfields were one of the largest families in the Big Sandy Valley, and the McCoys had farther to travel to get to Logan Courthouse (the town's name was actually Aracoma in 1880), we can probably assume that they numbered at least as many as the McCoys.

As Paris was arrested in July, 1880, and tried in September of that year, while Sam was not arrested until February, 1882, and tried shortly thereafter[14], King's "the day that Sam and Paris were brought to trial," is an imaginary day; there never was a day when both Sam and Paris were tried.

I wonder if King means that a hundred armed McCoys showed up in the tiny village of Logan Courthouse[15] on two separate occasions over a year apart, or if they only showed that impossible amount of support for one of the brothers. The other alternative is that King, after his years of research, and having access to Professor Waller's work, which he cites, just didn't know that the trials Paris and Sam were separated by more than a year.

The village, which G.T. Swain, in his History of Logan County, calls a tiny village in 1884, being something over a quarter of a square mile in area, with a population of something over one hundred, would certainly be crowded with two hundred armed men present.

Swain, who reported such details as the number of votes cast for each side in town elections, completely missed King's massive invasion of Swain's hometown. Robert Spence, writing his detailed history of Logan County several decades later, also missed the biggest peace time gathering of armed men in the history of the state up to that time. Were it not for Dean King, millions of Americans would know no more about Logan County history than did Logan historians George Swain and Robert Spence.

As I knew that fewer than ten Hatfields or McCoys were involved in the climactic Battle of Grapevine, I decided to consult the Census . Looking at the 1880 Census for Pike County, I began looking for McCoy males between sixteen and fifty, but I came up so short that I finally counted all males over fourteen who were still alive. These included one seasoned gent of ninety winters (Ran'l's father, Daniel), and came to a grand total of forty. When I added the numbers for Logan County, I found a total of sixty McCoys over age fourteen in the entire valley. It's hard to get a hundred men out of a total cohort of sixty, but King managed to do it somehow.

If Paris had been convicted, are we to assume that the hundred armed McCoys would have opened fire upon Josephine, daughter of Sally McCoy, and three of the children of Sally's brother, Allen McCoy,[16] who were among the eight McCoys who were listed as witnesses *against* Paris?

How could King write that a hundred armed McCoys invaded Logan at a time when barely sixty McCoy men over age fourteen existed in the entire valley, and some of them were witnesses *against* Paris McCoy? Why would he even attempt to run such a scam on his readers, knowing that all anyone has to do is consult the US Census to prove conclusively that he is prevaricating?[17]

The answer is that this twenty-first century feud supersizer is simply following in the footsteps of the New York newspaper reporters that he relies upon so much for "facts" in his "True Story." .

T.C. Crawford, one of King's favorite sources for historical fact, has a long chapter of more than forty pages in his book, *An American Vendetta*, entitled *The Commercial Traveller's* (sic) *Story*.[18] In this tale, we see an Austrian noblewoman named Von Bergen who is travelling through the wilds of West Virginia *in a coach with liveried attendants.* The Austrian noblewoman has come to find the deeds to five thousand acres near Logan town which her father, the Austrian General Steinmetz, who fought for the Union in the Civil War, had bought shortly after the war.

The lady ran into a feudist named Sam Hatfield, whose home had just been burned by an invading gang of McCoys. Enlisting the support of another Hatfield chieftain named John, who is said to have led a group of rebel raiders called both "The Logan Tigers," and "The Logan Wildcats," she was able to gain the cooperation of Samuel Hatfield. She retrieved her deeds and sold the land to a doctor named Parker.

This yarn was spun as part of Crawford's "history," and Crawford is a source of historical fact for the current "feud historian," Dean King, but there are problems, among which are:

1) No deed for such a tract of land in the name of either Steinmetz or Van Bergen exists in the Logan County records. 2) No man named Sam or Samuel Hatfield appears in the 1880 Census. There are two John Hatfields in the 1880 Census, but one is 7 years old and the other is four years old.

So, we see that when Dean King spins yarns that are easily proven false by official records, he is only carrying on a tradition that dates all the way back to T.C. Crawford and John Spears. Of course today's feud industry leaders claim that all three, Crawford, Spears and King are historians.

## The Pretty Girl:

Every good drama needs a love story, and we get a double dose of it in Costner's presentation of the affair between Johnse Hatfield and Roseanna McCoy. Most of the book writers also love the love affair, and get maximum mileage out of it. Virgil Jones has a chapter entitled, *Mountain Romeo and Juliet.* Lisa Alther demonstrates her originality by styling a chapter, *Montagues and Capulets of the Cumberlands.*

Johnse was a ladies' man; Johnse knew it, and all the ladies knew it. Roseanna was a very pretty young woman by any man's standards.

Our film's writers err in evaluating the affair and its relationship to the feud, because they look at the wrong end of the affair. The fact that the two young people got together was no big thing; it happened as often in the mountains as it did in more civilized climes. All the stories about Anse refusing to let Johnse marry a McCoy are just stories. There is not a bit of evidence that Devil Anse harbored any ill will toward the McCoys as a clan or toward Ran'l individually at the time Johnse and Roseanna got together.

Truda McCoy argues forcefully that Ran'l objected to Roseanna marrying a son of Devil Anse, and she might have been right. Ran'l might well have raised objections, being by most accounts — especially that of Truda McCoy — the type of person who might object to something for any reason or no reason at all. Simple jealousy over Devil Anse's success in the timber business could have caused Ran'l to object to his daughter marrying one of Anse's sons. In the case of Johnse Hatfield, however, he would have had other possible grounds for trying to scotch the romance. After all, at age eighteen, Johnse had a thriving business peddling his pappy's corn likker, and was wanted in Pike County for carrying a concealed weapon.[19]

If Ran'l objected to the marriage, he was almost surely the only person in either family who did so, as the marriage of Johnse and Roseanna's cousin, Nancy a year later proved. That marriage, which united the son of Devil Anse Hatfield and the daughter of Asa Harmon McCoy, took place in the home of Martha McCoy, Nancy's mother and the widow of Asa Harmon McCoy. The marriage bond was signed by Martha's brother, lawyer Perry A. Cline.

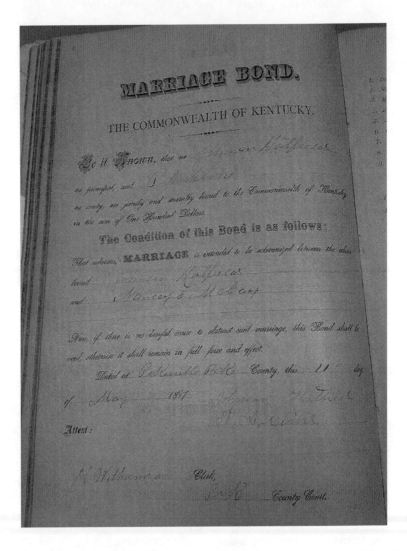

The only Hatfields and McCoys who had a reason to "feud" as of 1881 were the families of Asa Harmon McCoy and Devil Anse Hatfield. This recently discovered document,[20] along with the companion Marriage Certificate which shows that the wedding took place in the Peter Creek home of Nancy's mother, refutes entirely all claims that there was a "Hatfield and McCoy feud" ongoing in 1881. These documents prove that the wedding was accepted by Devil Anse and supported by both Martha McCoy and Perry Cline. This gives the lie to Dean King's claim that the Clines opposed the marriage and that Patty McCoy was "firmly opposed," and "forbade her daughter to marry Johnse." King says that the strong-willed Nancy "did it anyway, *in Pikeville* on May 14."[21](Italics mine)

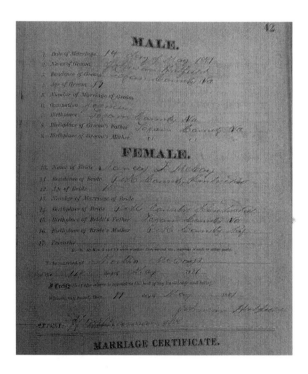

King knows the date of the marriage, so he must have seen the marriage certificate shown above. Yet King says that the marriage took place *in Pikeville*, over Martha's objection, when the document clearly states that the couple was married in the Peter Creek home of Nancy's mother, Martha (Patty) McCoy. The only motive I can see for this deliberate falsification is to maintain King's spurious contention that there was a blood feud between the two families underway in 1881.

About a dozen pages earlier, King told us that there were twenty-seven arrest warrants outstanding n Pikeville for Johnse. Now he tells us that Johnse came to Pikeville to get married. His more intelligent readers will know that at least one of those statements is false.  As is so often the case with King, both are false.

When I read Altina Waller's book, some twenty years ago, I checked her citations that referred to Pike County records thoroughly, and I can attest to the fact that she reported honestly, as befits a professional historian. Waller found one arrest warrant in Pike County for Johnse at that time. That warrant, which charged Johnse with carrying a concealed weapon, was served on Johnse in October, 1880, by Tolbert and Bud McCoy.[22] Tolbert testified in November, 1880 that Devil Anse and a gang took Johnse from his custody and cursed and abused him.[23]

King, who knows what Waller wrote, because he cites the passage from Waller, [24]says that it was Pharmer and not Bud who accompanied Tolbert in arresting Johnse.  The reason for this switch is apparent later, when we see him claiming that Bud was not involved in the Election Day fight. If the reader doesn't know that Bud was with Tolbert when he arrested Johnse, it is much easier to convince him that Bud was not in the fight against Ellison.

Of course the episode would not be sufficiently supersized without additional embellishment, so King says that when Johnse was arrested, he and Roseanna were "making love,"[25] clearly intending to convey to his reader that the couple was caught in flagrante. He cites Truda McCoy, but McCoy says that the couple was "standing and talking" when her brothers came upon them.[26] His other source is the New York reporter, John Spears, who says "they surprised their sister with her lover."[27] From Spears' words, they might have been playing checkers for all we know, but to King, the "deflator of legends and restorer of correct historical detail," they were "fornicating."[28]

When Devil Anse caught up with the Pikeville-bound party, King has Ran'l and "Big" Jim now accompanying Tolbert. Bud, whom the court record plainly says was there, is not present in King's supersized posse. At the end of the paragraph where the old man and Jim join the group there is a citation to Altina Waller[29]. On the cited page, 71, Altina Waller says what I am saying, contradicting most of what King says, yet he cites her for some reason. The only reason I can think of for citing Waller here is that if one is going to write fiction and call it history, he might as well cite a real historian to give it some credibility. It is obvious that all the recent supersizers depend upon their readers not checking their citations.

If one is constructing a multi-decade feud between two clan leaders, he must sooner or later bring them face to face. The Costner movie does it in the first scene, while King requires seventy-five pages. Both get the job done, and both are presenting fiction and selling it as history. When a writer cites a source and then writes something that disagrees with that source there are only a few explanations, none of which is complimentary to that writer.

Anyway, Johnse was arrested by Tolbert and Bud McCoy. Roseanna rode to West Virginia and told Devil Anse about it, and then Devil Anse, with a large group of backers, sprung the prisoner free, cursing and humiliating Tolbert in the process. Except for Roseanna's ride, this is in the sworn testimony of Tolbert McCoy in the cited case, and is true, no matter what some New York newspaper writer or modern supersizer says.[30] I say that Roseanna informed Devil Anse, because somebody had to have done it, and she is the only visible suspect.

Roseanna McCoy- West Virginia Archives and History

Johnse Hatfield — West Virginia Archives and History

The key to understanding the importance of the love affair to the troubles is to look at the end of the affair, and not at the beginning.

In the movie, the 1880 election was in West Virginia. We know this because when they left the election grounds for their little walk in the woods, Johnse tells Roseanna he is taking her to see the "second most beautiful thing in West Virginia." This implies, of course, that Roseanna is the most beautiful thing in West Virginia, but she was actually in Kentucky.

The second most beautiful thing in West Virginia, which Johnse took Roseanna to see, was — you would never have guessed — a moonshine still! I've seen moonshine stills, and they might be called interesting, but beautiful they aren't. I've tried to figure out why they used a still in this scene, but it eludes me. Surely Johnse didn't get the reputation of being the Valley's great lover by showing the girls *his still* on the first date.

Anyway, the deed was done — or we are led to believe it was — and it was done at such great length that they were late getting back to the election. Left with no choice but to drop her there with no way home other than to walk across the mountain, or take her home with him, Johnse boosted her up behind him and took her home to Devil Anse's place, where they lived in sin for several weeks.

Mountaineers of the late nineteenth century were not imbued with the Victorian prudishness of their Yankee betters. The distances involved in finding someone qualified to perform a legal marriage meant that many couples established a homestead and began a family without the blessing of a parson. They usually got around to it when a preacher came around later, but there was no hurry about it, and little social pressure to do so.

After enjoying the hospitality of the Hatfield home and Johnse's company — when he wasn't chasing some other woman — for several weeks, Roseanna had her fill of Johnse's philandering ways and left him. After a few days of listening to her disappointed father's scolding, Roseanna went to her Aunt Betty's house to live.

Truda McCoy tells the story of Roseanna staying with her Aunt Betty, where her baby was born and died, and where Johnse visited her. McCoy mentions "Aunt Betty's house" several times,[31] without referring to a husband a single time.

McCoy's editor, Leonard Roberts, states in a note that "Aunt Betty" was Allen McCoy's widow,[32] and I have faith in Mr. Roberts's integrity. Truda McCoy was writing the McCoys' story, but Leonard Roberts was a careful historian. So, I believe that Roseanna stayed with her widowed aunt, Betty Blankenship McCoy, and not with Betty and Uriah McCoy, as the feud industry now claims.

We have the court records of the arrest of Johnse and his rescue by Devil Anse as evidence that Roseanna was staying in Stringtown, and that is the only part of the story that is historically important.

Whether Roseanna had a boy or girl, a still-born child or miscarried is in dispute. My own family tradition agrees with what Cap Hatfield told John Spivak[33] — she had a girl, who died within a few months. Whatever the outcome of the pregnancy, there is little doubt that Roseanna came home pregnant.

I visited the McCoy homes in the Burnwell-Stringtown area in the late 1950s. The grave marker for the child of Roseanna that is shown to tourists today did not exist then. It is part of the feud industry that came into existence in the wake of the books by Truda McCoy and G. Elliott Hatfield in 1976. Leonard Roberts, the Editor of Truda McCoy's book, admitted that "no one can prove the child's birth, age or death."[34]

Most of the McCoy graves now shown to tourists have only the word of the feud industry as provenance. I know that Alifair was buried near Calvin's grave, because I heard it from persons who were at the burial. Calvin is the only one of Ran'l's children who died during the feud years for which an exact grave location can be established today, because his was the only grave that was marked with an engraved stone that still exists.

No one knows where or when William McCoy, whose name is on the large marker now at the cemetery, died; that does not prevent King claiming that William was a "feud fatality."

Dean King's handling of the story of William "Bill" McCoy is illustrative of the way the supersizers write "feud history." The reader will recall that King left Bud out of his account of the taking of Johnse Hatfield from the McCoys, and inserted Ran'l, Pharmer and "Big" Jim. King does this in spite of the fact that the court record shows that Johnse was arrested by Tolbert and Bud only, and that Tolbert swore that was the case.

Inserting Ran'l makes the feud bigger, which is the primary goal of the feud industry. Leaving Bud out makes it easier for King to falsify his later account of the stabbing of Ellison Hatfield by substituting Bill for Bud in the Election Day fight.

King carefully avoids making a categorical statement about the death of Bill McCoy. He says: "Bill, who should have been with them but instead *was said to have died* — of guilt and grief — because he was not."[35] He also says; "*Rumors* circulated that Bill had grown increasingly distraught until he had gone mad...Finally, *it was said*, he fell ill, took to his bed, and died without much of a fight."[36] King uses the phrases, "rumors circulated," and "it was said," never once stating categorically that Bill McCoy died, but he includes him in his list of feud fatalities nonetheless.[37]

King includes Bill McCoy among his feud fatalities, after quoting Sam McCoy saying that Bill McCoy was still alive three decades into the 20th century, and living in Mossy Rock, Washington.[38]

King also adds Mary Butcher McCoy, the widow of the timber tycoon, Tolbert McCoy to his list of feud fatalities, saying, "Mary refused to leave her bed; she grew weak and died, most said of a broken heart."[39] In the 1880 census, Tolbert was living and working on the John Maynard farm, while his wife, Mary Butcher McCoy was living with her aunt Zettie Butcher Williamson and Zettie's husband, Julius Williamson.

A man whom the Census shows to have been financially unable to establish his own home is presented to us by King as a wealthy timber man, whose brother, Calvin, made many trips to Pikeville in administering Tolbert's estate. King says that Mary was also involved in a lawsuit with Tolbert's partner in the timber business.

Of course, King does not name either the partner or the lawsuit, and for very good reason — no such partner or lawsuit ever existed.

Since King has been able to don the mantle of a historian while expanding the feud death toll in this manner, we can look forward to many more feud fatalities in the next *"True Story"* that the feud industry cranks out. We should soon eclipse the Rowan County feud's death toll of thirty-eight, on our way to the one hundred we saw reported in the Washington Post and New York Times. When the next generation of supersizers writes their books, we might even approach the total casualties at Gettysburg.

Ran'l McCoy's reported reaction to Roseanna's return home after tiring of Johnse's philandering ways is out of character for a father in that time and place, especially in light of the fact that Ran'l's own wife, Sally, had a daughter, Josephine, when they married. The 1880 census showed Josephine being 31 years old, with two illegitimate children of her own.

We cannot, however, dismiss Truda McCoy's version of this affair; after all, she is criticizing a McCoy (Ran'l), and we know that when a descendant criticizes her own side, we need to give it some weight. There is no more negative overall portrayal of the character of Ran'l McCoy anywhere in the literature than that of Truda McCoy. Therefore, it is quite possible that a combination of his own crankiness and his resentment of Devil Anse's business success caused him to mistreat his daughter.

Truda McCoy wrote that whenever Roseanna tried to speak to her father, "he would answer sharply and leave the room."[40]

Further, McCoy wrote:"He showed no signs of ever relenting... God forgives the sinner, but Ranel McCoy was not so lenient."[41]

While most writers, including Truda McCoy, say that Ran'l was bent out of shape because of his animosity toward the Hatfields, it could also have been that he was angry over the missed opportunity for his daughter to marry into the prosperous Hatfield family.

I don't believe the universal claim that Johnse and Roseanna met for the first time at the 1880 election. Johnse was a bootlegger, whose main market was Pike County, and Ran'l McCoy's sons liked their corn likker. It is virtually certain that Johnse knew Roseanna well before the election of 1880, as a result of his business.

Ran'l McCoy's sons were undoubtedly good customers of Johnse. Whether one or more of them also acted as a distributor is open to question, although the preponderance of the testimony that I have heard leads me to suspect that both Jim and Tolbert had acted in that capacity at various times.

The possible association of Ran'l' McCoy's sons with Johnse as distributors of Hatfield whiskey is inflated by Dean King, who says that Jim McCoy actually *worked at Devil Anse's still* in West Virginia, "an endeavor that required absolute faith among partic-ipants."[42]  King continues, saying that because Devil Anse's sons were too lazy to do the work around the still, and Randall's fam-ily was poorer than the Hatfields, Randall "was more than happy to have "Big" Jim fill in for them."[43] King has a vicious blood feud ongoing at the same time that the son of one of his clan leaders is working for the other clan leader!

King never explains why "Big" Jim didn't just go to work for his little brother, Tolbert, the timber tycoon rather than traveling all the way to Grapevine to help Devil Anse with his moonshine still. That Devil Anse could get forty kinsmen and neighbors to work in his timbering operation, which entails labor an order of magnitude harder than the labor around a still, does not seem to matter to King.

The very idea that anyone — much less someone as intelligent and cautious as Devil Anse Hatfield — would allow a non-kinsman out-of-state outsider to *look* at his still is preposterous.  From the day that Lincoln signed the law in 1862, making the distilling of untaxed liquor a federal offense until today, no operator of such a still would ever do such a thing.  King repeats at least three more times the ludicrous claim that Devil Anse, a member of one of the largest families in the entire Valley, had such a shortage of will-ing workers among his kin that he had to employ an out-of-state McCoy at his still.

King obviously read something about making moonshine and he impresses his readers by devoting several pages to describing how Devil Anse produced his renowned apple-jack.[44] He says that Anse ran his second run until the product no longer "tasted like brandy," then shut it off, at which time he had ninety-eight percent alcohol. As someone who actually watched moonshine being made on Blackberry Creek long ago, I can assure the reader that top quality double run apple jack would be far less than ninety-eight percent alcohol, and the stuff coming out of the still would have stopped tasting like brandy long before it reached that level of purity.

As Devil Anse was known for his fine apple-jack, his product would have been somewhere between forty percent and seventy-five percent alcohol (80-150 proof), and most likely much nearer the lower figure. Ideally one would want to retain as much apple taste as possible, which occurs at the lower proof levels. The problem is that at forty percent (80 proof), the brandy might have retained too much of the bad-tasting factors, and at alcohol levels higher than seventy percent it loses all its fruity taste. A ninety-eight percent alcohol drink tastes like pure alcohol whether it is made from apples, corn or sugar, and no one could tell the difference.

If Devil Anse had wanted to keep running his product until he got 196 proof alcohol, he wouldn't have gone to the trouble of toting three hundred bushels of apples a mile up the hill and processing them in the woods. He would have just used sugar, and run it until he got the virtually pure alcohol that King says he ran.

Ran'l and his sons were harboring ill will toward Johnse and his close kin when they went to the election a year later. This animosity was a combination of jealousy over the timber business, the embarrassing loss of Johnse after arresting him and the fact that Roseanna came home pregnant and still a McCoy.

Most feud writers tend to discard the love affair after they realize that Devil Anse really didn't prevent a marriage, but that is a mistake. The way the affair ended was definitely *a* contributing factor in the later troubles.

When Devil Anse took Johnse from their custody, Tolbert and Bud McCoy were shamed in a way that they would not soon be able to forget. Whether Anse told them to kneel and pray, as Costner did in the movie, is not certain. It probably happened, because I have heard it from several sources, and it is the kind of semi-sadistic prank Devil Anse was prone to do. Tolbert testified in a case a few weeks later that he was held prisoner for a long time and was cursed and abused.[45] As Tolbert swore that he was "cursed and abused," I can accept as true the claim that Devil Anse told him to "get on your damn knees...."

Whatever happened on the road to Pikeville that night, it was highly demeaning for the McCoy men, and it surely affected their mind-set on Election Day. As such, it was definitely *a* cause of the Election Day violence. The taking of a prisoner from law officers at gunpoint, while cursing and abusing them, is an act of violence.

In this part of the movie, the script writers are at least showing something that *could* have happened. They have the testimony from Tolbert and the writings of Truda McCoy and others to back them up. Best of all, it fits the character of the personalities involved.

I consider the arrest of Johnse Hatfield by Tolbert and Bud McCoy to have been the first overt act of the Hatfield-McCoy troubles. That Devil Anse did not harm the McCoys when he got the drop on them and took Johnse from their custody on the way to jail shows that Devil Anse did not have any great hatred for the McCoys in 1880. It also shows that Anse, despite his activities during the war, was not a psychopathic killer.

The movie misses the mark when it says that the McCoys intended to kill Johnse. If that had been their intention, they would have shot him as soon as they were out of sight of witnesses, taking no chance on Johnse either escaping or being rescued by his family.

This brings Tolbert McCoy to the 1882 election, filled with enmity toward Johnse for his mistreatment of his sister and needing revenge against Johnse's family for his humiliation when he lost custody of Johnse. It didn't take a lot of white lightning to get him in a killing mood.

The movie's introduction of Frank Phillips into the narrative, by way of him coming to West Virginia and killing two of Devil

Anse's cousins named Levinger, is another creation of Costner's writers. No such family existed in the valley, and no such incident ever occurred.

The scene showing Ran'l destroying Roseanna's hope chest is just one more example of the movie's trashing of Ran'l McCoy.

---

1 Hatfield and Spence, *Tale of the Devil*, 107.

2 Section 2252 of the Kentucky Statutes says: "A petit jury in the circuit court shall consist of twelve persons, and in all trials held in courts inferior to the circuit court, or by any county, police, or city judge, or justice of the peace, a jury shall consist of six persons; but the parties to any action or prosecution, except for felony, may agree to a trial by a less number of persons than is provided for in this section." Article 248 of the Kentucky Constitution incorporates the same requirements for juries in courts inferior to the circuit court.

3 He relented at least once, when Shirley Donnelly visited him in 1955.

4 King, 55.

5 McCoy, *McCoys*, 17.

6 A few people have expressed doubts to me over the years as to whether or not there actually was a hog trial. Some wonder what year it was held. There was a hog trial, in 1878. It was held in preacher Anse's front room, with six jurors—three each of Hatfields and McCoys, and the vote was four to two for Floyd Hatfield.

7 Rice, 73.

8 McCoy, Samuel, *Squirrel Huntin' Sam McCoy: His Memoir and Family Tree.* 27.

9 King's description of the killing of Bill Staton, including all the words herein quoted, is found in: King, *The Feud*, 61-2.

10 Rice, *The Hatfields and the McCoys,* 73.

11 Alther, Lisa, *Blood Feud*, 50.

12 Waller, Altina, *Feud*, 272, n. 31.

13 King, Dean, *The Feud*, 85.

14 Waller, *Feud*, 272, n. 31.

15 Swain, G.T., *History of Logan County*, 95.

16 *Ibid.* Uriah, Sylvester and Eva, all children of Sally's brother, Allen and his wife Betty Blankenship McCoy, were listed as witnesses against Paris.

17 I realize that *prevaricating* is a strong word, but King was obviously familiar with the 1880 Census, because he cites it in a footnote to his Prologue, in the very beginning of his book. Where I come from, when a man knows something to be true and deliberately states otherwise, he is prevaricating.

18 Crawford, American Vendetta, 93-135.

19 Waller, *Feud*, 272, n.42.

20 The records of the marriage, including the marriage certificate and bond were found at the Pikeville court house by feud researcher, Clifford Gene New.

21 King, 83. Shortly after New posted his findings, King put the marriage bond on his Facebook page, calling it a "cool document." Of course he said nothing about the fact that the documents proved his description of the event to be false in detail.

22 Waller, *Feud*, 273, n. 42.

23 Ibid.

24 King, The Feud, 361, n. 13.

25 King, *The Feud*, 75.

26 McCoy, *The McCoys*, 43-4. This is one of many places where King cites a source that refutes his words. How can a writer cite another writer who says the couple was "standing and talking" in support of a claim that they were "fornicating?"

27 Spears, *Mountain Feud*, 4.

28 King, 75.

29 King, *The Feud*, 361, n. 20.

30 *Commonwealth of Kentucky v. Andrew Hatfield, et. al.* November 26, 1880, Kentucky Department for Libraries and Archives.

31 McCoy, The McCoys, 39-56.

32 McCoy, The McCoys, 223, n. 5.

33 Rice, *Hatfields and McCoys*, p. 129, n.6.

34 McCoy, *The McCoys*, 224, n. 6.

35 King, *The Feud*, 195

36 King, 141.

37 King, 275.

38 King, 141.

39 King, 141.

40 McCoy, *The McCoys*, 38.

41 *Ibid.*

42 King, Dean, *The Feud*, 67.

43 King, 67.

44 King, 64-67.

45 *Commonwealth of Kentucky v. Andrew Hatfield, et. al.* Nov. 26, 1880, Kentucky Department for Libraries and Archives.

# CHAPTER 13.

# THE ELECTION NOBODY WON

The central event of the "Hatfield and McCoy Feud" was the killing of Ellison Hatfield by three sons of Ran'l McCoy, Tolbert, Pharmer and Randolph, Jr. (Bud) on Election Day, 1882. The supporting players were Preacher Anse and the two Elias Hatfields, one "Good" and one "Bad," and moonshine whiskey.[1]

The movie has it pretty well jumbled up, with Devil Anse's brother, who was "Good 'Lias" depicted as "Bad 'Lias" and the real "Bad 'Lias," Preacher Anse's brother, who had an early altercation with Tolbert McCoy that day, not on the scene at all.[2]

The movie has some people there who weren't there and some things happening that didn't happen. Devil Anse was not there, so the scene where he and Ran'l passed each other while everyone was wondering which of them would flinch, is just fiction. We see Johnse and Nancy still courting and discussing Roseanna's pregnancy, when in reality, Johnse and Nancy were already married at that time; the romance between Johnse and Roseanna had ended, and Roseanna's baby had been born and died.

The basic facts of what happened on Election Day, 1882 are very similar in almost all accounts. Given the large number of witnesses and the sworn testimony by both sides, most of the storytellers are somewhat constrained in the amount of supersizing they can get away with. The big exceptions are the New York Sun reporter, John Spears and Dean King. The former is of little import as no one has paid any attention to his scribbling for more than a century. The latter is a serious problem for real historians, because his fictional tale sold as history is a current best-seller, and its distortion of the Election Day, 1882 events literally *changes everything.* By changing two well established historical facts, i.e., that Tolbert was impoverished, and Ellison was unarmed, King makes everything different.

King adheres closely to John Spears' in his description of the Election Day fight—the most significant single event of the entire period. King explains his affinity for Spears' account, saying, "Spears likewise gave a detailed and descriptive account that, *while differing substantially* from other standard accounts, *had the ring of authenticity.*"[3] (Emphasis added)

Spears misspelled the names of all three of the Sons of Ran'l McCoy who were involved in the Election Day fight. Tolbert was Talbot, Pharmer was Farmer, and Bud was Budd. Spears says that Budd (sic), born in 1864, was *nine years old* at the time of the 1882 election. Yet King, after four years of intense research, accepts Spears' tale, which contradicts all eyewitness testimony by Hatfields, McCoys and neutrals—because *it sounds more authentic* to him!

The census of 1880 lists Tolbert as a farm laborer; the 1880 Agricultural Census says he is living on the farm of John Maynard, and working there. King says that Tolbert was a wealthy timber merchant who left his wife a sizeable estate. So intent is he upon impressing his readers with the wealth of Tolbert the timber tycoon that he states it in three separate places.[4] The deed books in the Pike County court house show no deeds in Tolbert's name. The County Court records show no will, no executor, no estate settlement and no lawsuits filed on behalf of the estate.

Everyone, McCoy, Hatfield or other that I talked to when I was growing up on Blackberry said Ellison was unarmed. All the testimony said he was unarmed. Even Truda McCoy says in her book that Ellison was unarmed. This simple fact formed much of the foundation upon which life proceeded in Tug Valley from that time at least until King's "True Story" came out. Everyone knew that Devil Anse had acted illegally when he lynched the three McCoy boys, but it was looked upon as justified or at least mitigated by the brutal butchering of his brother.

In King's version, Tolbert ceases being a poor farm laborer with little to look forward to, who comes to the election with a lot of resentment over his condition. He is not a man who is motivated by having been embarrassed by the Hatfields taking Johnse from his custody a few months before. He is also not a man who is envious of the fine horses and store bought clothes of Devil Anse's group, who gets likkered up and commits a foul deed. Instead, he is a wealthy timber merchant who starts a fight with the town drunk, Bad Elias, over a buck and change. Under this inverted set of facts, the work of Altina Waller is negated, and the feud was, indeed, as the yellow journalists of New York presented it in 1888—a series of mindlessly violent acts perpetrated by a depraved people.

My assessment of the state of mind of Tolbert McCoy on Election Day, 1882 is buttressed by the writings of the McCoy historian, Truda McCoy. As I wrote earlier, whenever a descendant of one of the families writes something that is derogatory to that writer's side in the feud, it can be given weight as being likely true.

Truda McCoy said: "The McCoys spent the evening before the election cleaning guns that were already clean and in sharpening knives that were already sharp...Tolbert McCoy, Ranel's son, age twenty-eight, married to Mary Butcher, sat on the stoop outside his house, cleaning and sharpening. Satisfied that his weapons were in perfect order, he laid them down..."[5] McCoy makes it perfectly clear that Tolbert McCoy went to that election expecting trouble of the kind that would require a sharp knife.

McCoy's story of how the McCoys prepared their weapons and carried them to the election contrasts sharply with the established fact that Ellison Hatfield was unarmed. Someone was loaded for bear on August 7, 1882, and someone wasn't.

Describing the Election Day events, McCoy says that Tolbert, realizing that he was losing his wrestling match with Ellison Hatfield, changed the nature of the fight by "reaching into his pocket, he pulled out the knife he had sharpened the day before. It had a long slender blade, razor sharp. Reaching backward, he cut time and again into Ellison's stomach and bowels."[6] This is in agreement with what everyone on Blackberry Creek said when I was growing up. It is especially important in that this comes from someone who says in the title of her book that she is telling *"The McCoy's Story."* King disputes the McCoy family story by making the outrageous claim that Ellison Hatfield started the fight with a knife. King's words are: "The bickering continued, and Big Ellison became more animated. He waved his jackknife in Tolbert's face."[7]

As I am probably the last person who knew many people personally who were alive on Blackberry Creek when the important feud events transpired who will write a book, I bear a special responsibility, both to my ancestors and to my posterity to refute that lie.

King even changes the size and shape of the knife as it was described by Truda McCoy[8] and by everyone who actually saw it, saying Tolbert's knife had a "broad two-inch blade."[9] "Truda McCoy described Tolbert's knife: "It had a long, slender blade, razor sharp." King gives no basis for his ridiculously shaped knife blade.

In an end note to Truda McCoy's book, her editor, the historian Leonard Roberts, describes Ellison Hatfield: "Ellison Hatfield, a tall, splendid man and soldier..."[10] Ellison Hatfield, who was presented as a *splendid man* in the definitive McCoy story and considered a splendid man by the people on both sides of Tug River, becomes a cowardly would-be-murderer in the *"True Story"* by Dean King.

If the movie had shown how voting was actually carried out, it would have been both entertaining and educational. As the Australian, or secret, ballot had not been adopted in Kentucky at that time, every voter had to approach the table where the election officers sat and announce his choice for each office in an audible voice.

Although neither Ellison nor Elias was armed, the mere presence of the West Virginia Hatfields, with their war reputations, their obvious wealth, and their standing in Logan County was enough to intimidate all but the most stalwart Republicans in most elections. Of course the chief Republican, Preacher Anse, would have tolerated no open interference in the vote by the Democrat Hatfields from across the river, but the implied threat was usually there. This day in 1882 was an exception, because Ellison and Elias were supporting the friend of the McCoys, Tom Stafford, in his candidacy for Justice of the Peace, making the fatal encounter not a political argument.

It certainly didn't happen the way Dan Cunningham said it happened. Old Dan says that Ellison Hatfield asked Pharmer McCoy how he was going to vote, and Pharmer answered that he was going to vote the way he pleased. Ellison, according to Cunningham, then told Pharmer, "You will vote to please me or you will not vote at all."[11]

Of course, Pharmer didn't vote at all. Born in 1863, he was a year short of the legal voting age of twenty-one. Once again Cunningham has it all garbled, as he says the scuffle started between Pharmer and Ellison, immediately after Ellison told the ineligible voter how he must vote.

As the free moonshine flowed, Tolbert McCoy was a fight ready to happen all day. He got into a tussle with Bad 'Lias Hatfield early in the day, over a debt he alleged was owed to him by Bad 'Lias, which Elias denied. As they came to blows, Preacher Anse stepped in and stopped the fight, saying, "Tolb, Election Day ain't no day to settle a debt."[12]

Toward mid-afternoon, Ellison arose from sleeping off his morning liquor, and an argument arose between him and Tolbert, during which Tolbert made the boast, "I'm hell on earth," to which Ellison replied, "You're a damn shit-hog." [13] Ellison's words, "You're a damn shit-hog," were spoken by Elias in the movie. This is just one of many places in the movie where history was twisted for no apparent reason.

A scuffle began, and Tolbert, unable to prevail in the fistfight against the stronger Ellison quickly went to his knife and opened a gash in Ellison's abdomen. Then he repeatedly stabbed Ellison, who was unarmed. Young Bud joined Tolbert in stabbing Ellison, who located and took up a large rock, but, before he could employ it, Pharmer shot him in the back, making Ellison the big loser in that particular election.

In King's "*True Story*" it is William, not Bud, who joins Tolbert and Pharmer in the killing of Ellison Hatfield. In this, he has the support of Truda McCoy and John Spears, who probably made the substitution of Bill for Bud to make the execution of the boys by Devil Anse at least partially cold-blooded murder. No one on Blackberry

Creek ever doubted that the three McCoys who were lynched were the three that actually killed Ellison Hatfield. Had there been a substantial number of Blackberry people who thought Devil Anse had killed an innocent boy, there would have been a great hue and cry for the Hatfields to be brought to justice. No one on Blackberry Creek even joined the posse that was formed in Pikeville five years later.

The most frequently asked question from folks learning about the feud is, "Why did the crowd allow the fight to go on so long? Why didn't someone break it up before Ellison was stabbed two dozen times?" It became apparent to me long ago that most people think it takes a long time for three men to stab someone two dozen times, but they are wrong, and the reader can easily prove this. Simply close one fist and strike the other open hand as fast as you would if you were trying to kill an angry bear, and count the seconds elapsed while striking a dozen blows. This simple exercise will show you that the time from the first slash until the bullet from Pharmer's revolver entered Ellison's back was probably no more than fifteen or twenty seconds.

Even if it were half a minute, that is not enough time for the number of men required to stop a four-man fight to assemble and act. There is no doubt that an effort was afoot to stop the stabbing, because Preacher Anse testified that he was close enough to Ellison to see his shirt twist as the bullet entered his back.

The Costner crew got it right on the size of the two combatants. Several books make much of the size differential between the two men, some saying that Ellison was well over six feet tall and nearly 250 pounds. His army record lists him as five feet ten inches tall.[14] The movie, which shows Ellison shorter and more powerfully built than Tolbert, is true to the facts.

Truda McCoy describes Tolbert as "tall and slender built, with fair complexion and light brown hair."[15] That sounds like the descriptions of all the McCoys in their service records.[16] The strong, burly Ellison Hatfield obviously had a great strength advantage over the tall, slender Tolbert McCoy, but Tolbert had an equalizer in his pocket.

Dean King's description of the Election Day fight changes the entire nature of the feud. King says Ellison was six feet six in his stocking feet,[17] but I think he knows better. Since he refers to the military records to correctly establish the height of Ellison's father, Ephraim, as six feet even, it is not logical to believe that he did not also see the five feet ten inch height of Ellison in those same records.[18]

King refers to Ellison alternately as either "Deacon Ellison" or "Big Ellison." The first moniker was never used by anyone in Tug Valley at any time. We know the source of the "Big" appellation,[19] which is King's extension of the true height of the man.

I was truly taken aback to see a purported *"True Story,"* make the preposterous claim that Ellison Hatfield was a Deacon in Preacher Anse's church. When I read the part about Ellison Hatfield being a Deacon in the Old Pond Church, my reaction was: "Just how dumb does he think we are?"

Preacher Anse, my great-great-grandfather, was a Union soldier and a Republican. The very idea that an ex- Confederate officer and Democrat from West Virginia would even be a regular attendee, much less a member and a Deacon in Preacher Anse's church is ludicrous; especially when there was a Primitive Baptist Church on Mate Creek, where Ellison lived, which was several hours ride from Preacher Anse's church on Pond Creek, in Kentucky.

I thought King had reached the outer limits of exaggeration with his "One hundred armed McCoys," but when he spun his yarn about "Deacon" Ellison, he went completely ballistic. King says that "on a fair day, eight hundred or more horses and mules were tied up to trees and bushes outside (Preacher Anse's church), and twelve hundred people were eager to hear the services, many more than could fill the pews inside the eighteen by thirty foot log structure."[20]

I am sure that the eight hundred horses will slip right by most of King's readers; after all, none of them has ever seen eight hundred horses in one place. When Colonel John Clarkson's eight hundred VSL cavalry — one of whom was Devil Anse

Hatfield — was on its way to kick John Dils's butt at Wireman's shoals in 1862, a Union scout reported that he had observed the rebel horsemen ride through Johns Creek. The scout said it took two hours for the eight hundred horses to pass his position.[21] Even a city-bred writer ought to recognize the practical impossibility of finding enough bushes and trees around that little mountain church to secure eight hundred horses. But, that's what he wrote.

Anyone can go to the website of the Mate's Creek Association and see that the Old Pond Church, where Preacher Anse was the preacher, and where Ellison Hatfield was *not a deacon*, had exactly twenty-eight members in 1890, and forty-three in 1905.[22]

As the increase between 1890 and 1905 was almost fifty percent, we can safely assume that the membership in 1882 was less than 28, so they would have fit nicely inside the little church. When I read stuff like this I wonder if the writer is unaware of written records that exist. One would think that a writer of a claimed "*True Story*," wherein he promises to "restore accurate historical detail," would at least be aware of things like Census reports and church minutes.

This mangling of history with the tale of "Deacon Ellison," is illustrative of the difficulty of writing history without actually studying history. Anyone who knows the history of the Primitive Baptists knows that, during the Civil War, the Primitive Baptists were generally rabidly pro-Confederate. In many of the Virginia and Carolina churches, members were "De-fellowshipped," (excommunicated) for supporting the Union.[23] Preacher Anse, as a pro-Union Kentucky Republican, was an anomaly within his denomination. An ex-Confederate from West Virginia would certainly not be drawn to his congregation, when virtually every Primitive Baptist Church in West Virginia was solidly Confederate in sentiment. Lastly, the Mate Creek Primitive Baptist church was within walking distance of Ellison's home.

Consider King's tale that Ellison Hatfield was a six foot six inch Deacon in Preacher Anse's Church, who started the Election Day fight with a drawn knife: Who is damaged by this lie?

First, Ellison Hatfield is libeled by it. He was a highly respected member of his community, and an elected constable in the Magnolia District, whom Truda McCoy's editor called "a splendid man." If he was a six foot six inch giant, who started a fight by drawing a knife on the much smaller Tolbert McCoy, then Ellison Hatfield was the lowest type of man, an assertion that would have been denied by everyone in the Valley, McCoys included.

This is the worst libel in a book that is teeming with libels. Next to Preacher Anse Hatfield, Ellison Hatfield was the most respected man in the Blackberry-Mate Creek area. It was respect and love for Ellison, and not fear of Devil Anse, that kept the people of Blackberry — Hatfields, McCoys and others — from trying to punish Anse for avenging Ellison's murder. Truda McCoy's editor was right; Ellison Hatfield was a splendid man.

Second, Preacher Anse is libeled by it. If King's tale is accepted as fact, then a deacon in Preacher Anse Hatfield's church started a fight, almost in the preacher's front yard, by pulling a knife on a much smaller man.

My great, great grandfather, Uriah McCoy and all his brothers, sons and nephews are libeled by it. Uriah McCoy, a confederate army veteran, never joined in "The Feud." Neither Uriah nor his sons, including my great-great grandfather, Asa, rallied to Ran'l's side, because they considered the execution of Ran'l's sons to be a crude form of justice. If Ellison Hatfield started the fight with a knife, then my great, great grandfather, Uriah McCoy, and his son, Asa, were either cowards or men without family loyalty or a sense of justice. Neither is true.

If Ellison Hatfield started the fight with a knife, then all my Kentucky ancestors, both Hatfields and McCoys were lawless and amoral people, since they took no action to see that the Hatfields who lynched the three McCoys were apprehended and brought to justice.

Of course the Randolph McCoy cult approves of King's twisting of the facts. By placing the knife in Ellison's hands, King makes Ran'l McCoy the only living victim of the event. They ignore what that does to all the other McCoys who refused to join Ran'l. If King was telling the truth, then at least eighty-five percent of all the McCoys in Pike County, and all the Kentucky Hatfields, were either cowards or men without either family loyalty or a sense of justice, since they had nothing to do with Ran'l and his "feud." Besmirching the memory of all those men who did nothing to avenge the three sons of Ran'l is a price the cult is willing to pay, just to cast Ran'l as a victim and Devil Anse as a villain.

The two leading *family* writers, Truda McCoy and Coleman Hatfield agree on the major facts of the Election Day fight, but King makes liars of both. Yet we see both Hatfields and McCoys helping King sell the great lie.

Distorting our history harms us all — the dead and the living — and it is obviously intentional, since this writer had access to the historical facts, but chose to go with the sensational lies of the yellow journalists of the day, in order to show the people as immoral and barbaric.

Lying about history is an intellectual act of terror, and we are all victims.

Although he was undoubtedly angry when Devil Anse took the three McCoy boys from his house to West Virginia,[24] Preacher Anse took no overt action to try to bring Devil Anse to justice. Preacher Anse himself was an eyewitness to the killing of Ellison, and he knew that it was a senseless butchering of a valued citizen in the community. He also knew as well as Devil Anse knew that the McCoys would not receive their just due in Pikeville.

Devil Anse, who showed no reluctance to use the legal system in dispute settlement throughout the remainder of his life, knew the same thing Ran'l knew. In addition to the power Colonel Dils had to sway the system, including witnesses, Anse undoubtedly knew that it would be virtually impossible to pick a jury in Pikeville that did not have at least one person who had either suffered from the wartime depredations of Anse's raiders or had friends or acquaintances who had. So he resorted to the law of Judge Lynch.

Remember that there was no court able to hear a murder case against the three sons of Ran'l within less than a day's ride, and probably no judge competent to preside over such a case within even that distance. The importance of Tug River as a state boundary, and the great distance between Tug Valley and the county seat of Pikeville are vitally important to an understanding of events during this period. A historian of the Preacher Anse Hatfield family, Ron G. Blackburn, found this petition.

### 1849 Pike County Kentucky Petition

I found this petition in a library at Huntsville Alabama in 1980. The title of the book was Petitions from the state of Kentucky. Unfortunately I do not remember the arthur. It seems ironic that the citizens of the area had these same thoughts and problems 30 years before the Hatfield and McCoy Feud. It is further noted that the majority of these individuals remained loyal to Virginia during the Civil War. Apparently the Petition was denied since this area is still within the state of Kentucky. I have no further information on the outcome of the petition.

*R B*

### January 31, 1849 Pike County Kentucky Petition

Residence of Pike County Kentucky intend petitioning the next legislature of Kentucky for a law ceding to Virginia that portion of the county of Pike including within the following boundaries: At the mouth of Big Creek on the west side of Tug Fork of Sandy River... to the top of the main dividing ridge between the tug and Lavica ... to the line between Kentucky and Virginia. They suffer many inconveniences in consequence of the present dividing line between the states. Violators of the law can in a moment of time pass from one state to the other and thus elude officers of the law. The present line divides neighbors, friends and relations.

#### *Signatures*

| | | | |
|---|---|---|---|
| John Ferrell | John McCoy | Wm. Tiller | Joseph Murphey |
| John Coy (Mc Coy) | Aly Hatfield | Daniel McCoy | Richard Furrell |
| John Murphey | Andrew Varney | Jacob Webb | John McCoy |
| M.G.B Davis | Asa McCOY | James Vance | Richard Maynard |
| David Maynard | Andy Murphey | Cummens Music | John Sanson |
| Samuel Mounts | Herndon Murphey | George Hatfield | Valentine Hatfield |
| Ferrell Hatfield | Mitchel Rumspsy | Asa Harmon McCoy | Richard Hatfield |
| John Hatfield | Thos Hatfield | Joseph Hatfield Jr | Joseph Hatfield |
| Ulysses McCoy | Nathan Pabnett | John Wolfred | Canly Blankinship |
| Ezekiel Blankinship | Fredrick Wolfred | Isaac New | William Blackburn |
| Henry G Davis | Peter M Alley | William T Cline | Randolph McCoy |
| Samuel Canada | William Davis | Madison Hatfield | Samuel Farley |

Refer to Court of Justices

The petition was signed by several Hatfields, James Vance, Asa Harmon McCoy and Randolph McCoy. Had the state government honored that petition, there would almost certainly not have been a vigilante execution of the three McCoys, and, therefore, no Hatfield and McCoy feud.

Preacher Anse was aware of all that, and, knowing Devil Anse's capacity for mayhem, he seems to have been willing to let his cousin slide on that one, hoping that would be the end of it.

Uncle Ransom said his father, who often said that Devil Anse had killed more people in Pike County during the war than consumption, witnessed the killing of Ellison, and simply wanted it to stop there; so he didn't do anything to try to get Devil Anse arrested. Preacher Anse continued to be a peacemaker as late as 1886, when he attempted to quiet tempers after the killing of Jeff McCoy.

Having surveyed Ellison's wounds, Preacher Anse decided that Ellison would surely die soon, and he ordered his Brother, Floyd, the Constable[25] and the two deputies[26] to take the three McCoys to Pikeville immediately. When Ran'l objected,[27] Preacher Anse told him that Devil Anse would probably be there shortly with a gang and that the Pikeville jail was the only safe place for his sons.[28] [29]

Preacher Anse told the officers[30] to take the boys directly to Pikeville, but after going a couple of miles up Blackberry, they decided to stop for the night and get an early start the next day, not relishing the prospect of riding all night in the dark. That decision cost the McCoys their lives.[31]

The movie then shows us an entirely fictional account of how the three McCoy boys were taken from the Kentucky law into the custody of the Hatfields. We see Devil Anse and Wall at the head of a large group of riders, intercepting the Kentucky party, which was headed by the sheriff. Anse demands that the sheriff release the McCoys to him, and then Wall does the same, drawing a gun and pointing it at the sheriff. The sheriff was in Pikeville—not on Blackberry Creek—and none of that happened.

Although the movie has Devil Anse and Wall at the election, Elias was actually the only brother of Ellison who was present.

The morning after the election, Wall and Elias went toward Pikeville, on the same track as the one taken by the officers with the McCoy prisoners. Wall and Elias did not force the surrender of the boys to them. Wall actually convinced the officers that they should take the boys back to Preacher Anse's place, and they all peacefully rode toward the preacher's house. On the way, they met Devil Anse and more than a dozen of his relatives and employees, who fell in with them on the trek to Preacher Anse's house.[32]

It is significant that the taking of the McCoys happened the day after the election, because it could not have happened a day earlier. Preacher Anse's standing in the community was such that he would have had the support of several dozen men in keeping custody of the McCoy boys, had it occurred while the election crowd was there On the day following the election, there were not enough of Preacher Anse's people at the preacher's house to oppose Devil Anse, and he rode away with the prisoners.

According to the trial testimony, Preacher Anse had dinner with Devil Anse and his brothers, Wall and Elias, while the three McCoys were in custody at his house. Uncle Ransom said that Devil Anse and his brothers wanted his father to keep the three nearby for a few days, to see how Ellison fared, and then have a trial for the McCoys there at his place. The preacher demurred, saying he had no authority to try a murder case. As he was an eyewitness, Preacher Anse knew that any such trial would be little more than a lynching, and he wanted no part of it.

The trial testimony says that Devil Anse stomped out of the house and called out his men from the porch.[33] Joined by several supporters, Devil Anse took the McCoy boys to West Virginia, and the rest, as they say, is history.[34]

Uncle Ransom said that Anse's taking the McCoy boys from Preacher Anse's home to West Virginia angered his father about as much as the later murders. It is obvious that the preacher felt responsible, having been unable to prevent Devil Anse taking the boys from his custody. Losing custody of the McCoys wounded his Hatfield pride.

The History Channel movie does a reasonable job in its treatment of the last two days of the lives of Tolbert, Pharmer, and Bud McCoy, after they fell into Hatfield custody. They were taken to the West Virginia side of the river and held under guard in an old schoolhouse, where their mother and Tolbert's wife came to plead for their lives. According to Sally McCoy's testimony, it was Wall and not Devil Anse, as shown in the movie, to whom her pleadings were made for the lives of her sons.[3536]

Preacher Anse Hatfield also visited in an effort to convince Devil Anse to turn the boys over to him, but he was rebuffed also.

Of course, the scene where Ran'l goes to Anse's home to plead for his boys never happened, but it continues the movie's theme of a long-term personal animosity between the two men.

Ellison, who had made a huge mistake by bringing his fists to a knife fight, and then compounded his error by taking a rock to a gunfight, died two days later. When Ellison expired, the Hatfields, under the leadership of Devil Anse, took the three McCoys back to the Kentucky side of the river, tied them to paw paw bushes, and executed them. The bodies of Tolbert and Pharmer were riddled with bullets, and the top of the head of the youngest, eighteen-year-old Bud, was blown away.[37]

An understanding of Jim McCoy's location and actions at this time is absolutely necessary in order to understand "the feud." Called "Uncle Jim" by virtually everyone in Pike County, Jim McCoy is "Big" Jim throughout Dean King's book. If you Google the name "Uncle Jim McCoy," you will get several results which show that the man was universally known as "Uncle Jim" — so much so that he is even referred to in that way in obituaries. Google "Big Jim McCoy" and the only relevant reference on the first page of results is from Dean King's book.

King knows where Jim McCoy was, and he tells us. Almost a hundred twenty pages into his tale of a violent blood feud that was so intense that it had led to the greatest peacetime concentration of armed men in the history of West Virginia two years earlier, King tells us that Jim McCoy was sitting smack dab in the middle of the

West Virginia Hatfields as his brothers were taken across the river to their place of execution.

Look at the map, and you will see that Jim McCoy, who was at the mouth of Sulphur Creek, had some two dozen armed Hatfields to his immediate right as he sat on Asa McCoy's porch and looked toward the river. To his rear and around to his left, were all the West Virginia Hatfields who were not in the execution squad, and the river was in front of him. The significance of the fact that Jim McCoy had no apparent concern for his own safety on the night of August 9, 1882 either eludes King, or else King ignores it because it does not fit into his story of a bitter blood feud ongoing at the time.

The Sworn testimony of Jim McCoy proves conclusively that there was no "Hatfield and McCoy feud" ongoing at the time of the execution of the three McCoy brothers.[38] Jim McCoy testified that he had been at the schoolhouse where his brothers were held prisoners. He left when word came that Ellison had died and went, not to the safety of his own home in Kentucky, but to the nearby West Virginia home of his cousin, Asa McCoy. Jim and Asa sat on Asa's porch and heard the shots that killed Jim's brothers, some 300 yards distant. Asa was a partner with Devil Anse in land investments at the time.

According to the uncontested sworn testimony of Wall Hatfield, both Wall and Elias Hatfield were literally within a pistol shot of Asa and Jim McCoy at the exact instant when the shots were fired, killing the three McCoys—brothers of Jim and the first cousins of Asa. King knows that neither of the McCoys feared any harm from the two Hatfields, and vice versa. Yet he would have us believe that there was a furious "Hatfield and McCoy feud" underway, and that was the moment of its highest intensity!

King never explains to his readers how it came about that the man whom Truda McCoy identifies as "the bravest of the McCoys, and the leader of the clan," was sitting within rifle range of dozens of armed Hatfields, with the river between him and the safety of Kentucky. King would have us believe that, even though Ellison Hatfield started the fight with a knife, and there was an ongoing blood feud between the two families, Jim McCoy sat there in the middle of Hatfield country, unconcerned about his own safety *doing nothing,* while his three brothers were being taken across the river.

The fact of the matter is that Jim and Asa McCoy, like most of the McCoys, knew that the three sons of Ran'l had brutally butchered Devil Anse's brother, Ellison, and that what was happening was actually a kind of rough justice. That same belief was held by the other McCoys and the general population of the Valley from that time at least up until the publication of King's book, and that belief made it possible for the families to live in relative peace after Devil Anse capitulated to the Pikeville power structure in January, 1888.

I asked Uncle Ransom why the people who knew Ran'l McCoy didn't rally to him after his three sons were killed on the river bank. Him He said it was because everyone knew that his sons would have been let go in a trial in Pikeville. He said that many people thought that Ran'l was just mad because his boys didn't get away with murder.

He said that everyone was really sorry for what happened to Ran'l and his family on New Year's, 1888, but that most folks thought he had at least partly brought it on himself by continually talking about how bad the West Virginia Hatfields were, and frequently going to Pikeville to try to stir up the law against Devil Anse and company.

Ransom Hatfield always stressed how shocked the community was at the murder of Ellison Hatfield. Contrary to the claims of the feud supersizers, Tug Valley was a peaceful place from the earliest settlement until 1880, except for the war years. The Hatfields and McCoys had lived there since the turn of the century, and the killing of Ellison Hatfield in 1882 was the first known peace-time case of murder on Blackberry Creek. Their revulsion toward the McCoy brothers for their breaking of that record of peace and harmony contributed much to the acceptance by the people of the area of Devil Anse's punishment of the McCoys.

I was confused about it at the time, but when I read Truda McCoy's book about twenty-five years later, one statement brought it back to me. Truda McCoy wrote: "Ran'l did not worry too much, for he knew that no Kentucky jury would convict a McCoy for killing a Hatfield."

Unless Truda McCoy lied to the detriment of her own family, then that is exactly what Ran'l McCoy wanted—his sons to get away with murder. Again, Ransom Hatfield was proven right. Once that is understood, then the actions of the non-feuding McCoys and the Kentucky Hatfields following the events of August, 1882 are easy to understand. They thought that Devil Anse had delivered a form of justice that was extreme but that the alternative was likely to be no justice at all.

Truda McCoy says that the sons of Asa Harmon McCoy were known as dangerous men, and she was right.[39] Waller said that Bud McCoy had a reputation "similar to that of Frank Phillips," and she was also right on that. While Bud was killed in 1892 by two of his McCoy cousins, Lark lived to a ripe old age. From what I heard from the older folks who knew him, Lark McCoy was believed to be at least as dangerous a man to cross as any of the Hatfield cohort. The four sons of Asa Harmon McCoy were all dangerous men, who lacked only a leader to make them active feudists against the men who killed their father.

If Jim McCoy had asserted leadership against Devil Anse when his brothers were taken prisoner, he probably could have enlisted the support of the sons of Asa Harmon and either freed his brothers or shed a lot of Hatfield blood in the effort. Jim McCoy and his brothers, accompanied by the four sons of Asa Harmon, would have been able to meet Devil Anse's execution squad on relatively equal terms and force them to release the three brothers or pay a heavy price in blood. It did not happen, because Jim McCoy knew that his brothers had committed a brutal crime, and he held a glimmer of hope that Devil Anse would not kill them.

The actions — and the lack thereof — by Jim McCoy at the time of the August, 1882 events prove conclusively to all except the supersizers of the feud story that there was no Hatfield and McCoy feud under way in 1882.

I talked to only a few witnesses who were at that election in 1882 and saw the fight, but I heard many stories from people who got it second hand. I talked to dozens of people who said, "My pappy saw it, and he said...." The story they all told of that day's events does not conflict materially with the writings of most feud writers, or with the sworn testimony in the cases.[40] Of course, Dean King's version conflicts with everyone else's version, except for that of the New York journalist, John Spears.

One story I heard that I believe to be true, because I heard parts of it from several people, is one told by Vicy Stafford McCoy who was a teenager selling gingerbread at the election. She actually saw the fight, but her story adds nothing to the accepted story. What she said happened the following day is interesting, because it gives an insight into how the people were thinking, and what they were doing as the momentous events unfolded.

Vicy said that her father, Mont Stafford, a neighbor of Ran'l McCoy and a brother to Tom Stafford who was elected Justice of the Peace on that fateful day, owned a horse that was the envy of the Valley. Mont had been offered several hundred dollars for the horse on many occasions, but had refused to sell his prize animal. Devil Anse Hatfield was one person who had tried to buy the horse, offering more money than anyone had ever paid for a horse in the area.

After Devil Anse stomped out of Preacher Anse's house and called his troops to order, Mont Stafford approached him and offered to give him the finest horse in the valley, in exchange for the prisoners. Devil Anse dismissed the offer summarily, and proceeded to take the boys down the road to their eventual doom.

Vicy Stafford McCoy also told a story that would be very significant if any corroboration could be found. She said that Sally McCoy was on her way back to Mate Creek to visit her sons, and was close enough to the pawpaw grove to hear the shots when her sons were killed. Sally did not say that in her trial testimony, but she didn't say otherwise either. I don't think one unsupported testimony is enough to enter something into the historical record, because Jim McCoy gave an account of his activities that night in his sworn testimony, and did not mention his mother being there. As it would add to the emotional impact of that night's doings, Vicy's story would be valuable, if true. I wish I could substantiate it, but wishing does not make a historical fact, so I include it as folklore only, although I believe it to be true.

Many writers treat the Election Day killing of Ellison Hatfield as an indication that Tug Valley men were singularly violent. This is rubbish. Election-related killings are interwoven in the fabric of American history, from the beginning until well into the twentieth century. Virgil Jones gives us several newspaper reports of violence at other elections the same day Ellison was killed.[41]

Reporting on the 1897 election, the *Glasgow, Kentucky, News* said: "Twenty men were killed...in the election fights on Tuesday. Frankfort led off with five killed...."

None of these deaths was in Pike County. The death toll in the civilized state capital was much higher on Election Day 1897 than it had been in Pike County fifteen years earlier.

Four decades after Ellison lost at the Blackberry election, twenty-one people were shot, nine of them fatally, at a polling place in Breathitt County, Kentucky, in a dispute that arose over a woman exercising her recently won right to vote.[42]

As late as 1933, seven people were killed and four more wounded in Election Day fracases across Kentucky, none of them in Pike County.[43]

In 1895, a powerful Kentucky state senator, William Goebel, and a former Confederate general and banker, John Sanford, met in front of the general's bank. They simultaneously drew pistols and fired. The senator's clothes were penetrated, but he was unhurt. The banker's skull was penetrated, and he fell dead. Despite the provision in the Kentucky Constitution, barring anyone who had ever participated in a duel from holding any public office, Goebel was elected governor five years later.

As he walked toward the Capitol on the day before his inauguration, with a bodyguard on each side, Goebel was shot from a nearby state office building. He was sworn in on his hospital bed and died three days later.[44]

In 1937, a man who had formerly been both lieutenant governor and adjutant general was tried for killing his fiancée. After the trial ended in a hung jury, three of the murdered lass' brothers confronted the accused murderer on the main street of Shelbyville. They shot him three times in the back and then administered the coup de grace to his head after he was down. They were acquitted at trial.[45]

The Hill-Evans feud took place in Garrard County, Kentucky, which is in the middle part of the state. That feud featured factions which were both headed by physicians. The Darnell-Watson feud, from which Mark Twain derived his feud in *Huckleberry Finn*, took place in the far western part of the state, along the Mississippi River.

The tales about Tug Valley being inordinately violent for their time are nothing but propaganda. The propaganda is old enough to be considered "history" by many, but it is still just propaganda.

---

1 Altina Waller gives a good description of the events of August 7–9, 1882 in *Feud*, 70-76.

2 Jones, *The Hatfields and the McCoys*, 40–41.

3 King, 364-5, n. 4.

4 King, Dean, *The Feud*, 47, 92, 124. While King makes many statements that are easily disproved by the public records, he also frequently says that things exist which should be public records, such as deeds and lawsuits on behalf of Tolbert's estate, and twenty-seven warrants for Johnse Hatfield, when, in fact, no such records exist. King is either exaggerating when he says he did four years of diligent research, or else he misrepresents the results of his research.

5 McCoy, *The McCoys,"* p. 70.

6 McCoy, 74.

7 King, *The Feud*, 94.

8 McCoy, 74.

9 King, *The Feud*, 94. As a former long-time collector of Case knives, I never saw a blade that would be described as a broad two inch blade, and neither did Dean King.

10 McCoy, *The McCoys*, 225, n. 10.

11 Cunningham, Daniel, *"The Horrible butcheries of West Virginia*, Ludwell Johnson, ed., West Virginia History, Volume XLVI, 1985-1986, 29.

12  Waller, 72.

13  Jones, *The Hatfields and the McCoys*, 42.

14  Osborne and Weaver, *Virginia State Rangers*, 200. I doubt the accuracy of the military records on the heights of the Hatfields, based on the photos I have seen of them, and the descriptions I heard from people who knew both Anse and Ellison. Of course it can never be proven, but I believe that Ellison was at least six feet tall, and Anse was nearer to six feet than the five feet-six seen in his army records. Anse was not often referred to as tall by anyone who knew him personally, while Ellison was.  A man was not normally called "tall" in those days unless he was six feet tall. My best guess is that Ellison was six feet or maybe an inch or so above that, and Anse probably about the same amount under six feet.

15  McCoy, *McCoys*, 73.

16  All the McCoys who were described in their military records had light hair and skin, and all had blue eyes, except for one, whose eyes were gray.  Preston, 448-9. The "black, curly hair" ascribed to Asa Harmon McCoy by Lisa Alther did not exist in the McCoy line at that time.

17  King, True Story, 94.

18  Osborne and Weaver, 200.

19  The practice of naming children after their progenitors resulted in some names appearing in every succeeding generation. This resulted in people referring to the older person as "big" and the younger as "little." It was not to denote size. The practice continues to this day. It is sometime used to differentiate kinsmen of different generations who do not have the same names, but are of the same sex. The family I grew up next door to referred to their mother as "Mommy" and their grandmother as "Big Mommy," even though they were about the same size. Jim McCoy was referred to occasionally as "Big Jim" to distinguish him from younger Jim McCoys. Ditto for Ellison Hatfield. Our family referred to my Uncle Tom as "Big Tom" and to his son as "Little Tom."  This continued after the younger Tom became a 250 pound tackle in high school. Going all the way back to the original settlers in the valley, I know of only one person who was commonly referred to as "Big" for any reason other than to differentiate him from someone else of the same name. James Elias Dotson, Jr. was referred to as "Big Junior." He weighed over 400 pounds.

20  King, Dean, The Feud, 89.

21  Preston, John D. *The Civil War*, 141.

22  http://www.matescreek.com/minutes/matescreek_1905.pdf

23  McKnight, Brian, *Contested Borderland*, 146-8.

24  Uncle Ransom said that Preacher Anse "Always did like Devil Anse," but he got mad at him for taking the boys from his custody, and never got completely over it.

25  Not "Hog Floyd."

26 The two deputies were also Hatfields—Matthew and Joseph.

27 That Ran'l objected to his sons being arrested at the scene of the bloody crime shows that he had the intense family loyalty that goes with the feuding mindset. Although this mindset never moved him to initiate violent action, it was nevertheless present, as shown here and elsewhere during his life.

28 Rice, *The Hatfields and the McCoys*, 25.

26 Testimony by Preacher Anse Hatfield in *Commonwealth of Kentucky vs. Valentine Hatfield*, Case #19594, KCA

30 The officers were Constable Floyd Hatfield and Deputies Matthew and Joseph Hatfield.

31 *Ibid.*

32 *Ibid.*

33 Testimony of Randolph McCoy, case# 19601 KCA.

34 Rice, *The Hatfields and the McCoys*, 26.

35 Rice, *The Hatfields and the McCoys*, 27.

36 Case #19601, KCA.

37 Rice, Otis, 27-8.

38 Rice, 102.

39 Waller, *Feud*, 156 and 186.

40 See especially these Kentucky Court of Appeals cases, which are in the Kentucky Department for Libraries and Archives, in Frankfort: *Commonwealth of Kentucky v. Valentine Hatfield*, Case #19594, *Commonwealth of Kentucky v. Plyant Mayhorn*, Case #19601, *Commonwealth of Kentucky v. Ellison Mounts*, Case #19602

41 Jones, *The Hatfields and the McCoys*, 39–40.

42 James C. Klotter, *Kentucky: Portrait in Paradox, 1900–1950.*

43 *Ibid.*

44 Klotter, *William Goebel: The Politics of Wrath* (Place: Publisher, Year), 100–02.

45 Klotter, *Portrait in Paradox*, 70.

# CHAPTER 14.
# A FIVE-YEAR CEASE-FIRE

In the period between the murder of the three McCoys in August 1882 and the arrest of the first Hatfield partisan in October 1887, the killing of Jeff McCoy was the only fatality that was in any way connected to "the feud." This means that after three days of violence in August, 1882, there was not a single documented violent encounter between Devil Anse Hatfield or his immediate family and Ran'l McCoy or his immediate family until the raids into West Virginia by the Pikeville posse began in December, 1887. There is not a single death certificate, no new indictments and no documented wounding of any member of either family. The Louisville Courier journal, with its editor, Henry Watterson, leading a virtual crusade against "feuding" in an effort to entice outside investment, never referred to a "feud" in Pike County until 1888.

What is a writer of a "feud story" to do with all this dead time?

While five years with only one fatality was a blessing to the two families, it was a curse to us as readers and viewers of feud stories. The quiet years required something to fill the gap, and the supersizers took to the task with enthusiasm, beginning with the yellow journalists of 1888. When the reporters were preparing their reports, they couldn't tell their city readers that there had been a murder and a retaliatory lynching over five years before, and then nothing at all for over four years, until a man wanted for murder was killed while trying to escape from custody, followed over a year later by an illegal invasion of West Virginia by a gang composed mostly of men with no connection whatsoever to the 1882 events. The last thing that the owners of the papers, who represented the same big eastern money that was snapping up the coal lands in Tug Valley, wanted was for their readers to start wondering why the feud was revived after so long; therefore, enough filler material was generated to make "the feud" a long and continuous conflict.

The newspaper writers filled those years with cross-border sniping, cases of mistaken identity, battles between forces who couldn't hit anything they shot at, visits to isolated mountain whorehouses, and other similar fantasies, each of which was of a nature that showed the Tug Valley to be inhabited by barbarians. Their only constraint was the lack of death certificates, so the battles and ambushes needed to be non-fatal farces involving people who couldn't shoot straight. They sometimes went ahead and said someone was killed, even though no documentation of the death was available.

There is no better way to get a titillating story than to turn loose a creative writer with four vacant years to fill with his imagination. And that's what they did, working mainly from stories told to the reporters by Perry Cline and others in Pikeville who were trying to make the West Virginia Hatfields the arch-villains.

Imagine the consternation of the people at the Kentucky and West Virginia papers when they read the 1888 reports from New York chronicling a vicious blood feud that occurred right under their noses, without them even knowing about it.

As ludicrous as it is, that is precisely what one must believe in order to believe the writings of the supersizers, from Spears and Crawford right up to Alther and King. One must accept as true, the proposition that Spears, the New Yorker could visit for a few days, only briefly passing through the area where most of the action supposedly transpired, and discover an entire feud's worth of trouble that the Kentucky and West Virginia newspapers never got wind of. That's a tall order, but the feud supersizers have successfully accomplished it from 1888 until 2013.

The historians Rice and Waller give those years scant mention. Rice has his shortest chapter — only six pages — covering the entire period.

Rice's meager attempt to fill up the years from August, 1882 when the Blackberry Creek killings occurred, until November, 1886, when Jeff McCoy was killed illustrates the problem writers have with this period.

There is absolutely no real evidence that anything that could possibly be part of "the feud" happened during the four years between the execution of Ran'l's sons and the incident at the Daniels home. There is no evidence that Devil Anse Hatfield did anything during this period that was even remotely connected to an alleged feud. He was totally engrossed in his efforts to sustain his business in the face of growing competition from the big out-of-state timber concerns, and the perfidy of some of the suppliers he did business with, who repeatedly sued Anse for alleged debts owed for timbering supplies.

The supersizers face a Herculean task in filling up the quiet years with violence and gore, but they are equal to the task, some having dozens of pages devoted to the period, when Otis Rice had to pad his account to come up with six pages. Truda McCoy has those years chock full of events, and Dean King has even more, filling over fifty pages with stories gleaned from old newspapers and prior writers who cited either folklore or those same old newspapers.

While Truda McCoy has a lot of action during these quiet years, her editor, Leonard Roberts, says in an end note on this period, "Not much of the material given here has been proved."[1] What the historian, Roberts, is saying in so many words, is: "You have just read dozens of pages of very exciting stuff, but it's all just a *story*."

## The Death of Jeff McCoy

The killing of Jeff McCoy in 1886 arose out of a domestic squabble, and did not involve Ran'l and Anse in any way other than the fact that Cap was Anse's son, but because it involved a son of Devil

Anse and a son and a daughter of Harmon McCoy, it should be considered.

Something happened at the home of Bill Daniels shortly before Jeff McCoy was killed, because Jeff had to have been highly motivated to go to the home of Cap Hatfield in search of his niece's husband, Tom Wallace. Jeff McCoy, son of the slain Union soldier, Asa Harmon, was known generally as one of Pike County's bad men, as were his brothers, Bud, Lark and Jake. While it is likely that none of the sons of Asa Harmon were afraid of Cap Hatfield — or anyone else for that matter — it is also not likely that he would have approached Cap's home and shot into it, had he not been highly agitated about something. That Jeff indeed shot into Cap's home is supported by the words of Devil Anse in his letter to Perry Cline.

As I do not believe that Jeff would have done that without provocation, I accept the story that something happened between Jeff's niece Victoria and her husband, Tom Wallace, at the home of her father, Bill Daniels. Whatever actually transpired in the Daniels home, it undoubtedly is what motivated Jeff McCoy to shoot into Cap Hatfield's home, thus forfeiting his own life.

Jeff was staying at the West Virginia home of his sister and brother in law, Nancy and Johnse Hatfield, while avoiding arrest for killing a mailman in Kentucky. Jeff McCoy approached the cabin of Cap Hatfield, where Wallace was working as a farmhand. After ascertaining that Cap was away, Jeff opened fire upon Wallace, who had barricaded himself in Cap's house, along with Cap's ill wife, producing the "aggravating circumstances" referred to in Devil Anse's letter to Cline.

Upon returning to his bullet-riddled cabin, Cap must have been infuriated. Most writers say that Cap went to Logan Courthouse (the name of the town was Aracoma, but it was generally referred to as Logan courthouse) and swore out a warrant for Jeff, and had himself appointed a special constable to serve the warrant.[2] I don't believe this, because I think that if Cap had been a duly sworn officer Devil Anse would have said so in his letter to Cline. Anse said that Cap had "arrested Jeff to hand him over to a peace officer." This would make no sense if Cap had been a peace officer himself.

I don't think that Cap Hatfield had any intention of taking Jeff McCoy to Logan. When Jeff McCoy shot into the home of Cap Hatfield, where his wife was sick abed, I think he signed his death warrant. It is highly unlikely that Cap Hatfield would have made the eighty mile round trip to Logan, just to have Jeff McCoy tried for wanton endangerment.

Of course Jeff knew this, too, and was no doubt on the lookout for a chance to escape. It is the route that Cap took that convinces me that he intended to kill Jeff McCoy. If authors and scriptwriters would consult their maps now and then, they would stay out of a lot of trouble. They would have known that Ran'l McCoy would not have passed Devil Anse's timbering site on his way home from Camp Douglas, Illinois, and Cap Hatfield would not have traveled downriver from Grapevine to Thacker if he really intended to go to Logan. Cap's failure to go up Grapevine and across at the head of the creek, and go instead down Tug River makes no sense unless you keep in mind one of Devil Anse's cardinal rules: A West Virginia Hatfield never commits a major crime in West Virginia.

Devil Anse was neck-deep in business problems in 1886, thus making his rule against committing crime in West Virginia even more binding. His quick response to the Jeff McCoy shooting — the conciliatory letter to Perry Cline — proves that he wanted above all to avoid anything that might excite his Kentucky enemies to take action against him on the old warrants for murder. His entire life gives the lie to the "feud writers" who portray him as a man who had only contempt for the law, because he never did anything that would set his neighbors against him, or expose himself to the sanction of a West Virginia court — with the exception of bootlegging, of course.

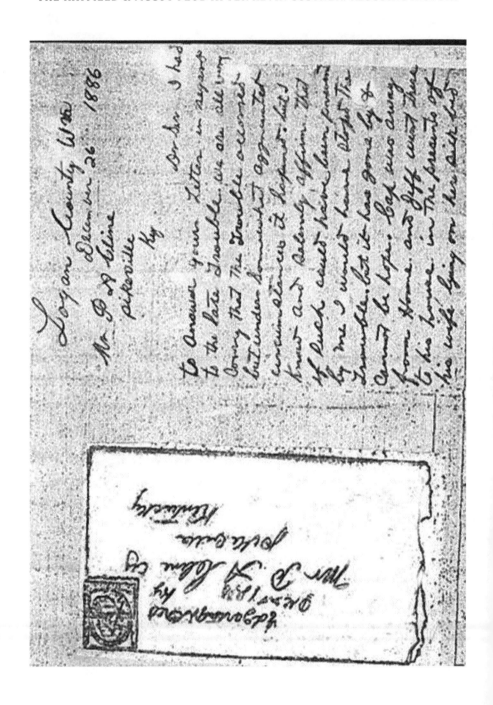

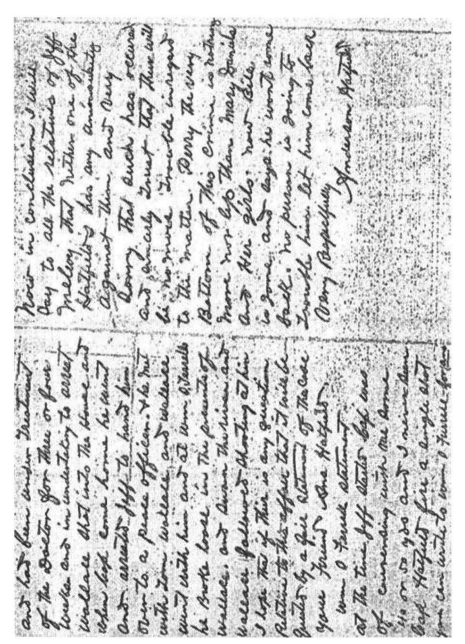

The original letter is owned by Ron G. Blackburn.[3]

Most writers say that this letter was written for the illiterate Devil Anse by Cap's wife, Nancy. I disagree. After comparing the letter to known samples of the handwriting of Preacher Anse, I believe the letter was written by my great-great Grandfather, Preacher Anse Hatfield. The claim that the preacher was the scribe is bolstered by the fact that the Cline family gave the original to the son of Preacher Anse, my great-great Uncle Ransom Hatfield. Why else would the Cline family part with such an important family artifact?

This is important because it shows that in December, 1886, Preacher Anse was trying to keep the peace in the Valley.

As the Kentucky Court of Appeals said in the Wall Hatfield case, if someone is shot with the shooter standing in one state and the victim in another state, the crime is in the state where the victim is when shot. If Cap started through the head of Grapevine on the direct line to Logan, and shot Jeff on the way, he would be liable for a charge of murder in West Virginia, which would mean he would have to leave the Valley. As he was already under indictment for three murders in Kentucky, another such charge in the bluegrass state would be of little concern.

So, Cap marched Jeff McCoy down the West Virginia bank of Tug River, where Jeff could see Kentucky and freedom with every step. When he stopped at Shanghai Ferrell's place at the Mouth of Thacker, Cap surely had an eagle eye on Jeff as he transacted his business with Shang. Although we can't know for sure, I doubt if the rope binding Jeff was tied very tight; at least not so tight that he couldn't easily slip his bonds.

Don't believe any of the stories about Cap Hatfield or Cap and Tom Wallace firing a multitude of shots at Jeff while he was swimming the river. In the first place, it wouldn't require the aim of a mountain hunter to hit a man at the distance involved, but most importantly, Cap wanted Jeff McCoy to fall dead in Kentucky. There is no way that Cap would have shot at Jeff—or allowed Tom to shoot at him had Cap been nearby-- before he was sure that the crime would be a Kentucky crime.

In spite of Devil Anse's claim of Cap's innocence in the letter, buttressed by calling upon Shanghai Ferrell as a witness, I believe that Cap Hatfield shot Jeff McCoy. Had it been Wallace — with Cap fifty yards away as Devil Anse claimed — I believe Jeff would have been shot while swimming the river. It was an easy shot with a Winchester rifle. Waiting for Jeff to emerge onto Kentucky soil before shooting him, making any potential criminal charge a Kentucky case, fits the Hatfield template.

Of course Cap had the "Rooster Cogburn" defense of "stopping a felon in flight," but it would be much easier to assert that defense against a Kentucky extradition requisition than against a West Virginia murder charge.

There is a small coterie of anti-Hatfield feud enthusiasts who claim that the revival of the conflict in 1887 was simply because the Pikeville elite wanted to see the law enforced. Of course, they can't explain why Perry Cline didn't go before the grand jury and indict Cap Hatfield for killing Cline's nephew, Jeff McCoy, opting instead to pursue a five-year-old indictment against Devil Anse.

They also overlook the fact that the invasions of West Virginia by the Phillips posse were unauthorized and the resultant kidnappings and killings nothing but vigilante acts, in defiance of the law. The crossing of the river by the Pikeville posse to murder Jim Vance was the legal equivalent of the crossing to raid the McCoy home by the Hatfields. Such vigilante violence is hardly the hallmark of a group seeking only to see that the law is honored. Neither can they explain why the "feud" ended when Devil Anse gave up his land.

As this incident involved a son of Devil Anse and a son of the slain Union soldier, Harmon McCoy, and as I believe that the second phase of the feud was, as far as the sons of Asa Harmon McCoy were concerned, a continuation of the war by other means, I count the killing of Jeff McCoy as a feud event, albeit of a hybrid nature. It did not involve the family of Ran'l McCoy, but it involved the son of the slain Union soldier, Asa Harmon McCoy, and was part of the larger conflict between Devil Anse and the Pikeville elite, which was connected to the war.

The killing of Jeff McCoy was not connected to the previous "feud incidents" in any way. Jeff McCoy shot into Cap's house because Tom Wallace, who had abused his niece, was there. It was not because Cap had helped lynch his cousins four years earlier. Cap Hatfield shot Jeff McCoy because--as Devil Anse said in his letter--Jeff had shot into Cap's house, where Cap's wife was lying in her sick bed.

## The Tale of the Cow's Tale

The tale of the whipping of the two Daniels women with a cow's tail appears in most feud books, including the two recent best-sellers; however, it was unheard of on Blackberry Creek before the appearance of the Virgil Jones' book in 1948. Of course we had other "front porch tales" that were just as gruesome and just as apocryphal that we heard many times growing up, but some of them never made it into the "histories."

The tale of Jim Vance greasing his boots with the brains of Bud McCoy when the three boys were killed in the paw paw grove had wide currency, as did its counterpart, wherein the other Bud McCoy — the son of Asa Harmon McCoy — not only greased his boots with Jim Vance's brains, but actually licked his fingers when he finished with his shoe shine. This last tale made it into my Cousin L.D. Hatfield's 1944 book, "The True Story of the Hatfield and McCoy Feud,"[4] but for some reason did not make the grade for recent supersizers, such as Alther and King. I actually resent King leaving these shoe-shining tales out of his tale. He included almost every other tall tale I ever heard, and of all the tall tales about the feud, those two brain-matter shoe shines were most widely told in my family.

Virtually every writer since Jones in 1948 has told of Cap Hatfield and others — ranging from one accomplice to a dozen — beating two women with a cow's tail. Most writers say that the beating was administered because Mary Daniels, the wife of Bill Daniels and sister of Nancy McCoy Hatfield, was relaying information from Nancy to the McCoys about the mysterious and unnamed doings of the Hatfields. Some offer an alternative motive, saying that Tom Wallace, who accompanied Cap on this raid, had lived with Daniels' daughter for a time and she had left him.

I believe that something happened in the Daniels home in the fall of 1886, because I don't think Jeff McCoy, who was on the lam from a murder charge in Kentucky, would have antagonized Cap Hatfield by coming to Cap's house in an attempt to get Tom Wallace,[5] unless he was severely provoked — and mistreatment of his sister would have done it.

The question is what really happened at the Daniels house? Was there a verbal confrontation between Tom Wallace and his estranged wife? The answer is "almost surely." Did either Wallace or Cap Hatfield or both physically assault one or more of the women? The answer is "very likely." Did either Cap Hatfield or Tom Wallace beat the women for forty minutes with a bludgeon the size and weight of a baseball bat? Of course not!

If Tom Wallace, who was working for Cap on Cap's farm at the time, wanted to go to Kentucky to try to get his wife to return to him, it is likely that Cap accompanied him. If she rebuffed Tom, it is quite possible that Tom became physical with her. If Tom became physical with her daughter, it would be only natural for Mary Daniels to intercede, and it is just as likely that Cap restrained Mary.

Most feud writers eschew documentary evidence in favor of the much more exciting folk tales and newspaper reports. In many cases, they don't even use it when it would bolster their tales. I have been amazed that the supersizers have not used the letter that Kentucky Governor Buckner wrote to West Virginia Governor Wilson on January 30, 1888, as documentary evidence for the cow's tail tale. The governor says of the Hatfields: "They have, on several occasions, while in Kentucky, *unmercifully whipped defenseless* women and inoffensive men, whose only provocation was some alleged remark in disapproval of their lawless conduct."[6]

I hesitated about citing this, lest it pushes the feud story supersizers to even greater heights, but there it is for what it is worth.

Of course, the Governor could have been referring to other incidents, as he said "on *several* occasions." The governor's failure to mention Cap's name — he used the Hatfield names in the letter — weakens the case that he is referring to the incident at Bill Daniels' home. The connection to the Daniels incident is further weakened by the Governor's stated reasons for the Hatfields' beatings of defenseless women. He mentions neither stopping excess gossip, nor a domestic dispute, and gives as the reason for the beatings only that the victims had chided the Hatfields about their outlaw ways. The Governor omitted any mention of a cow's tail in his letter.

I consider Governor Buckner's failure to mention the cow's tail to be further proof of my position. The Governor had surely read the Spears articles, which had appeared earlier the same month. His failure to mention the bovine appendage is surely due to the fact that, as a man who was knowledgeable about farm animals, he gave no credence to Spears' claim that two women survived a forty minute thrashing with a cow's tail.

I'd bet dollars to doughnuts that, now that I have publicized it, the next "True Story" will cite this as documentary proof that Cap beat the Daniels women with a cow's tail for the greater part of an hour.

I cited Mutzenberg only because he is the only writer who reproduces the letter in its entirety. Knowing where to find it will save interested readers — or writers of "True Stories" — a trip to the Frankfort archives. I hesitated to cite Mutzenberg, because he was one of the earliest supersizers. Mutzenberg says that Mary Daniels was killed in the attack, but she must have been miraculously resurrected, because she showed up three years later in Pikeville to sign one of Cottontop Mounts' confessions, had four more children, and was around well into the 20th century. Mutzenberg further claimed that Mary Daniels' mother, who was Asa Harmon McCoy's widow, Patty Cline McCoy, was crippled for life in the beating. Patty Cline McCoy also lived into the 20th century, with no apparent disabilities.

In grading Mutzenberg's effort, I would normally flunk him for his whoppers, but I add a few points back to his grade because he did not claim to know how many invaders entered the Daniels home, nor did he name any of them. I would restore enough points to bring him up to a passing grade, despite the whoppers, for one reason: Writing originally in 1899, when memories were fresh, Mutzenberg *did not mention a cow's tail!*

I was puzzled by certain aspects of the cow's tail tale, as there is no precedent for the employment of such an instrument of torture. In his note on the cow's tail tale in Truda McCoy's book, her editor, Leonard Roberts, says: "These reports are unproved. The use of a cow's tail on gossipers is a first in the annals and folkways of feuding."[7] Roberts, the historian, is obviously with me on the cow's tail tale, else he wouldn't have included that caveat in his notes.

I wondered which end of the appendage Cap would have grasped as he administered the punishment. Did he grip the bony end and deliver sharp, whip-like cracks with the hairy end, or did he grasp the hairy end and lay on crushing blows with the heavy end of the tail? None of the writers said, and I really wanted to know.

Having been raised a country boy, I knew that a cow's tail was a formidable instrument, being at least as long and as heavy as a major league baseball bat. As a beating with such an implement would result in at least great bodily injury, and quite likely death for the recipient, I tried for years to figure out where the tale of the tail came from.

The claim by many writers that the beating was to teach the women a lesson made no sense at all to me. A man might attempt to teach a woman a lesson with his open hand, or in extreme cases, with his fist. He might even employ a belt or some kind of small whip, such as the one employed in whipping Nancy Hatfield by Jim Vance in the movie. When the attack is made with a bludgeon that is longer and heavier than the bat Hank Aaron used to hit seven hundred fifty-five home runs, his intention is not to teach a lesson, but, rather to cripple or to kill his victim, depending on the number of strokes.

In support of the cow's tail tale, many writers cite Virgil Jones, who cites no one. Truda McCoy's book was published in 1976, and she has the tale, albeit with a dozen invaders of the Daniels home, where Jones had only Cap and Tom Wallace.[8]

Mutzenberg says only that the women were "cruelly beaten"[9] and does not mention the cow's tail, so I was right back to square one in my search for the origination of the tale of the cow's tail.

Truda McCoy cites no one, so whether her tale of the tail is part of her McCoy family history, or came from her collection of old newspaper articles, we will never know. Ms. McCoy couldn't have gotten the story from Jones, because her book was actually written in the 1930's, although not published until 1976.

Desperate for material to fill the quiet years, Otis Rice tells the tale of the tail, citing both Jones and McCoy.[10]  When the grandson of Cap Hatfield, Coleman Hatfield, published *The Tale of the Devil* in 2003, I rushed to get a copy, expecting to finally have the cow's tail tale straight from the horse's mouth.  Sure enough, it was there, along with two footnotes.[11]  Imagine my dismay when I read the footnotes and learned that the grandson of the alleged wielder of the cow's tail gave Otis Rice and Truda McCoy as sources.

Lisa Alther also includes the cow's tail tale in her compilation of prior writings presented as a "history" of the feud, in which she informs us that the cow was "recently butchered,"[12] which means it retained its full and un-dehydrated weight, which would make it at least as heavy as Bobby Bonds' Louisville Slugger.

Now Dean King comes with the supersized version.  In his account, the beating with the cow's tail lasted more than forty minutes.  Assuming an equal division between the two women, and a slow, methodical stroke of about one lash every three seconds, this gave each woman over 400 lashes with this meaty bludgeon.  In the old British Royal Navy, the punishment of flogging through the fleet was so severe that it was sometimes offered as an alternative to hanging, because only a small percentage of the sailors thus honored survived the torturous punishment, which was between 300 and 500 lashes with a whip.

The contention that a woman survived hundreds of strokes from an instrument the size and weight of a baseball bat is unworthy of a novel, much less a purported history.

King, like Alther, has the appendage fresh and of full weight, but he says that Cap had cut off the cow's tail for the purpose of employing it in his visit to the Daniels home.  This means that King, like Truda McCoy, wants readers to know that Cap was a torturer of animals as well as a murderer.

In desperation, I checked the newspapers, which I knew had carried a lot of the contemporaneous feud news, and there it was! On January 1, 1889, one year to the day after the raid on the Ran'l McCoy home, the *Wheeling Register* reported the death of Tom Wallace, and it had the tale of the cow's tail!

"Captain Hatfield wrapped the hairy part of a cow's tail around his fist and beat the invalid woman with the heavy stump till she was almost dead."[13] The Register not only makes Cap, who was born a year before the war ended, a veteran, it also gives him a rank higher than the one attained by his father!

Not only did I have the tale as told by an early teller, I also solved my problem of trying to figure out the exact method of employment.

I then searched further back, and found that the Wheeling writer actually got his story from an Article in the *New York Sun*, published three months earlier, on page 9 of the October 7, 1888 *Sun*. This article by John Spears is the original version of the cow's tail tale. There is none earlier, so we can safely conclude that the story of Cap Hatfield beating the women with a cow's tale was told first to the public by a New York reporter.

Spears says the invaders included only Cap and Tom Wallace, who entered the Daniels cabin and held Bill Daniels at rifle-point. Spears says: "...(Cap) grabbing Mrs. Daniels by the hair, forced her to her knees in front of the fireplace, and began beating her across the back, using the heavy bone end of the cow's tail to strike her with. The blows were delivered with a will. The woman screamed in agony, for the first two blows broke two ribs, while to her cries were added those of her daughter and several children."

That sounds about right to me; one broken bone for each blow with a tool about the same size and weight as a baseball bat. Then Spears spoils it all by saying that the beatings of the two women lasted over 40 minutes! Although Spears says the blows were "delivered with a will," he reports no additional broken bones. Spears says the women were beaten unconscious during the forty minute beating, but no physical damage beyond the two broken ribs caused by the first two blows is mentioned.

Spears says the younger woman recovered completely, but Mrs. Daniels would probably die within a year. Mrs. Daniels went on to have four more children after that and lived well into the 20th century, but Spears' story is what it is.[14] Spears' account is closely followed and sometimes copied almost word for word in Dean King's "True Story."[15]

The degree to which King copies from Spears is remarkable. Spears says: "When it was over both women lay on the floor unconscious — dead, Daniels supposed."

King renders it: "When they finally ended, both women lay on the floor unconscious — dead, the helpless Daniels supposed." By changing "When it was over" to "When they finally ended," and adding the words "the helpless" in front of Daniels, King absolves himself of the duty to put Spears' words in quotation marks and give him credit, even though King follows Spears so closely that he even has the same dash between "unconscious" and "dead."

King has the helpless Bill Daniels observing the torture of his womenfolk at gunpoint. His source is, of course, John Spears. Had he consulted a real source, he might have left that part out. In his letter to Perry Cline, Devil Anse mentions Bill Daniels, saying: "Now Bill *is gone* and says he won't come back. No person is going to trouble him—let him come back."

This is clearly not a reference to Bill Daniels being held at gunpoint while his womenfolk were beaten. Had that been the case, Anse would surely have addressed it, but Anse says that Bill *is gone*. The obvious conclusion is that Cap and/or Tom Wallace, or someone else had run him off, and Anse was addressing that in his letter.

Does Dean King, obviously a very intelligent man, actually believe that two women sustained several hundred blows from an instrument as long and as heavy as a baseball bat and survived? Or is he just writing a story?

King uses some real sleight of hand to connect the cow's tail tale to the feud. After telling how the Daniels women were divulging Hatfield strategy to the McCoys, King says: "Cap and Tom were told to deal with the situation."[16] He does not say who told Cap and Tom to deal with the situation, but knowing that only one man could give orders to Cap, King's intention with this unsubstantiated statement is clear; he wants his readers to believe that Devil Anse, in 1886, was carrying on operations against the McCoys, and that those operations were of such a serious nature that in order to stop the women talking about his operations he would order an attack on the wife of a man who was listed as one of the witnesses against him in the killing of the McCoy boys.

King doesn't tell us what those Hatfield operations were that were thwarted by the gossipy women, which is understandable, as there is no record of any such operations.

So, after reading dozens of accounts, each of which cited previous accounts, I was finally led back to a New York newspaperman, who probably never was close to either Cap Hatfield or a cow in his life, and who attributed his yarn about the cow's tale to no one.[17] This is the "daisy-chain" to which I referred earlier, in spades. So many writers have re-told John Spears' 1888 tale of the extended beating of two women with a cow's tail that I expect to hear any day that some senator from New York or California is introducing a law to ban cow's tails; or to at least register them.

There is another explanation for the intrusion into the Daniels home by Cap and Tom — and I believe it did take place — that makes a lot more sense to me: Tom Wallace had been living with the daughter of Mary Daniels. Some say Tom had deceived the poor lass into thinking they were married, using a fake marriage license and an ersatz preacher, but there is a record of their marriage in Logan, with Wallace's last name misspelled. Whether legally married or not, the girl tired of Wallace and went home to Mama.[18] Wallace, accompanied by Cap, went to the Daniels home to attempt reconciliation, and it turned bad. This seems more reasonable to me than the spy vs. spy version seen in most accounts.

I believe that any beating that took place that night involved only Tom Wallace and his wife, Victoria, and that Cap did nothing worse than possibly restraining Mary. I am convinced that if Cap had beaten either of the women, Anse would have either denied it or tried to justify it in his letter to Cline. I also believe that if Cap had beaten either of the women, he would have been charged with the crime by either Mary Daniels or Perry Cline.[19]

The invasion of the Daniels home, whatever it involved, is tangentially related to the feud, in that Bill Daniels was on the list of prosecution witnesses for the Commonwealth of Kentucky against Devil Anse and his gang in the murders of the three McCoy boys, and it involved a son of Devil Anse and a daughter of the slain Union soldier, Asa Harmon McCoy.

Devil Anse, an intelligent man, had done absolutely nothing since August, 1882 that would in any way further antagonize the McCoys. Devil Anse would not have sent Cap to Bill Daniels' house to whip his wife and daughter, thereby further antagonizing a potential witness against him. Devil Anse was far more likely to offer Daniels a job on his timber crew than to have his womenfolk whipped in his presence.

Whatever happened in Bill Daniels' cabin was far less serious than most writers portray it, and certainly not even on the same planet with the description by Spears that is reproduced by King. While it was not serious enough to lead to Cap being indicted for the offense, it was, bad enough to cause Jeff McCoy to attack Tom Wallace in Cap Hatfield's home, forfeiting his life in the process.

## The McCoys who couldn't shoot straight

The movie shows Sam McCoy taking a shot at Devil Anse from a tree stand, missing him completely from a distance of less than fifty yards. The movie-makers couldn't show anything that is more unlikely than that. At the distance shown in the movie, the real Sam McCoy couldn't get drunk enough to miss completely. Squirrel Huntin' Sam could have shot Anse in either eye he chose from that distance.

A few scenes later, we see Paris taking the necessary steps to remedy the poor McCoy aim, by procuring a scope for his rifle. Paris tells Sam that the scope will make a hundred-yard shot look like twenty-five. The brothers then proceed to West Virginia to use the new scope in assassinating Devil Anse.

The brothers take a position about a hundred yards from their target, who is unwarily going about his business of running a sawmill.

It was not Sam, who could shoot as straight as any Hatfield — except when shooting at a Hatfield — it was Paris who took the shot.

Normally you would expect a man planning an assassination from a distance to zero in his scope, and then carefully carry the scoped rifle to the site, making sure he didn't bump against anything and throw his scope off-center. But this nineteenth century Lee Oswald took the scope along in his pocket and attached it after reaching his sniper's nest. It's a wonder he didn't shoot one of the mules standing a few yards from Anse!

Then, from a distance at which the real Sam McCoy could have hit Devil Anse between the ears a hundred times in a row with open sights, Paris takes aim through his scope — and misses Anse completely again!

I ran it back a couple of times in an effort to see what went wrong, and the only thing I could come up with is that when Paris told Sam, "Get behind me on the ground — don't even breathe," Sam did not comply. What effect Sam's position or breathing could possibly have on Paris' aim is beyond me, but that's what he said.

What I think went wrong here is that, while he was concerned about Sam being perfectly still and not even breathing, Paris himself was talking and vigorously masticating what must have been a mouthful of jerky as he took aim. This shows us once again that one should never talk and chew at the same time. Of course, one should do neither while taking aim to shoot someone.

After Paris muffed this second chance to kill the Devil, Cap shouldered his Winchester and, taking aim over its open sights, plugged Paris through the breastbone. Of course, this didn't happen either because both Sam and Paris McCoy survived the feud in vigorous health.

So, according to our movie, Devil Anse lived another three-plus decades and died in bed of pneumonia, only because when they tried to kill him neither Squirrel Huntin' Sam McCoy, one of the best marksmen alive, nor Paris McCoy with a scope, could hit a barn door.

Neither of these events happened, but they do make good scenes in a movie.

## The Hatfields Who Couldn't Shoot Straight

Some writers say that some Hatfields, probably Johnse and Cap, laid in ambush to kill Ran'l on his way to Pikeville. Learning that the old man was planning a trip to further his efforts to get action from the Pike authorities on the old warrants, they positioned themselves on the hillside above the road downstream from Ran'l's house and waited for him to ride by. Fortunately for Ran'l, he was delayed in starting, and the assassins mistook two Scotts, John and Hense, for Ran'l and Calvin. The hapless Hatfields fired a volley of shots at the wrong men, killing both horses and wounding Hense.[20] [21] [22]

That did not happen. It is not the way Devil Anse would have gone about killing Ran'l McCoy, if he were of the mind to do so. Anse had no reason to eliminate Ran'l after the triple murders, because in Anse's mind, the scales were balanced. Had Devil Anse wanted to eliminate Ran'l, he would have placed a sharpshooter in the woods around the McCoy homestead.

I also doubt the story of the shooting of the Scotts by the Hatfields because of the poor marksmanship. It is hard to believe that both Cap and Johnse fired several shots at the Scotts from close ambush, and not a single bullet found its target in a Scott torso.

Dean King has several more men shooting at the Scotts along with the Hatfield brothers in this ambush, which is a level of sorry marksmanship that is just not believable for men of that time and place.

I was really shocked to learn from Mr. King that the Hatfields used Mose Christian(Cline) as one of their shooters for the botched ambush of Randolph and Calvin as they rode home from their court appearance in the case involving the estate of the recently deceased timber magnate, Tolbert McCoy. I could see no good reason to employ a man nearly my own age in such a venture. The only thing I could come up with is that since Mose was old enough to be on Medicare, he wouldn't be a drain on Devil Anse's finances should he be wounded in the ambush.

It behooves us to consider all possibilities: Maybe having the superannuated Mose on the team explains the mistaken identity, which led to the wounding of two McCoy neighbors, and the slaying of two fine horses. Maybe Old Mose was posted as the lookout, responsible for alerting the strike force as the McCoys approached. Being over sixty-five, it is quite likely that Old Mose had failing eyesight. As there was no practicing ophthalmologist in the area — not even a Walmart Vision Center — Old Mose might well have made the tragic misidentification. Don't laugh too hard, because this is far more believable than the claim that Cap and Johnse didn't know the McCoys well enough to identify them from a position thirty feet above the road.

The terrible marksmanship of the Hatfield ambush team is also a matter of some concern. Being posted only thirty feet from the road with Winchester rifles, and having three men riding abreast, you would think that a seven man hit squad comprised of New York newspapermen could score at least one torso hit, much less seven mountain hunters. Shooting at three men riding abreast from that distance would be even easier than the proverbial "fish in a barrel," but, alas, in King's version, all the inept Hatfields could accomplish was one knee-capping, a minor shoulder wound and two dead horses.

King says that the Hatfields, obviously too obtuse to know that Ran'l was a sitting duck every day as he went about his farm chores, "resolved to keep an eye out for an opportunity and saw it come that June. Randall had been summoned to the Pikeville courthouse to appear at a public hearing regarding Tolbert's timber interests."[23]

When I was in high school, during the mid 1950's, I visited the site where Ran'l McCoy's children who died during the feud were buried. I saw only one marker with an inscription, a simple dornick with Calvin McCoy's name on it, with no dates. The stone had "Cal Mc" on the top line and "Coy" on the line below it. As I had not read the "True Story" at that time, Dean King not yet having even born, I had no idea that I was looking at the headstone of a man who served as administrator of the estate of a timber magnate, whose own grave somewhere nearby was not visibly marked at all.

Nearly a century after the McCoys died, supersizing occurred, with the installation of the large and ornate marker seen above.

The marker says that six of Ran'l's children are buried there, even though there is no record of the death of William McCoy in the Pike County records. In fact, no one knows for sure the time or place of the death of William McCoy, or even if he died anywhere in Kentucky. This did not prevent the adding of his name, with no date of death, to the marker. The people who commissioned the marker had no idea when or where William McCoy died, but they were sure enough that he died of feud-related grief to add him to the list. The latest supersizer, Dean King, lists William McCoy as one of his feud fatalities,[24] even though King has no evidence of how, where or when William McCoy died.

According to King, the Hatfields, being too dumb to pick Ran'l off at home while he was slopping his hogs, began an intelligence-gathering operation to learn when Ran'l might be away from home and vulnerable to ambush.

Upon learning that Ran'l and Calvin would be going to court in the matter of the estate of Tolbert McCoy, the Hatfields set up an ambush along the roadside. King goes Truda McCoy several men better, having his ambush party comprised of a "Heavily armed Johnse, Cap and Bill Tom Hatfield, Cotton top Mounts, Mose Christian and two other men."[25]

King says that after the ambush was in place, the son of the local magistrate came by and Cap exited his hiding place and instructed the boy to "go to the courtroom and bring back a description of the clothes Randall and Calvin were wearing."[26] Mr. King is obviously either unaware, or unconcerned with the fact that it was a hard day's ride from there to the courtroom in Pikeville. Are we to believe that the gang stayed in place all day, through the night and the next day, while waiting for the boy to complete his round trip to Pikeville?

Are we also expected to believe that the son of the magistrate would not have gone only far enough toward Pikeville to get out of sight of the West Virginia hit squad before doubling back to tell his father of the impending crime in his district? King says the boy made the sixty mile round trip in time to describe the clothing of the McCoys to Cap, before the intended targets arrived at the ambush site.

Mr. King says: "By the time the hearing ended, it was dusk. The participants filed out."[27] There you have it. The McCoys and their neighbors, the Scotts, left the courtroom, which was a hard eight hour ride from the ambush site, at dusk.[28] The Hatfield gang is waiting for them. In fact, according to King, they had already waited all day! Luckily for the intended murderers, the McCoy group made the trip in record time. Leaving the courtroom, some thirty miles distant at "dusk," they reached the ambush site "as the sun sank below the ridgeline."[29]

Then the Hatfield incompetence that we see so often in King's book crops up to bite them again. So poor was the Hatfield gang's vision as the sun set in the West that they couldn't recognize them, even though the boy had completed the sixty-mile round trip that day and described the clothes being worn by the McCoys.

After all that superhuman effort, where the boy made a sixty-mile round trip in a day, and the court case participants travelled thirty miles between dusk and sunset, the same poor marksmanship that caused Cap to miss Jeff McCoy repeatedly at a distance of ten yards or so showed up again. The gang unleashed a fusillade at the unfortunate Scotts, whom they mistook for the McCoys, despite the heroic boy's description. The poor marksmanship of the Hatfield clan resulted in one man being shot in the shoulder and another shot in the knee. Not a single ball found its way into a torso. Like Glen Campbell in "True Grit," they did succeed in killing the horses. Unlike the other versions, King has Cap being wounded in the chest during the ambush. King's source for this Keystone Kops fiasco is the estimable John Spears, reporter for the New York Sun.

The filler material supersizers add to their tales always makes the feudists look either bloodthirsty or stupid, or both. The Hatfields engaging in an elaborate roadside ambush for men they could have picked off at home at their leisure makes them look somewhat bloodthirsty and immensely stupid. It is filler material and not history.[30]

From 1952-1955, my Sister Wanda and her husband, Francis Hatfield, rented a small home from Pricy Scott, widow of Crit Scott. At that time, Pricy Scott lived on the old Ran'l McCoy home place, along with her daughter, Mertie, directly across Blackberry Fork from the house my wife grew up in. Pricy Scott grew up just two houses above the McCoy home. She married in 1889 and moved to Johns Creek. In 1902, she and her husband, Crit Scott, bought the McCoy home place and she lived there until she died in 1965.[31] The little house that my sister lived in sat very near where the original McCoy home sat. Part of the chimney and the super-structure of the original well still stood as they were on January 1, 1888.

Mrs. Scott, who sold baked goods at the 1882 election, was a friend and neighbor of the Ran'l McCoy family who certainly had no reason to shade the facts in favor of the West Virginia Hatfields.

Several times when I visited my sister after reading the Virgil Jones book, I discussed it with Pricy and her daughter, Mertie. They had the book, and Mertie was familiar with its contents. She considered it the same as Uncle Ransom did — mostly fairy tales.

The details of the Election Day 1882 killings, and the New Year's raid of 1888, as told by Pricy and Mertie, were essentially the same as I have related them here.

Pricy Scott said that she slept through the New Year's 1888 raid on the McCoy home, but her mother told them the next day that there were thirteen horses, carrying fourteen men — two men riding double on one horse — in the returning raiding party.

Her father, Aly Farley and her brother, John B. Farley were the first to arrive at the McCoy home the morning following the raid. Her father told her that Sally's hair was frozen to the ground. She saw Calvin and Alifair laid out at Jim McCoy's house later that day, and attended the burial the next day. She said it was "The awfulest time ever."

I remember asking the Scott ladies about John and Hense Scott being ambushed by mistake by the Hatfields. Pricy said that she remembered at least three John Scotts and at least three Hense Scotts living on Blackberry or Pond Creek when she was growing up, but she had no memory of any of them being shot by Hatfields. She said that there was a John Scott who had been shot and wounded on Blackberry Creek, but she didn't think it had anything to do with Hatfields.

Sometime around the turn of the last century, I came across a lawsuit involving a John Scott versus Pricy and her husband, Crit Scott. The case lasted for years and was appealed to the Kentucky Court of Appeals *twice*.[32] As there were three John Scotts in the Blackberry-Pond Creek area, I don't know if this was the John Scott who was said to have been ambushed.

Pricy's daughter, Mertie, who was living with her mother, was a little more astute than is today's average reader of "feud histories." While discussing the Hatfields planning an ambush while Ran'l traveled to Pikeville, she pointed toward the base of the hill in back of the house, and said, "If they wanted to kill Ol' Ran'l, why didn't they just sneak through the woods and do it right back there? They could have got close enough to him to knock him in the head while he was slopping the hogs." That has been my own position on the matter for about fifty years, and it would take hard evidence to convince me otherwise.

Truda McCoy says that the Scotts were ambushed, along with Ran'l McCoy's son, Sam, while carrying sacks of corn — *on foot* — from main Blackberry through the head of Dials Branch to Blackberry Fork of Pond Creek. McCoy's version places the ambush on the wrong side of Ran'l's home for it to have been where King places it, on the road to Pikeville. McCoy said that there were five in the Hatfield gang involved in the ambush, including three Hatfields, Cap, Elias and Wall. Johnse is absent from Truda McCoy's gang. There is nothing in Truda McCoy's story about going to Pikeville for a court hearing or anything else. She had the Scotts approaching Ran'l's home on foot from the opposite direction, with sacks of corn on their backs.[33]

Truda McCoy's version of this farcical incident brings up an interesting question: How in the world did the Hatfields know when the McCoys would be carrying corn from main Blackberry to Blackberry Fork of Pond Creek? That would require an even better intelligence network than would discovering when Ran'l would be going to Pikeville.

Dean King added Truda McCoy's five shooters to the two shooters reported in most other versions, to come up with a seven-man hit squad — not one of whom could hit the side of a barn — with the two Scotts plus Sam McCoy *on horses.* King places the hapless Scotts on the Pikeville side of Ran'l's home, riding horses and not carrying corn on foot.

King tells of Cap later mistaking a Hatfield relative for Ol' Ran'l, at a distance of less than seventy yards, and shooting him through the knee.[34] King's source for this is a newspaper interview of a Hatfield relative, who did not claim to be an eyewitness. The interview was almost a century after the claimed incident.

After reading of these repeated knee-shootings, I wonder if the modern Cosa Nostra copied their kneecapping thing from Cap Hatfield.

As unbelievable as it may seem, the Hatfields never caught onto the idea that they could hide in the edge of the woods less than fifty yards from Ran'l's house and dispatch him at their leisure.

Kevin Costner's movie omits the farcical ambush of the innocents, and I commend him for that.

## Devil Anse Electioneering

Multiple sources also say that Devil Anse rode into Logan on Election Day in 1886, with a large force of armed men, in an attempt to intimidate supporters of the opponent of Devil Anse's man, John B. Floyd.[35] This fits the character of Devil Anse and I believe that it happened. It also fits with the vital support Floyd gave in helping Anse fight extradition to Kentucky two years later. I am just as sure that there were not a hundred armed men with devil Anse, as some writers claim. There was never a documented case of more than twenty armed men with Devil Anse at any time.

This reported election maneuver by Devil Anse is rendered even more credible by the memoirs of Governor William McCorkle, who reported that during his campaign for the office in 1892, the Democratic Caucus in Logan County reached an impasse in deciding whom to endorse. Governor McCorkle said that Devil Anse broke the logjam by telling the assembly that if they didn't vote forthwith to endorse McCorkle, he would go home and get his Winchester and come back and see that the caucus did the right thing. McCorkle said that he received the endorsement very quickly after Devil Anse's speech.[36]

Another 1886 event, far from Tug Valley, was much more important to the feud story than any of the events discussed above--the decision by the N&W railroad to build a line connecting the Ohio River with Virginia.[37] When this decision was reported in the company's annual report for 1886, Dils, Mayo, Williamson, Nighbert, Sergeant, and all the other vultures swooping over the coal-rich lands of the valley became aware of the impending explosion in land values along the route of the new railroad, and they acted to gather up as much land and mineral as possible, in a dog-eat-dog fight for coal lands. Hence, the five thousand acres Devil Anse owned right in the heart of the "billion-dollar coal field" came into the sights of all the big gunners, including John Dils in Pikeville.

1 McCoy, *The McCoys*, 227, n. 13.
2 Rice, Otis, *The Hatfields and the McCoys*, 33-35.
3 The original letter with its envelope was given to my great-great Uncle, Ransom Hatfield, by the Cline family. It now belongs to Ransom's grandson, Ron G. Blackburn.
4 Hatfield, L.D., True Story of the Hatfield and McCoy Feud, 32.
5 Jones, Virgil, *the Hatfields and the McCoys*, 75-6.
6 Mutzenberg, 39-45.
7 McCoy, *The McCoys*, 227, n. 12.
8 McCoy, McCoys, 114–15.
9 Mutzenberg, *Famous Feuds*, 28.
10 Rice, *The Hatfields and the McCoys,* 33.
11 Hatfield and Spence, *The Hatfields and the McCoys,* 126–27.
12 Alther, *Blood Feud*, 77.
13 *Wheeling Register* January 1, 1899.
14 Spears, *Mountain Feud*, 19-20.
15 King, the Feud, 144-45.
16 King, 144.
17 I do not believe that Spears made this one up himself. Although I never heard that tale growing up, I believe he heard it during his visit to Pike County, probably from Perry Cline. The creativity of some of our old mountain storytellers is remarkable.
18 Rice, *The Hatfields and the McCoys,* 33.
19 Although there is no record of either Cap or Wallace being charged with a crime in the invasion of the Daniels home, there may have been a warrant issued for Tom Wallace, because in his letter to Cline, Devil Anse referred to Jeff McCoy's attempt to "arrest" Tom Wallace. I conclude that there could have been a warrant for Wallace, but not for Cap, and I therefore believe that Cap's involvement was minimal. Cap's participation certainly did not involve beating the women to the point of death, or else Jeff would have been trying to arrest both men.
20 Rice, Hatfields and McCoys, 31.
21 Jones, Hatfields & McCoys, 69
22 McCoy, *McCoys*, 96.
23 King, 124.
24 King, *The Feud*, 274-5.
25 Ibid.
26 King, 125.
27 Ibid.

28 King tells us when the hearing ended, and who attended it, but he does not give us any reference to the case to allow us to check the records. Neither does he inform us of the size of the estate, nor when it was finally settled. According to King, the estate was so vast and complicated that Calvin had to file multiple lawsuits and make many trips to Pikeville in settling it. We are told only that the estate was still in the court two years after Tolbert's demise. As I can find no records of any of it in the Pike Court house, maybe it is still unsettled, in which case I, as a distant relative, might be well advised to retain Pikeville counsel and demand my rightful share of Tolbert's wealth.

29 ibid

30 While the writers for the Costner movie invented many incidents in constructing their long feud, they did not include two of the most ludicrous "events' seen in the supersized accounts—the tale of the cow's tale and the shooting of the Scotts by mistake. For this they are to be complimented.

31 In 1950, my older brother, George W., bought a 1928 Buick from Pricy Scott. The car had been bought new by her husband, Crit Scott, and had not been started since he died in 1932. G.W. paid $40 for the car and got it running again. As many as a dozen neighborhood boys would pile into that big old sedan and tool around Blackberry Creek.

32 Scott v. Scott, 190 S. W. 143, and, Scott et. al. v. Scott et. al., 210 S. W. 175.

33 Truda McCoy says in an endnote that John Scott told her the story of the ambush nearly forty years after it happened. McCoy, The McCoys, p. 225-6, n. 10. Truda McCoy should have asked John Scott why the Hatfields would have thought that Ran'l McCoy would be carrying corn from Main Blackberry toward his home on Blackberry Fork, and how the Hatfields found out about it in time to set up an ambush.

34 King, 126.

35 Waller, Feud, 151.

36 McCorkle, William A., Recollections of Fifty years in West Virginia, New York: Putnam's Sons, 1928, pp. 285-86.

37 Waller, Feud, 153–54.

# CHAPTER 15.

# THIS LAND IS WHOSE LAND?

When the movie shows Perry Cline approaching Devil Anse at his timber-cutting operation with lawsuit papers as the beginning of the contest for the Grapevine land, the film begins a segment that is entirely fictitious. Again, what really happened would have made for better drama, but, so far as I know, you are about to read the first published description of new evidence as to what really happened.

Whereas the movie shows that Cline was caught trying to swindle Anse with a forged document, the opposite is actually closer to the truth, as it was Anse who might have been dealing in forged documents at that time.

Devil Anse might have, as the movie shows, cut timber on land belonging to himself and his brothers in the beginning of his post-war timbering activities, but by 1868 he was logging on the five thousand acres that Perry Cline and his brother Jacob had inherited from their father in 1858.

The movie is not alone in getting the Grapevine lands fight wrong-- most writers miss the point. Everyone wonders why Perry Cline was cutting timber on Anse's three hundred acres, when he had five thousand acres of his own,[1] but that is not what it was about.

I was also puzzled about this for decades, until I read a case decided by the West Virginia Supreme Court of Appeals, called Ellison v. Torpin.[2]

The case arose when a land speculator named Ellison did some research and found that the Grapevine lands had been left in a moiety (undivided interest), one half to Jacob Cline and one half to Perry, his brother. Ellison then went to Jacob Cline's two surviving heirs and bought their half interest. In 1892, Ellison brought suit to enforce his claim to half the land against the Eastern financiers, the Torpin Trust, to whom J.D. Sergeant had flipped the land after buying it from Anse in January of 1888.

It certainly would have been beneficial for readers if the best-selling "histories" by Alther and King had delved into this subject. King gives little coverage to the land dispute, having said that economics had nothing to do with "the feud."

In 1872, Anse sued Perry Cline for cutting timber land that Anse claimed belonged to him. The lawsuit by Anse was not a claim that Perry Cline was logging on land that Devil Anse previously owned, but rather a claim by Anse that the five thousand acres on Grapevine Creek that Cline inherited from his father in 1858 actually belonged to Anse. The Torpin decision is the only place where this can be learned.

It is not clear from the record what Anse's original grounds were for claiming the Cline lands. One witness testified that Anse went there in 1867 under a survey done by Anse's father in 1860. Then he said that Anse had bought the land from the Cline Brothers in 1868.

The testimony of a family outsider about Ephraim Hatfield's survey introduces an interesting question: What if Ephraim did survey the land and claim it? If so, then it is possible that Devil Anse actually believed he was the rightful owner all along. That would make him not a land grabber, but simply a man claiming what he believed was rightfully his.

Rich Jake Cline filed two separate deeds on the land, twenty years apart. This is evidence of some level of insecurity on the part of Perry Cline's father as to the validity of his title. Perry Cline's signing over of his interest in the land in 1877, without contesting it in court, requires us to consider every possibility, and the testimony regarding Ephraim's survey certainly raises questions. The dissenting opinion of Justice Brannon makes it clear that at least one justice questioned the title of Perry Cline's brother, Jacob, Jr. If Jake, Jr. did not have a secure title, then the same applies to the title held by Perry.

The 1855 deed from the heirs of David Mounts to Jacob Cline bore the names of ten heirs of David Mounts, but two names were missing.[3] David Mounts' daughter, Martha, who married John Steele, did not sign the deed, and neither did David Mounts' surviving widow, Margaret (Peggy) Mounts.[4] Martha Mounts Steele had a son who married Wall Hatfield's daughter, Nancy. Another son of Martha married Wall's daughter, Sarah Ann, after her husband, Doc Mayhorn, went to jail for his part in the killing of the three McCoy boys. When Doc got out of prison fourteen years later, Sarah Ann divorced Rafe Steele and remarried Doc. Mayhorn.[5]

DAVID MOUNTS HEIRS

**Deed Book C, pg. 432, Logan County, WV**

This Indenture made and entered into this the twenty sixth day of July 1855, Jacob Cline of the County of Logan and State of *Virginey* of one part and the *hars* of David Mounts *decest* of the County of Logan and State of *Cantucky* of the second part *witnesseth* that the *sd. hars* for and in consideration the sum of Two hundred Dollars to them in hand paid by the sd. Jacob Cline the receipt where is hearby *acnoledg* have granted *barganed* sold and by these presents do hereby grant bargain and sell the sd Jacob Cline his *hars* and *assins* part of a survey granted to John Green for Thirty thousand acres lying and being on Grape Vine Creek and bounded as follows *Comencing* at the line between Jacob Cline and the said *hars* of David Mounts including all the land on the waters of the Grape Vine *Creeke* running with the top of the dividing ridge around the same including a certain tract *witch* was *willd* to Harrison Mounts a *sun* of Michael Mounts white the said Michael Mounts *dos warrent* and defend from the claim of his son Harrison with all *singelar* ...*appertances tharun* to belonging or in any wise appertaining. To have and to hold the sd. Tract or parcel of land with its *appertainences* unto the said Jacob Cline his *hars* and *assins* against them the *sd hars* of David Mounts and against all and every person or persons lawfully claiming the same by from or with them *shal* and will warrant and forever defend. In witness wherof wee have set our hands *seels* the day and year first written the said William Mounts does *hearby* warrant and defend the *hoshon* of land *wild* to *Sarly* Mounts hars.

| Attested by | signed |
|---|---|
| Alexander Mounts | Alexander Mounts (seal) |
| Wm. T. Cline | William Mounts (seal) |
| Richard Daniels | Peter + Mounts (seal) |
| Matason Hatfield | Charles + Mounts (seal) |
| Weslley Mounts | Sary Mounts  (seal) |
| Jackson Mounts | Alexander Trent (seal) |
|  | Jackson + Mounts (seal) |
|  | Eligh + Mounts (seal) |
|  | Asbury + Hurley (seal) |
|  | Michal Mounts (seal) |

+ his mark

---

Notes on Signers:
1. Alexander Trent married David's daughter Elizabeth
2. Asbury Hurley married Davids's daughter Nancy, b. 1816 or so.
3. Sarah Mounts married Daniel Christian in Tazewell Co. Va, 1850

Notable Omission:
daughter Martha Mounts, b. abt. 1825 d. 1909, who married John Steele

Notable Exception:
The surviving widow of David Mounts did not sign the deed.

As Margaret (Peggy) Mounts was living in the household of Devil Anse's employee, Selkirk McCoy, in the 1880 census, Devil Anse likely had an ace in the hole in challenging the Cline title to the land.

Perry Cline might have thought he owned a one-half interest in the Grapevine land, but this deed brings his ownership into question, as Jacob Cline's deed to the land from the heirs of David Mounts lacked the signatures of one daughter and the surviving widow.

The 1877 settlement might have been brought about by Anse simply showing Cline's lawyer the deed, without all the required signatures. What we do know for sure is that Perry Cline never owned whatever interests was owned by the two Mounts heirs who did not sign the deed. This means that the lone dissenting judge in *Torpin* was probably right when he said that Jacob Cline's title was imperfect, and, if so, Perry Cline's title was also defective.

Two of the heirs who signed that deed, Charles Mounts and Asbury Hurley, were men whom Devil Anse is said to have killed during the Civil War. David Mounts' daughter, Sarah, who signed her name "Sary," was said to have had four children who were fathered by Uncle Wall Hatfield.[6]

The Court majority clouds the time-line further by saying: "In 1870 or 1871, Perry Cline traded all the lands devised to him by his father to one Anderson Hatfield for lands on the other side of Tug River, in Pike County, Ky., and Hatfield, who had been cutting timber as a trespasser, and building cabins on said Grapevine creek, claiming some sort of survey made by his father, left Grapevine Creek and moved to the old (Cline) home place."[7] So, according to the Supreme Court, Devil Anse was already living in the Cline home place when he filed the suit claiming the Grapevine lands in 1872.

This land trade of 1870-71, involved only the Cline home place, which was some 1500 acres, and which was left to Perry Cline alone. It must be distinguished from the Grapevine lands, which were left to the two brothers in a moiety.

We have additional evidence for dating Anse's entrance into the Grapevine lands in the appointment of Colonel John Dils as legal guardian of Perry Cline in 1868. This appointment brings up several interesting questions. Why, one might ask, would an outside guardian be appointed for a young man of eighteen years, when he had lived quite well for a decade with family and no legal guardian appointed? Why would a young man of eighteen ask the court to give him a guardian who had, just months before the appointment, been removed as guardian of other minors because the guardian had misused the assets of his minor charges?[8]

As the Supreme Court said in 1892, his land had been invaded by a trespasser, who was taking the valuable timber from said land. We see this in Cline's own words, in a letter he wrote to Governor Buckner some twenty years later, wherein Cline said of the Hatfields, "These men has (sic) made good citizens leave their homes and forsake all they had, and refuse to let any person tend their lands."[9]

As Perry Cline is the only person who ever left his home under pressure from Devil Anse, there is no question about whom he is writing. And how did Devil Anse move him off the land? Was it because he sued him, or was it because "they (the Hatfields) are the worst band of meroders (sic) ever existed in the mountains, and have been in arms since the war...."[10] Could it have been that Cline had grave doubts about proving his title?

*Why* did C line choose a man who had recently been found by the Pike County courts to have stolen from his charges?[11] Perry Cline needed a man who had both the power to oppose Devil Anse and the inclination to use his power. John Dils, Devil Anse's wartime adversary and the most powerful man in postwar Pike County, uniquely fit the bill.

Devil Anse's efforts to get Perry Cline to sign a title bond for the land is probably what drove Cline to Colonel Dils in 1868. This was not known for nearly a quarter century, when the bond was produced in evidence in the Ellison v. Torpin case. Devil Anse had a title bond, dated August 24, 1869[12] covering the Grapevine lands, and with the signatures of both Perry Cline and his brother Jacob affixed thereto, he filed the bond away and never recorded it himself. We would have never known of its existence, had not the

Torpin Trust lawyers discovered it in a search of Anse's papers in his home. The court says it was found wrapped in an old shawl, where it had been for twenty years.[13]

Unable to sustain their claim to full ownership under the 1877 deed, the Torpin Trust fell back upon the 1869 title bond, claiming that Devil Anse had owned all of the five thousand acres since that time. The fact that Perry Cline was under the age of majority, and thus not competent to transfer his ownership was never brought out in the lawsuit.

The case is further complicated in the concurring opinion by Justice McWhorter, who says that Anse had given an affidavit in the case, wherein Anse admitted that the signature of Jacob Cline on the title bond *was a forgery*! The justice further stated that the Torpin lawyers had tricked Ellison's lawyers into thinking that Anse's testimony would somehow be adverse to him, and thereby kept the deposition testimony of Devil Anse out of the case.[14]

It appears that Devil Anse might have secured the signature of Perry Cline in 1868, and left the date off, pending Jacob's signature. Then in 1869, realizing that Jacob was not going to sign, *someone* forged Jacob's name to the document and dated it. If that is true, then Perry Cline had already signed the title bond when he went to Colonel Dils for protection.

Devil Anse never recorded the title bond, so the question arises as to why he procured it in the first place. Although we can only surmise, I am of the opinion that this title bond is the key to the mystery posed by Altina Waller in relation to Devil Anse's dealings with suppliers and bankers during the years prior to receiving the deed from Perry Cline in 1877. All Anse had to do was show the signed title bond, and he would be treated just like anyone else who owned over five thousand acres.

The Supreme Court majority rejected the title bond, without even considering Anse's own sworn deposition, wherein Anse said that the signature of Jacob Cline was a forgery.

In his dissenting opinion, Justice Brannon accepted the validity of the title bond. The justice said he would reverse the lower court and allow the Torpin Trust to keep all the land, based on the title bond. The justice said that the Jacob Cline heirs, as well as Ellison, knew that what Ellison was buying from them was an imperfect title, because he paid only a tiny fraction of the worth of their supposed one-half interest, a total of two hundred dollars. To Justice Brannon, the payment of $200 for "2,000 to 3,000 acres of coal land traversed by the Norfolk & Western Railroad, on which were vast operations in the mining of coal" was a red flag he could not ignore.[15]

Justice Brannon certainly has a point: Why would the heirs of Jacob Cline sell a half interest in five thousand acres for two hundred dollars, unless they had serious doubts about their title?

The judge is also telling us that a few years after Anse capitulated to the pressure from the Pikeville posse, the railroad had been completed and "vast operations in the mining of coal" under way. Once the land was in the hands of the Torpin trust, there was no further interest in Devil Anse Hatfield, murder warrants or no, on the part of the Dils/Cline gang in Pikeville. The "feud" was over.

Assuming his signature on the title bond was genuine, one explanation for Perry Cline's action (Jacob never signed the bond) is simple fear. Bearing in mind his statement to the governor twenty years later that "these men has (sic) *made good citizens leave their homes and forsake all they had*, and refuse to let any person to even tend their lands"[16] (emphasis mine), it is possible that Perry Cline feared that if he resisted, he would be shot by a sniper as he traveled through the wilds of the Valley.

An alternate explanation is that Anse paid him five hundred dollars, as the testimony of one witness said.

If Cline had already come under the guardianship of Colonel Dils when he signed the title bond, then the Colonel might well have told him to go ahead and sign it, for the sake of his personal safety, knowing that the signature of a minor on such an instrument would be meaningless anyway Colonel Dils, knowing first hand from war experience the capacity for mayhem possessed by Anse Hatfield, could have been concerned for the safety of his new foster son in 1868.

The Cline lands Devil Anse eventually owned consisted of two main tracts. One tract, just upriver from the mouth of Grapevine

Creek, was known as the home place. The common practice in those days was for the family home to descend to the youngest son, and Rich Jake Cline followed tradition by willing the home place to Perry alone. We can deduce from the evidence in the lawsuit that this comprised some 1,500 acres and was the land that Devil Anse sold tracts from to various kinsmen and employees during the following decade or so. There was never any question about the title to the home place, but I did not know that until I read in the Torpin case that there had been an exchange involving the home place between Devil Anse and Perry Cline before the lawsuit over the Grapevine land was filed.

Most of the tracts that Devil Anse sold to various kinsmen and employees were from the home place tract. This reflects well on the man, since he took care to give his associates good title on land he knew he legally owned, rather than on the Grapevine land, which he knew had title problems.

We know from the Torpin case that when Devil Anse sold out to J.D. Sergeant, the home place tract was actually purchased from Devil Anse and several of his kinsmen, whereas the Grapevine lands required only Anse's signature. There was never any question about the validity of the title on the home place land passed to Sergeant and to the Philadelphia financiers a little later. Not so with the Grapevine land.

Anse did not win the Grapevine land in a court decision; Anse filed a lawsuit, which in some manner not known to me, was settled in 1877 by Cline signing over his entire inheritance to Devil Anse. The 1877 settlement is much harder to explain than is the 1869 title bond or the 1870-1 land swap, because Anse is now dealing with a man who has been elected sheriff of his county, and is the protégé of the most powerful man in the Valley, and not a fearful eighteen year-old living among enemies.

As the 1877 deal cannot be explained on the basis of Cline's fear of Devil Anse, we should examine the known facts look for what makes sense. The main facts of the situation in 1877 are: 1) Cline is now safely ensconced in a powerful position in Pikeville, with the most powerful man in the county in his corner; 2) Devil

Anse has in his possession a title bond, bearing the signatures of both of the Cline heirs; 3) Anse has at least one witness who will testify that Anse's father surveyed and claimed the land; 4) Anse has the backing of some of the most influential and respected men in Logan County, who signed a six thousand dollar bond to allow Anse to prosecute his suit; and, 5) Cline is facing a lawsuit in Logan County, where he would likely lose and be assessed damages which might reduce him to penury. Therefore, it was a smart move for Cline to sign over his part of the Grapevine lands.

The widely held view that Perry Cline signed away most of his personal wealth when he was actually "in the right," does not hold water. A man in the position of power Perry Cline held in 1877 does not sign away five thousand prime acres unless he sees more downside in fighting than in surrendering. Perry Cline must have thought that the odds were very high that he would lose the case, and be assessed damages. One may argue that Cline thought he would lose only because the Logan court would be biased in favor of Devil Anse, but the fact that Cline had the backing of Dils, meant that he had the wherewithal to appeal to a higher court, beyond the influence of the Logan County Hatfields. I can see no logical reason for Cline settling by surrendering other than that he was convinced that he would lose the case on its merits.

The fact that Dr. Elliott Rutherford, George Steele, William McCoy and Richard Phillips signed a bond in the huge — for that time — amount of six thousand dollars shows that Anse had at least a reasonable chance of winning. Those men would not have signed that large bond if the only thing Anse had going for him was his reputation, because the record shows that Anse lost a majority of the lawsuits he was involved in. Those men thought that Anse had a case; otherwise they would not have exposed themselves to the liability. Knowing that the deed from the Mounts heirs to Rich Jake lacked two of the required signatures might well have been what convinced that group of substantial citizens to sign the bond for Devil Anse. It is also noteworthy that, at a time when many feud industry writers would have us believe that there was an ongoing

Hatfield and McCoy feud, a man named McCoy signed a large bond for Devil Anse Hatfield.

It is also noteworthy that Mary Daniels, a daughter of Asa Harmon McCoy and niece of Perry Cline was active in the Grapevine land case, giving depositions for Cline. The actual record of the period shows more friction between the Asa Harmon McCoy/Perry Cline faction and Devil Anse than between Ran'l McCoy and Devil Anse. Yet, whatever the conflict was, it is always presented by the feud writers as a blood feud between Ran'l McCoy and Devil Anse.

All that said, the fact that Perry Cline signed the marriage bond for Johnse Hatfield and his niece, Nancy McCoy in May of 1881, proves to me that there was not a "feuding enmity" even between those two factions until at least the time of the killing of Jeff McCoy, in late 1886.

Most feud writers assume that the Grapevine land contest was extremely bitter, but there is evidence that it was not; Cline signed the marriage bond for Johnse and Nancy. No one knows for sure how the lawsuit was settled. It could very well be that Cline realized the weaknesses in his title, and that Devil Anse greased the skids with a thousand or so. After all, Anse had been running a profitable timber business for nearly a decade, and could easily have come up with the dough.

Although losing the five thousand acres—no matter how it came about—must have left a bitter taste in Cline's mouth, he signed the 1881 marriage bond for Johnse Hatfield and his niece, Nancy McCoy. Cline's approval of his niece's marriage to Devil Anse's son showed that there was not a feuding enmity between Perry Cline and Devil Anse four years after the land settlement, and six years before Cline helped to organize the posse that raided into West Virginia in search of Hatfields. This leads further credence to my argument in the following pages that Perry Cline was acting under the direction of his foster-father, John Dils in 1887-8.

Devil Anse could have gotten many times the seven thousand dollars he received (plus paying off all Anse's creditors) if he could have held out for a couple of years. Nevertheless, the court's decision in the Torpin case means Anse's deal was twice as good as it appeared in 1888 because he only transferred a one-half interest in the Grapevine land. Of course, Mr. Ellison made the best deal of all, getting one half of the five thousand acres for two hundred dollars, plus his lawyer's fee.

What did Anse do to try to get Jacob Cline to sign the title bond? One thing is to give sworn testimony in 1869 for Jacob Cline in a lawsuit. The old saying, "Truth is stranger than fiction," certainly holds true in this court case. The issue being contested in the case is even stranger: Jacob Cline, a Union Army deserter, was with the Confederate raiders in November, 1864 when they cleaned out John Dils and the Sowards brothers, and they sued Cline, along with Devil Anse and several more of the rebel raiders.[17]

Jake, Jr., was one of nearly two hundred deserters from Colonel Dils's former regiment, the 39th Kentucky Mounted Infantry, who deserted in August 1864, when the 109th Colored Regiment joined the federal forces at Louisa, where the 39th was based. Most of the Pike County members of Dils's former outfit went home rather than serve with colored soldiers, and Jake Cline, a slave owner himself, was among the deserters.[18] He was easily identified when he showed up among Bill Smith's raiders at Peach Orchard.

Devil Anse swore that he was on that raid and that Cline was with the Confederates *against his will*. Devil Anse swore that Cline had been told by the rebels that if he did not join them on the raid, they would kill him. Devil Anse said that the threat to young Jacob came from "men who did kill sometimes."[19] I suspect that the man giving the deposition for Cline in 1869 might very well have been the man "who did kill sometimes," who scared the youngster into going on the raid.

By 1887, much of the prime coal along the Tug River had been secured for Eastern money. Several mountaineer political and business leaders became rich by buying up the land and mineral rights of their kinsmen and neighbors and flipping them to the Big Money. Knowing in 1887 that the Norfolk and Western railroad would be finished up the Tug Valley within a few years, the pressure on the land and coal grabbers was intense. They knew that the price of land and mineral rights would skyrocket when the locals saw the track being laid, and they reacted accordingly.

Devil Anse, who, by exploiting the timber, had helped his own family escape the poverty that results from too many people on too little land, undoubtedly counted on his minerals taking the place of the timber, once that resource was depleted, and he held onto his land. West Virginia did not have Mayo's *broad form deed*, so outside money bought the land, both surface and mineral. They paid taxes on the land as if it had continued to be used for subsistence farming.

Absentee corporate owners now own a majority of the land in twenty-seven coal-rich counties in West Virginia. In Mingo County, where Devil Anse's Grapevine land is located, four corporations own 177,000 out of 270,000 total acres in the county. US Steel, which owns the Grapevine lands, owns 36,000 acres of Mingo County My brother-in-law worked for US Steel's Old Ben mine on Grapevine in the 1980s—a century after Devil Anse gave it up.

## How Did the Moguls Do It?

When discussing this history with outsiders, the first question I am usually asked is, "How could those hillbillies have been so dumb?"

I say they were ignorant of certain things, but not that they were dumb. I'm sure that many would be surprised to see the results of an IQ test, if one could be posthumously given to the Tug Valley people of the feud era. Devil Anse's mother was an illiterate midwife, but eight of her grandchildren were physicians.

All the falsehoods inserted into the feud story by the supersizers either make the people involved look dumb or ultra-violent or both. The obvious intent is to make all of us who are descended from the feudists the inheritors of the wickedness and stupidity they ascribe to the feudists. While Dean King has us still a violent people today, Lisa Alther says we are dumb.

Alther quotes a statement saying our 19th century ancestors were "strange, half-civilized natives who live in the blood-stained wilderness."[20] She then describes our condition today, referring to the "Appalachian Brain Drain, during which any resident who could figure out how to leave the region did so."[21]

So, according to this novelist masquerading as a historian, my Blackberry Creek ancestors were "half-civilized," and the only people remaining on the creek are those who are too dumb to find Route 23 North.

The brain drain is very real, as we have had at least three fourths of the top twenty percent of students leave the hills for three generations. But, is Alther right about what remains? On September 27, 2011, the Lexington Herald-Leader carried the following: "Leading the way was tiny Blackberry Elementary, which put 100 percent of its students in proficient or distinguished in four of five tested subjects: reading, math, science and social studies. Blackberry, which has just 144 students in grades K-5, was the only Kentucky public school of any size to do that."

That school sits less than two miles from where Ellison Hatfield was killed, and five miles from where the three McCoy boys were shot. At least three fourths of those students are directly descended from the Hatfields and the McCoys, and they lead the entire state. After three generations of continuous brain drain, Blackberry still leads the entire state in the intellectual accomplishment of its children, but the feud writers will never say we are anything other than violent near-imbeciles.

Harry Caudill summed it up thus: "On one side of the table sat an astute trader, more often than not a graduate of a fine college, and a man experienced in the larger business world — across the table sat a man and woman out of a different age. Unable to read the instrument or able to read it only with much uncertainty, the sellers relied upon the agent for an explanation of its contents."[22]

Smart as he was, Preacher Anse Hatfield sold his coal rights and urged all his friends, relatives, and church congregants to do the same. He obviously believed that most of the titles would not stand up under a court challenge and that the isolation of the valley meant the coal would never be mined anyway.

The big club that the land-grabbers held over the heads of the mountaineers in Eastern Kentucky was the Virginia Compact.

Most of the land in the area had been granted to soldiers in the French and Indian and Revolutionary wars by the government of Virginia. When the Hatfields, McCoys, and others settled on the land, they received patents from the state of Kentucky on the same lands covered by the prior Virginia patents. They were relying on the old common law concept of *seizin,* which required a landowner to physically set foot upon the land to perfect title. As the Virginia patent holders had never even seen the mountain land they had been granted, the mountaineers felt safe. Their confidence was unfounded, because when the new state of Kentucky was formed out of part of Virginia, the founders had incorporated a section in Kentucky's Constitution saying that the Virginia grants would be honored by Kentucky forever.

In 1823, in the case of Green v. Biddle,[23] the US Supreme Court upheld the rights of the Virginia grantees. An interesting sidelight in the Green case is that the Supreme Court's decision allowed Humphrey Marshall, the first cousin of the Chief Justice, John Marshall, to hold onto thirty thousand acres of Kentucky land covered by one of the old Virginia grants.

I am sure that someone sat at Preacher Anse's table and read with him the relevant sections of the Virginia Compact, the Kentucky constitution, and the Green v. Biddle decision, and convinced the patriarch that he and his kin would be much better off with a few hundred or, in some cases, a few thousand dollars in cash than to hold onto land to which their title would be proven worthless someday. What Preacher Anse and the other natives didn't know was that Mayo, Dils, and others were already setting up a constitutional convention that would write a section explicitly declaring the Virginia Compact language on land titles null and void.

The Hatfield-McCoy violence took place during the decade when the men mentioned in this chapter were most active in grabbing the wealth of the area. These men had money and the political power that goes with money.

## Where Did the Money Come from?

The best exposition of the sources of the money that was used to gobble up the mineral riches of Southern Appalachia is Harry Caudill's *Theirs Be the Power*. The money came from industrialists and financiers from New York, Boston and Philadelphia; much of it accumulated over decades of slave trading, dope dealing (the China opium trade), and war profiteering.

Some of the names in Caudill's book are Mayo, Camden, Delano, Forbes, Watson and Roosevelt.

The Delano riches found their way into the coal lands of Eastern Kentucky after Warren Delano's daughter, Sara, married a member of the board of Consolidation Coal Company, James Roosevelt.

In *Theirs Be the Power*, Harry Caudill devotes several pages to reproducing letters written by Franklin Roosevelt to his wife during an extended trip to Eastern Kentucky with his uncle, Warren Delano, inspecting the thousands of acres of coal lands the family owned there.

The Uncle Warren referred to in FDR's letters was Warren Delano, Junior, who traversed the hills of eastern Kentucky, and bought up huge swaths of it. He was later one of the original members of the Federal Reserve Board.

Their company, Kentenia Land, actually owned the mineral that was being mined in Harlan County during 1933-35, when several dozen miners were killed by company thugs during what is known as Bloody Harlan. FDR's family owned tens of thousands of acres in three states, Kentucky, Tennessee and Virginia; hence the name, Kentenia.

Before one can really understand what was happening in Pike County during the 1880s, one must know a little of the history of a remarkable man named John Caldwell Calhoun Mayo. Calhoun (as his family and close friends called him) Mayo began his acquisition of coal land and leases during the mid-1880s, when the power and influence of John Dils was at its zenith. He went on to eclipse Dils and become, according to the New York Times, the richest man in Kentucky before he died at 49 years of age.[24]

Mayo studied the geological surveys done by the State of Kentucky while at college, thereby gaining knowledge of the location of the best coal lands in Eastern Kentucky. "Both the geology and mineralogy courses at Wesleyan were taught by Wesleyan's President, Dr. D.W. Batson, who later wrote articles about the scholarship of J.C.C. Mayo while Mayo was his student..."[25]

Perhaps anticipating what your writer says here thirty years later, Mayo's biographer says: "Detractors of John C.C. Mayo say that he used his education and knowledge of the value of minerals in an unfair manner."[26] Truer words were never spoken.

Knowing that the coming of the railroad was a simple matter of time, Mayo began to buy options on mineral rights in the early 1880s. He paid anywhere from ten cents to fifty cents per acre for these options, most of which gave him ten years to complete the deal. Thus Mayo held the rights to the mineral coal, oil and gas at a mere pittance, with *no* tax liability.

The real stroke of genius was Mayo's use of the broad form deed, which relinquished the owners' rights to everything on or below the surface, and permitted coal operators to do whatever it took to extract the coal, and, absolved coal companies of all responsibility for damages caused by mining, such as the diversion of water, pollution, etc., even downstream.

The coal companies Mayo sold the deeds operated under those deeds for nearly a century, until the Kentucky Legislature finally passed a law in 1972, restricting the rights of the mineral owner to only the methods of extraction employed at the time of the original sale.

Mayo actually picked governors and senators in both states, and turned down offers of both positions himself on several occasions. Harry Caudill quotes a West Virginia legislator as saying, after Mayo secured a seat in the US Senate for his fellow consolidation Coal Corporation board member, Clarence Watson: "It does beat hell how a coal operator from Kentucky came over here and took a millionaire from Maryland and sent him to Washington as a United States Senator from West Virginia."[27]

Mayo had associates in every county, using their local knowledge, kinships and personal relations with land owners as levers to pry the wealth from the hands of the ill-informed mountaineers. These included Devil John Wright in Pike and Letcher counties, John Dils in Pike County, and J.D. Sergeant in Logan County, West Virginia, among others.

In especially tough cases, he sent his enforcer, Devil John Wright, to close the deal. Devil John Wright, one of only two men in the region[28] who had a worse reputation for violence than Devil Anse Hatfield, was an agent and sometime partner of John C.C. Mayo for more than fifteen years.

Devil John, said by Mayo's biographers to have killed twenty-eight men and fathered twenty-seven children, once went to Tug Valley to try to collect the bounties on the Hatfields, but, after surveying the situation around Anse's house through a telescope from the Kentucky side, decided there were too many armed Hatfields, and went back to Letcher County.[29]

Mayo's biographers tell us that Devil John was a very effective agent for Mayo, buying coal rights for bottom dollar. They cite records showing that Devil John was actually the owner of one of the coal companies that Mayo acquired along the way.[30] The headquarters of Mayo's main corporation, the Northern Coal and Coke Company, was located on Devil John Wright's farm.[31]

Wright's son, William (Chid) Wright, wrote a biography of his father, wherein he said that his father sired thirty-five children, but only killed sixteen men. William Wright said his father and other men like him rendered invaluable service to Mayo's company with the mountaineers for "they bought land from these rustic backwoodsmen that no outsider could have bought, and the price they paid for it was almost negligible."[32]

Devil John was also a feudist — a real feudist — since his feud with the Claiborne (Clabe) Jones family lasted almost his entire adult life. It is told that they raided each other so many times that they sometimes unknowingly passed each other in the night on the way to raid the opposition. Devil John Wright fared much better than his fellow feudist, Devil Anse. In 1905, when both men were in their sixties, Anse was still cutting a little timber and making a little moonshine, while Devil John was President of one of Mayo's coal companies.

A man who is rich and powerful enough to pick governors and senators for two states and has a long-term relationship with one of the worst murderers in American history might perceive a need to cover his tracks, and Mayo did just that.

The story is that Mayo invited a novelist to be his long-term guest in Mayo's Paintsville mansion. The writer enjoyed Mayo's hospitality for several months, during which time he produced one of the bestselling books of the early 20th century.[33]

*The Trail of the Lonesome Pine,* published in 1908, at the peak of Mayo's power, features a hero who is a buyer and developer of mountain coal lands, whose close associate is a mountain bush-whacker and feudist named Devil Jud Tolliver, whom Fox admitted was based on Devil John Wright. This story is buttressed by the fact that John Fox, Jr.'s brother James was hired by Mayo the year following the book's publication.

*Trail of the Lonesome Pine's* hero, John Hale (same first name as Mayo, with a four letter surname), is a highly educated mining engineer, who uses his knowledge of what lies beneath the land owned by the mountain feudists to build a fortune. The hero is a man of outstanding character. Literary whores, serving the rich and powerful have been around a long time.

The relationship between Mayo and Devil John gives weight to something I heard from several people, but could never substanti-ate: Many oldsters said that Bad Frank Phillips was an enforcer for his foster father, John Dils, closing the hard deals for Dils with recalcitrant land owners. Though there is no solid evidence for this, it is not a great reach to think that if John Mayo, who had a much better reputation than Dils, would use a man who was "bad-der" than Bad Frank, then Dils may have employed Phillips in the same way.

That Mayo knew he was cheating honest men is proven by his own actions. It is well known that he travelled throughout the mountains, on horseback, or in a buggy, carrying thousands of dollars in cash and gold. His wife carried as much as ten thousand dollars in gold, concealed beneath her skirts.[34] You can rest assured that Mayo would not have taken his young wife through the mountains, carrying a fortune in gold in her petticoats if he were not 100% convinced that he was traveling among honest men.

Mayo held options on hundreds of thousands of acres of Eastern Kentucky minerals as the 1890s began. It also happens that, in 1890, a commission was busy writing a new Constitution for the State of Kentucky. As Harry Caudill recounts in his *Theirs Be the Power*, while Mayo was gathering all the wealth of the mountains to himself, he was busy agitating for a new Constitution, which would not contain the onerous "Virginia Compact," which clouded the title to much of his optioned land.

Dean King's contention that economics did not influence feud events borders upon the ridiculous. Economic issues underlay all the Eastern Kentucky feuds of that era. Most historians who have studied the feuds agree that the French-Eversole feud, in Pike County's neighboring county of Perry, grew out of the very same thing I say was at the root of the revival of the Hatfield and McCoy troubles in 1887 — the greed for the coal under the land of the feudists.

Fulton French and Joe Eversole were both lawyers and businessmen in Hazard, Kentucky, the county seat of Perry County. Fulton French was the John Dils of Perry County, buying the coal rights from hundreds of farmers, and then flipping them to Eastern capitalists. Joe Eversole warned all who would listen of the terrible consequences that would come from signing broad form mineral deeds, and Fulton French set out to silence him. Joe Eversole died — in vain, as it turned out — trying to keep French from stripping his friends and neighbors of their wealth.[35]

With a clear view of the big picture, we can better understand what happened in Tug Valley, as all the financial and political power in the country funneled down through local men like Dils in Pikeville and Nighbert and Sergeant in Logan, bearing finally on people like the two Anderson Hatfields.

1 Waller, *Feud*, 41.

2 *Ellison v. Torpin, Southeastern* Reporter, Volume 30, 183. And 44 W. Va. p. 426.

3 Logan County Courthouse, Deed Book C, p. 432.

4 This brings up the very interesting question of whether the heirs of the two non-signatory heirs of David Mounts own an interest in the lands US Steel owns today. Could they be entitled to a payment for the millions of tons of coal US Steel has mined from property in which Margaret Mounts had an interest which she never signed away?

5 Special thanks to Brenda Ferrell Sampsel for her assistance in researching this transaction.

6 Cline, Cecil, *The Clines and Associated Families*, 74.

7 *Ibid.*

8 Waller, *Feud*, 174.

9 Waller, *Feud*, 177.

10 *Ibid.*

11 *Pike County Court Order Book E*, p. 109. Dils was dismissed by the court as guardian for certain Ratliff children, after evidence of misuse of funds was produced. He was ordered to surrender all funds of the Ratliff estate, and removed as guardian.

12 *Ellison v Torpin, Southeastern Reporter, Volume 30*, p. 184.

13 *Ellison v Torpin, Southeastern Reporter*, Volume 30, p. 186.

14 *Ellison v Torpin Southeastern Reporter, Volume 30*, p. 190.

15 *Ellison v Torpin, Southeastern Reporter, Volume 30*, p. 195.

16 Rice, *The Hatfields and the McCoys*, 54.

17 Pritchard, *The Devil at Large*, 68–69.

18 Preston, *Civil War*, 210

19 Pritchard, The Devil at Large 69.

20 Alther, Lisa, *Blood Feud*, xv.

21 *Ibid.*

22 Harry M. Caudill, *Night Comes to the Cumberlands* (Place: Publisher, Year), 73.

23 Green v. Biddle, 21 US 1, 1823.

24 Turner Carolyn and Traum, Carolyn, *John C.C. Mayo, Cumberland Capitalist*, 127.

25 Turner and Traum, 8.

26 Turner and Traum 11.

27 Caudill, Harry, *Theirs Be the Power*, 76-7.

28 The other was "Bad" Lewis Hall, who was reputed to have killed more than twenty men.

29 Turner and Traum, 44.

30 Turner and Traum, 50.

31 Turner and Traum, 44.

32 Wright, William T., *Devil John Wright of the Cumberlands*, p. 276.

33 Turner and Traum, 45.

34 Turner and Traum, 28.

35 Pearce, John Ed, *Days of Darkness: The Feuds of Eastern Kentucky*, 75-94.

# CHAPTER 16.

# REVVING THE ENGINE

## Pikeville Captures a Governor

The plain truth is that the second and most violent phase of "the feud" was initiated by the Pikeville elite, with the aid of the state government, and not by anyone—Hatfield or McCoy—, who lived in Tug Valley. Knowledge of this truth is vital to understanding the "Hatfield and McCoy feud." The supersizers never recognize this central fact. Dean King actually reverses it, by stating very early—in his *Author's Note*—that, by 1889, "The fighting grew so bitter and became such a threat to public safety that it almost brought the two Civil War border states back to war."[1]

The people of the Tug Valley, having enjoyed a five-year period of peace following the events of August, 1882, were taken by surprise by the re-opening of the violence when the Pikeville posse illegally invaded West Virginia in December, 1887. With the exception of the handful who joined Dils's posse, they were so alarmed that they successfully pressured Sheriff Basil Hatfield to remove Frank Phillips as a deputy.

By stating that the invasion of 1887 was a result of the State of Kentucky being forced to act to stop "bitter fighting" and remove a "threat to public safety," King profoundly distorts the record. As the invasions began five years after the last violence between the families of Devil Anse and Ran'l McCoy, it is almost as bad as his twisting of the facts of the Election Day, 1882 fight.

The movie shows Perry Cline as the Chief and Frank Phillips as the War Chief planning the first raid into West Virginia. All books on the feud also name Perry Cline as the top dog on the Kentucky side of the feud from 1887 onward. Most of them use the fact that Anse sent the conciliatory letter addressed to Cline in December 1886, after Jeff McCoy was shot, as proof that Anse viewed Cline as the man calling the shots.[2] That letter, which I believe was written for the illiterate patriarch by Preacher Anse Hatfield, was mainly an attempt to remove the killing of Jeff McCoy as a reason for reviving the old warrants. Secondly, it laid the basis for a defense should Cap be charged in that killing.

A year later, after the governor had issued extradition requests and offered rewards for the Hatfields, push had come to shove for Devil Anse, and the way he went about trying to stop this very real threat to himself and his family is one of the strongest pieces of evidence for my position that the man in charge in Pikeville was Anse's old Civil War nemesis, Colonel John Dils.

Within days of Phillips' first raid into West Virginia, there was a meeting in Pikeville to try to settle the conflict. As one of his two representatives, Anse chose attorney A.J. Auxier, one of the few men in Pikeville who would oppose John Dils. In addition to the lawyer, Anse used a trusted Kentucky cousin named Johnson Hatfield. This was a Pike Countian, who owned a hotel in Logan.[3] The reason for Anse choosing him was that Johnson Hatfield, a brother of Preacher Anse, was, like Dils and York, a Republican, and he had served as a sergeant in Colonel Dils's 39th Kentucky.[4]

Across the table from Anse's representatives sat Perry Cline and James York. Everyone who watched the Costner movie knows the name "Perry Cline," but James York is undoubtedly a mystery. Who was he, and what was he doing in a meeting that was called to try to settle the "Hatfield and McCoy feud"? The answer is that James York, attorney, was married to Augusta Dils York, the daughter of Colonel John Dils. Dils was not there, but the family consigliore was.

While Cline had been Ran'l McCoy's lawyer, and York would later be Ran'l's lawyer after Cline started representing Wall Hatfield, the first allegiance of both these lawyers was to the man who was foster father to one and father-in-law to the other — Colonel John Dils. Although it is not vital to the story, I don't believe that Cline was representing Ran'l McCoy in this meeting. Had he been being paid to represent Ran'l, his litigious client would have surely sued him for taking a bribe from the Hatfields.[5]

The meeting resulted in an agreement that the Hatfields would pay Perry Cline $225, and the proceedings against the Hatfields would cease. Cline took the money, but Phillips' raids into West Virginia continued.[6] Two hundred twenty-five dollars doesn't sound like a lot of money, but it was probably nearly as much as a deputy jailer made in a year.

Governor Buckner clearly stated in his letter to Governor Wilson that he: "had been fully apprised of the efforts on the part of P.A. Kline (sic) to secure a withdrawal of the requisitions and rewards in this case."[7]

The only mentions of Perry Cline in the Governor's letter relate to the bribe. Governor Buckner names the names of the people who approached him to request that he take action against the Hatfields after five years of peace between the families of Ran'l McCoy and Anse Hatfield; it was the County Judge, the District Court Judge and the Commonwealth's Attorney. To believe that these three high officials were motivated to approach the governor by a deputy jailer strains credulity. That the governor didn't even know the correct spelling of Cline's name is further evidence that he was not working closely with the deputy jailer.

Further on the subject of the Cline bribe, the governor said, "...even admitting the truth of the affidavit...that the friends of the indicted parties succeeded in bribing Kline (sic), their former enemy...I cannot see why this should cause your Excellency to hesitate..."[8] This language, appearing in a letter wherein virtually every factual statement is heavily slanted in favor of the Pikeville group is as close to an admission of Cline's guilt as it could be, without coming right out and saying that Perry Cline was guilty of a crime.

Governor Buckner's letter is explicit proof that the Governor is not acting at the behest of Perry Cline. In fact, it shows that he is not paying any attention at all to Perry Cline in the matter.

The governor's words prove that Cline did what Johnson Hatfield swore he paid him the bribe for, so I don't see how anyone can claim that Cline did not accept the bribe. I think he accepted the bribe, and then kept his promise to Johnson Hatfield by asking the governor to withdraw the requisitions, knowing that the governor would pay no attention him. It was a win-win for Cline. He got two hundred twenty-five dollars, while knowing all the time that the Hatfields would receive nothing in return, because he knew that his request would carry no weight with the governor.

It is obvious that Perry Cline could not stop the process, but we are still asked to believe he started it. The fact is that the bribe to Perry Cline availed Devil Anse nothing. The only way Anse could have stopped the invasions of West Virginia would have been to either bribe John Dils's lawyer son-in-law, James York, or surrender his five thousand acres. As there wasn't enough money in the entire Hatfield clan to bribe York, the "feud" continued until Devil Anse sold his land.

In most feud stories, it seems as if Perry Cline was the only person there for the Kentucky crowd. Think about it: there were two men on that side of the table. One was Perry Cline, who was struggling so hard to make a living that he was working as a deputy jailer and taking two hundred twenty-five dollars as a bribe. The other was James York, whose wife was so rich that she gifted her sister the house that now serves as the Historic Mansion Bed and Breakfast.[9] She also designed and built for herself and her husband, James York, the house shown below.

**6. Augusta Dils York Mansion**

There is an organization dedicated to the restoration of the mansion. The organization does not style itself the Foundation for the Restoration of the *James York* Mansion. Rather, it is the Foundation for the Restoration of the *Augusta Dils York* Mansion.[10]

Which of the two was calling the shots at that meeting? I say York was the most important man at that table, and he was there, not representing a ferry-boat operator, but as a surrogate for the man whose wealth and power put him in that mansion and his later position as county judge — Colonel John Dils.

There is general agreement among feud historians that Devil Anse would not have received the support of his state's governor, had not the Kentuckians invaded the state, and had not the assistant secretary of state, John B. Floyd, gone to bat for Anse. Yet, we are to believe that a deputy jailer could move the governor of Kentucky to revive a feud at a time when he had several feuds ongoing. It boggles the mind!

The year after the N&W Railroad announced the imminent building of a railroad up the Tug River, the state of Kentucky produced a new geological survey, which showed some of the best coking coal in the world in the Tug Valley. Of course, the richness of Eastern Kentucky in general had been widely known since the first such surveys were published shortly after the end of the war, but this one, in 1887, drew a bull's-eye over the section bordering the Tug.

Just as the juices started to flow in the speculators, a gubernatorial campaign was underway in Kentucky. Everyone knew it was a close race, and the Democratic candidate, former Confederate General Simon Bolivar Buckner, was desperate for votes. In any close election, cross-over votes from members of the opposition party are highly sought after. The large Republican vote of the former Union adherents in Pike County represented a treasure trove for a Democrat in a close race. The deep pockets of John Dils could provide much of the money needed to run Buckner's campaign.

If Buckner did nothing, the voters in Pike County would have done what they almost always did; they would vote their straight party ticket. It was not necessary for Buckner to make any commitment to anyone to secure the Democrats that Perry Cline had influence over. The large Republican vote in the Pikeville area was another thing altogether. The switch of a hundred of those Republicans into Buckner's column might mean the difference between victory and defeat and Perry Cline had next to zero influence over those voters--but John Dils did.

So, are we to believe that Buckner somehow decided that he ought to contact the Democrat deputy jailer to try to sew up those Republican votes? The simple fact is that if John Dils had supported Buckner's opponent, virtually all of the Republicans of Pike County would have voted their party ticket.

Although we are working with incomplete information, a recap is in order to try to make sense of the political situation in Pike County in 1887.

Perry Cline came to Pikeville in 1868 and petitioned the County court to appoint as his guardian the richest and most powerful man in the county, Colonel John Dils, who was a Republican. Three years later, Perry Cline attains voting age and registers as a Democrat. Does anyone believe that he would have done so if Colonel Dils were opposed to it?

Colonel Dils, the most ardent Unionist in Eastern Kentucky, and a man who considered former Confederates his enemies for life, obviously found it impossible to join the Democratic Party, even though it had a solid majority in the county in the post war years. So, he did the next best thing, which was to set his foster son, Perry Cline up to become an influential Democrat.

Pike County, which produced about three times as many Union soldiers as it did Confederates voted solidly Democratic in the post war period. The harbinger of things to come politically was the mass desertion among the Pike County members of the 39th Regiment when the 109th Colored Regiment showed up at Union Headquarters in Louisa.

While Pike County produced over 600 Union soldiers, only 92 of them showed up to vote for their old Commander in Chief, U.S. Grant, when he ran for President in 1868.[11]

Only five voters showed up for Grant in District 7, which included Blackberry and Peter Creek.[12] One of the five stalwarts who voted for Grant was my great grandfather, Ransom Dotson, whose father's house was robbed by Devil Anse's partisans, and whose brother Reuben was wounded by the same gang during the war.

It is important to note that the former Union soldiers in Pike County--District 7 in particular--did not vote for the Democrat. They simply stayed home. The absent Republicans on Election Day, 1868 included Preacher Anderson Hatfield and all of his Republican Hatfield relatives on Blackberry Creek. Not one of them voted in that election.

Any doubt that Colonel Dils was simply setting himself up to control both parties is removed quickly, as Perry Cline runs for Sheriff the very next year, when few people in the county even know his name, and is elected, winning a large share of the Republican vote in Pikeville. Does anyone believe a new 'immigrant' could accomplish that on his own?

When Perry Cline, a Democrat, was sworn in as Sheriff, the bond required of a Sheriff was signed by none other than the pre-eminent Republican in the county, Colonel John Dils. Elected

Sheriff at age 25, the youngest in the history of Pike County, it was all downhill for Cline from there, as he dropped to the state legislature next, and finally was serving as a deputy jailer in 1887.

While Cline had personal reasons to seek revenge against Devil Anse Hatfield, Cline's signature on the marriage bond for Johnse Hatfield and his niece, Nancy McCoy, four years after the 1877 settlement, makes it less likely that Cline was acting for personal vengeance only. Although Cline's scathing denunciation of the Hatfields in his 1887 letter to the governor could argue for a personal vendetta, it could also be simply a lawyer arguing a case.

Perry Cline by himself could do nothing to put the state of Kentucky into action. John Dils, striking at a time when the iron was hot, could get the ball rolling. At the time Simon Buckner was sworn in as governor, industrial development — especially in the resource-rich eastern part of the state — was the paramount interest among the movers and shakers in Louisville, Lexington and Frankfort. The big impediment to development in Eastern Kentucky was the newspaper-created image of the violent mountain feudist, which had been created by the reporting on other feuds in Kentucky, with no mention at all of a feud in Pike County.

Even though none of the dozens of articles that had been printed in the Louisville Courier Journal over the preceding three years had been about Pike County — no one recognized a feud in Pike County at that time — Dils and company had the perfect deal for the Governor. He could deflect the eyes of the world away from his own Kentucky feuds in Rowan, Perry and other counties — feuds that had claimed many times as many lives as had been lost in Pike County at that time — *and direct attention to West Virginia!* Putting his office behind an effort to extradite almost two dozen indicted feudist murderers from West Virginia was just what the governor needed; he issued the requisitions and upped the rewards for the West Virginia villains.

There were nearly forty casualties in the Perry County feud, including a battle that shot up both the courthouse and the jail, during a five year period when the only death in Pike County was Jeff McCoy, who was wanted for murder. One might think that the attention of the writers would focus on Perry County, but all their attention was directed to Pike County, where the talk was all about getting the murdering feudists from West Virginia.

Beginning with an Election Day killing (sound familiar?) in 1884, over twenty men were killed in three years in the Tolliver-Martin feud in Rowan County. In the summer of 1887, just as Buckner was taking office, there was a gunfight in the streets of Morehead between the feudists, involving over sixty fighters. The battle lasted two hours and claimed at least four lives.[13] Yet the attention of the Governor and all the big city newspapers was on Pike County's war with the wanted criminals in West Virginia.

Perry Cline was the front man in the 1887 revival of the feud, but only because Colonel Dils opted to remain in the background. Dils wanted to take no chances by openly antagonizing Anse, who, as the record shows, was thought to be capable of mounting a raid on Pikeville at any time. Colonel Dils, who said in the autobiography he wrote for Ely's book that he had moved his wife and family out of the mountains during the war out of fear for their safety, was not about to risk it again.

Many are perplexed by the transition of Perry Cline from the fearful victim of Devil Anse in 1868 to the apparently fearless pursuer of 1887-89. His position in the Pikeville elite has already been covered, but I think something else was also involved. I think that the same thing was working in Perry Cline that made Doc Holliday totally fearless in the face of Johnny Ringo and the Cowboys of Tombstone; the same thing that made Leander McNelly the most fearless of all the Texas Rangers. Cline, Holliday and McNelly all died within a few years of their apparently heroic actions of the same disease. Men who knew that they had tuberculosis, called consumption in those days, sometimes performed dangerous deeds that amazed others. It was called *consumption courage.*

I think some diligent researcher will someday find proof that Perry Cline learned that he had consumption in 1887. He died of the disease only a year after Ellison Mounts was hanged. During the violent last phase of "the feud" Devil Anse faced the most dreaded of all enemies—one who has nothing to lose.

Devil Anse obviously had pretty good intelligence sources in Pikeville, because he sent a letter to Perry Cline the day before the new governor was inaugurated. Unlike the one eight months before, this was not a friendly letter from "Your friend Ans Hatfield." It was, instead, a stern warning that unless the effort to revive the old warrants was stopped, the Logan Regulators, forty-nine in number according to the letter, would string up the Pikeville lawyer. The letter closed with: "We take no particular pleasure in hanging dogs, but we know you and have counted the miles and marked the tree."[14]

Did Cline take that letter seriously? His willingness to accept a small bribe and attempt to get the governor to withdraw the requisitions and rewards three months later might mean that he did, indeed, take it seriously.

Ten days after taking office, Governor Simon Bolivar Buckner, at the urging of either a deputy jailer or Colonel John Dils — take your pick — issued formal extradition requests to the governor of West Virginia for the twenty men indicted in the 1882 murders, posted large rewards on them, and appointed Bad Frank Phillips, a man generally reckoned by the people of Pike County to be a stone-cold killer, as his agent to "receive the prisoners."[15]

Although Perry Cline grew up on the West Virginia side and knew the topography well, he had no fighting experience. Now, what if he and Phillips could get help in their raid plans from someone who had not only been there but had fought there and who also had just as much experience as a war leader as their enemy? What if that person had actually raided on Grapevine Creek? If such a person were available, would they not avail themselves of his knowledge?

Of course they would, and they did, because that man was the foster father of both Perry Cline and Frank Phillips: Colonel John Dils. To believe that John Dils did not sit with Frank Phillips, with a map spread in front of them, and plan the details of Phillips' raids, is just not rational. .

A month after the governor issued the requisitions for the Hatfields and appointed Frank Phillips as his agent to receive them; Phillips was appointed a deputy sheriff of Pike County.[16] Basil Hatfield was sheriff of Pike County at the time. Although he was a cousin of Devil Anse, he was also the brother of Preacher Anse — and a Republican. Basil Hatfield was, like his brother, Anderson, a Primitive Baptist preacher. As his brother, Anse was already known as Preacher Anse at the time Basil started preaching, Basil was commonly referred to as Deacon Basil.

Basil Hatfield is the only Hatfield of that era who was commonly given the title, Deacon. Whether John Spears heard someone refer to Basil Hatfield as Deacon Hatfield, and was confused when he called Ellison Hatfield Deacon Ellison cannot be known for sure. What we do know is that Spears mistakenly attached Deacon to the name of Ellison Hatfield, and Dean King followed suit.

Basil Hatfield was a close ally of John Dils, as indeed any Republican who ascended to the sheriff's office during that time had to be. There is no way that Basil Hatfield would have allowed a man of Frank Phillips' character and reputation to wear a deputy's badge unless he was forced to do so. Basil Hatfield was county judge before he became sheriff and was, by all accounts, an honest and upright man. Of course, I am sure he bent whenever Dils applied pressure because that was necessary to hold the positions he held.

West Virginia Governor E. Willis Wilson, a populist Democrat, delayed his response to the request to deliver the Hatfields up to Phillips. The Governor was undoubtedly responding to pressure from his assistant secretary of state, John B. Floyd, on whose behalf Devil Anse had led the armed party into Logan town during the previous election.[17] In mid-November, Perry Cline sent Wilson the famous letter, in which he laid out his charges against the Hatfields. A reading of that letter, replete with misspellings and jumbled grammar, should be enough to convince anyone that this "lawyer" was not the caliber of man who could move a state government.[18]

In this letter to the governor, we see *affidavit* spelled *affidavid*, *requisition* as *reqision*, *employed* as *employd*, *raised* as *rased*, *marauders* as *meroders*, *remand* as *remain*, and *earliest* as *earlest*. This is the letter containing the critical claim that the Hatfields had forced people to leave their homes and would not let them tend their lands.[19]

Frank Phillips's letter to Governor Wilson a month later, written on Cline's letterhead and signed by Phillips was almost surely written by Cline, as it contains many of the same errors.[20] When you compare the composition of that letter to Frank Phillips's holographic will, which is on file at the Pike County courthouse, it is apparent that Frank Phillips, who was educated under the care of Colonel Dils, was much more literate than was the lawyer, Perry Cline.[21] No one who reads the letter to Governor Wilson and the holographic will of Frank Phillips could possibly believe that the two documents were written by the same man.

Bad Frank wasn't the only literate feud personage. Look at the letter from Devil Anse to Perry Cline. That writer was more literate than lawyer Cline.[22]

The top of the literary stack among the feudists was Cap Hatfield. In 1891, only a few years after his wife taught him to read, he says in a letter to the editor: "The war spirit in me has abated.....I sincerely rejoice at the prospect of peace....We being, like Adam, not the first transgressors...."[23]

That is incredible phraseology for a man who couldn't even read 5 years earlier. Wouldn't it be something to hear the thirty minute closing plea he made to the jury on behalf of his brother, Willis, two decades later? That must have been some speech that Cap made to that jury. Willis was charged with first degree murder for pumping six slugs into the town doctor, and he got off with involuntary manslaughter.[24]

Uncle Jeff Davis, a justice of the peace and store proprietor on Blackberry Creek when I was young, spent a considerable amount of time in Cap Hatfield's house, while reading the law. Uncle Jeff was a nephew of Joe Davis, a friend of the Hatfields who was a major witness in the 1889 trials. Uncle Jeff said that Cap Hatfield could quote lengthy passages from the Iliad and the Odyssey and the Longfellow poem, Evangeline. Altina Waller makes a similar statement about Cap.[25]

The claims by the yellow journalists of yesteryear and the sensationalist writers of today that the feudists were all both moral and mental dwarfs are libels.

## Bad Frank's Raids

On December 12, 1887, after more than five years of peace broken only by the killing of Jeff McCoy, Frank Phillips led a posse of some forty men, only about a fourth of whom were connected to the McCoys (many of those were Harmon's Peter Creek kin), on a blatantly illegal invasion of West Virginia. This foray reaped a small harvest, consisting only of Selkirk McCoy, the turncoat juror at the hog trial, who worked for Devil Anse. The scene in the movie where Selkirk is in a nearby town under an assumed name is bogus.

**Bad Frank Phillips — <u>Vera Kay Fink Hankins</u>**

There is a bit of irony here that also shows that the feud was not simply a matter of blood relatives choosing their family's side. As we already know, the 1880 census has an eighty-six-year-old woman named Margaret Mounts living in the household of Selkirk McCoy.[26] Margaret (Peggy) Mounts' maiden name was Cline. She was a sister to Rich Jake" Cline, and therefore the aunt of Perry Cline. So, the first person nabbed by Perry Cline's posse was a man who cared for his aging aunt during her last years.

On the Kentucky side, we have two foster sons of Colonel John Dils; Perry Cline, who had a slave and several in-laws killed during the war by Devil Anse or an associate,[27] and whose brothers were Union Home guard officers; Frank Phillips, whose father fought the rebels[28] and died in Confederate captivity;[29] and the sons of Asa Harmon McCoy, who was gunned down near the war's end by men under Anse's command, riding into West Virginia to exact vengeance for wartime actions by the Hatfields. On the West Virginia side is Devil Anse Hatfield, who had participated in actions where Colonel Dils had been defeated, wounded, and captured, and whom some say shot and seriously wounded Harmon McCoy early in the war[30] and had been present (and, possibly, the triggerman) when Asa Harmon was killed. Thus, for many of the participants, the 1887-8 raids by the Kentucky posse were a continuation of the War, disguised as a feud.

All of this was, of course, planned, financed and directed by a man, John Dils, who was intent upon getting the five thousand acres of valuable coal land from Devil Anse Hatfield.

The residents on the Pike County side of Tug River, seeing this illegal raid as reopening the Feud by the Pikeville elite, applied so much pressure on the county government that Phillips' badge was pulled. This didn't faze Bad Frank because he was still the governor's appointed agent to *receive* the Hatfields,[31] and he continued to raid into West Virginia, eventually *receiving* a total of six of the Hatfield gang. Dan Cunningham added three, making a total of nine of the Hatfield contingent residents of the Pikeville jail.

Frank Phillips was a man of considerable inherited wealth, who had a reputation of being a *bad* man from his teen years until he was shot dead at age thirty-six. Phillips married a first cousin at age sixteen. He later married twice more, the last time to Nancy McCoy, Johnse Hatfield's ex-wife, who left Johnse for Frank during the 1887-8 troubles.

Frank Phillips was the son of William (Billy) Phillips, who was a member of Company H of Col. John Dils's 39th Kentucky regiment. Billy was captured on January 9, 1864 at the battle of Turman's Ferry by Virginia partisan cavalry. Devil Anse was probably among the victors in that fight. The 39th Kentucky Regiment website reflects little or no research on Billy Phillips, saying that he was "captured and presumed dead." When his widow, Mary, applied for a pension, she had witnesses who said they were with Billy in Belle Isle prison, where he contracted smallpox. The records show that Billy Phillips died in Howard Grove General Hospital, and he is interred in Richmond National Cemetery.

Frank Phillips' grandfather, Jesse, ceded his guardianship of Frank to Colonel John Dils in 1868. Frank Phillips' ties to Colonel Dils and his 39th Regiment go far beyond Frank's father's service as a private. William King, a first cousin of both Billy Phillips and his wife, Mary King Phillips, was a Captain in the 39th. Richard King, a first cousin to both of Frank's parents was a 1st Lieutenant. Franklin and Samuel King, both brothers of Frank Phillips' mother, were members of the 39th Regiment.

As it is doubtful that there was another man in Pike County in 1887 who would dare lead a posse into West Virginia in search of Hatfields, it may be argued that the last bloody phase of the feud would not have happened had Bad Frank not been around. I don't agree with that because I believe that once the N&W Railroad announced in its 1886 report that the railroad would come up the Tug River, John Dils would have tried to wrest the five thousand acres from Devil Anse, no matter what it took. He would most likely have hired someone like Devil John Wright or Dan Cunningham, both of whom regularly rendered such service, and either of whom would have taken the contract.

---

1  King, ix.
2  Rice, *The Hatfields and the McCoys*, 35.

3 Hatfield and Spence, *Tale of the Devil*, 140. This section of Hatfield and Spence's book is the same in all important particulars as the story related to me by Ransom Hatfield. It is also in agreement with the sworn affidavit of Johnson Hatfield, who was a respected man, not likely to swear a lie.

4 Preston, *Civil War*, 442.

5 Although the affidavit of Johnson Hatfield on the bribe to Cline leads one to believe that Cline represented himself as Ran'l's lawyer at that meeting, I don't believe that, simply because I believe that had Cline been the paid attorney of Ran'l McCoy at that meeting, Ran'l would have sued him. After all, Ran'l was a litigious man, and the Johnson Hatfield affidavit would likely have won his case against Cline.

6 Hatfield and Spence, *Tale of the Devil*, 140.

7 Mutzenberg, 41.

8 Mutzenberg, *Famous Feuds*, 41-2.

9 http://www.pikevillehistoricmansion.com/

10 http://companies.findthecompany.com/l/24374468/Foundation-For-The-Restoration-Of-The-Augusta-Dils-York-Mansion-Inc-in-Pikeville-KY

11 Preston, John D. *The Civil War*, 240.

12 As the secret ballot had not been adopted in Kentucky, it was possible for John David Preston to find the names of every voter. The entire list for Pike County is in "The Civil War in the Big Sandy Valley, pp. 259-63.

13 Rice, *The Hatfields and the McCoys*, 42–44.

14 Waller, *Feud*, 172

15 Rice, *The Hatfields and the McCoys*, 52.

16 Waller, *ibid.*

17 Waller, *Feud*, 151.

18 Jones, *The Hatfields and the McCoys*, 84–85.

19 The letter is reproduced in its entirety in Jones, Virgil, *The Hatfields & the McCoys*, 84-5.

20 Jones, *The Hatfields and the McCoys*, 86–87.

21 I do not have the Will Book and Page number, but I read the will about 20 years ago, and can attest that it is on file in the Pike County Courthouse, and available for inspection.

22 Waller, Altina, *Feud*, 157.

23 Wayne County News, February 24, 1891.

24 Hatfield and Spence, *Tale of the Devil*, 273

25 Waller, Altina, *Feud*, 243.

26 Cline, *The Clines and Associated Families*, 51.

27 Pritchard, *The Devil at Large*, 62–63.

28 McCoy, *McCoys*, 129–30.

29 The roster for Company H says he was captured, supposed dead." http://www.reocities.com/rmbaker66/index.html

30 G. Elliott Hatfield, *Hatfields*, 14.

31 Rice, 52.

# CHAPTER 17.

# THE NEW YEAR'S MURDER RAID

Two weeks after the first cross-border raid by the Pikeville posse, the Hatfields retaliated. On January 1, 1888, a group of Hatfields and associated men conducted a raid on the home of Ran'l McCoy which ended in disaster—for *both* families! The raid was led by James Vance and Cap Hatfield.

Despite all the ink he gets in various feud books, Jim Vance actually only appears in the conflict on two occasions — first when he led the New Year's raid, and a week later when he was murdered by Frank Phillips.

Tom Berenger won my "Best Actor" award for his portrayal of Old Jim, but he did such a good job that Vance is now seen as a much worse character than he actually was. I don't cut Vance any slack for what he did during that raid, but the nickname bestowed upon him by Dean King, "Crazy Jim," is certainly uncalled for. In a cast of characters that includes Cap Hatfield, Frank Phillips and Dan Cunningham, a man who killed no one after the end of the Civil War does not deserve the sobriquet "Crazy."

Vance, who was called either Jim or James Vance, and sometimes the avuncular "Uncle Jim" by Truda McCoy in her highly partisan version of the McCoy story, is initially just "Jim Vance" on page 33 of King's book. Three pages later he has become "Crazy" Jim Vance. There is no explanation given for the transformation; with a few simple strokes on a keyboard, a man who was never even accused of killing a single person during the entire conflict is magically transformed into a psychopath.

Other than his possible clubbing of Sally McCoy[1] during the heat of battle on New Year's Day, 1888, the worst accusation in King's book is that Vance had a mistress in the 1880s.[2] I guess you could say that a man who had reached Social Security age was a little bit crazy if he thought he could keep both a wife and mistress satisfied at that stage of his life, but it hardly justifies the permanent sobriquet. According to King, Vance offset his marital infidelity by being otherwise a good citizen, putting up his own money and labor to build roads in the area.[3]

I am sure that some of his contemporaries sometimes called him "Crazy Jim," just as some people no doubt sometimes referred to Ran'l McCoy as "Crazy Ol' Ran'l," but it is not honest to find a few such references among hundreds of more benign references, and posthumously tag a man as a psychopath for all eternity. To make matters even worse, one of the laudatory blurbs I saw for King's book is by a man who claims to be a direct descendant of James Vance.

We see Devil Anse in the movie addressing his gang by firelight when he outlines the objectives of the raid on the McCoy home. Anse tells them that the feud must be ended, saying, "I would give my life if it would end this." The truest line in the movie comes when Jim Vance interjects at that point, "He would not."

Costner's Devil Anse tells Jim Vance that Frank Phillips was "just the fangs," which was true. Then he says, "We gotta get Randall McCoy," as if Ran'l were the head. In reality, when Devil Anse sent his representatives to attempt to settle things at that point, Ran'l McCoy wasn't even in the meeting and probably didn't even know of the meeting.

I think that the movie has it right on the purpose of the raid; Anse told them to harm no one unless it was necessary, and to bring Ran'l to him unharmed. Costner's Anse repeated it, telling them that *if they didn't bring Ran'l to him unharmed, they would have to answer to him for it.*

Then the movie's scriptwriters blew it all to hell by having Anse say that once he got Ran'l to his place in West Virginia, he would execute him. That would be the dumbest act imaginable. Devil Anse was a free man as he spoke, only because he had assiduously avoided being charged with a crime in West Virginia.[4] He would have been better off had he gone to Kentucky and killed Ran'l in church than to kill him anywhere in West Virginia.

The movie goes along with the majority of the books in saying that Anse intended to lead the raid, but caught some kind of bug that incapacitated him. I disagree. If Anse had intended to lead the raid, he would have postponed it for a day or two until he got over his malady.

Charles Gillespie made three confessions, neither of which directly associated Devil Anse with the raid. Gillespie placed the number of raiders at either nine or ten. Both Uncle Ransom Hatfield and Pricy Scott told me there were fourteen men involved. Leonard Roberts says that Pricy's mother said there were fourteen raiders.[5] Since no one except Truda McCoy says Devil Anse was among them, the number is probably not important, but I will go with fourteen. Truda McCoy also said that Devil Anse was at the Blackberry election, and we know that is in error, so I discount her claim that he was on this raid. Preacher Anse Hatfield, who knew exactly how Devil Anse "sat a horse," said Devil Anse was not in the party, and that's good enough for me.

One newspaper reported that Gillespie said the purpose of the raid was to kill Ran'l and Calvin, and thereby get rid of "every material witness against the men who had taken part in the killing of the McCoy boys."[6] Since neither Randolph nor Calvin could testify to the boys being in Hatfield custody just before they were killed, this is a sublimely stupid statement. The only material witness at the McCoy home that night was Sally McCoy, and no one ever claimed that she was the target of the raiders. Therefore, the removal of witnesses could not have been the purpose of the raid. The purpose had to have been either to kill Ran'l, or to kill as many as possible or to kidnap one or more persons.

A murder raid is beyond stupid. Given the political situation, where Governor Wilson was supporting Anse, his only problem was to fortify the border against the Phillips raiders and wait it out. Nothing could possibly be done that would be more damaging to Anse and his family than killing a McCoy in Pike County at that time. Nothing!

As it turned out, the raid cost Devil Anse his political position with the governor, his home and land on the Tug, and his moral standing in the Valley. Had Frank Phillips not gone into West Virginia and murdered Jim Vance a week later, I believe that Devil Anse, Cap and most of their gang would have been in Pikeville jail within a month or so, or else "on the lam." Luckily for Anse and the rest of the crew, the Old Man Vance's life bought them theirs. After the January 8, 1888 murder of Vance, Phillips and his men were indicted for murder in West Virginia, giving Governor Wilson the ammunition he needed to maintain his resistance to the extradition request from Kentucky.

Some writers say that Devil Anse was not involved in the raid at all. That is possible, but only if I am wrong about the purpose of the raid. If the outcome of the raid was the intended outcome, then I agree that Devil Anse knew nothing about it. With the State of Kentucky pressing for extradition of Anse and a dozen of his men, and Governor Wilson wavering in his resistance, the last thing Devil Anse needed was the publicity resulting from such a raid. There is no way that a murder raid was planned by Devil Anse. He was much too smart to do such a stupid thing.

A murder raid into Kentucky at that time is so monumentally stupid that I have trouble believing that even Vance and Cap would do it. How bad an idea was it? Well, it was so bad that only the trigger-happiness of Frank Phillips saved Anse, Cap, and probably more from the noose. Had not Vance been murdered, there was no way that Governor Wilson could have held out against Governor Buckner's requisitions for more than a few weeks after the raid on the McCoy home. Whatever one may think of Old Jim Vance, the fact is that because he died, several men lived and remained free

My hesitation to accept the idea that Anse knew nothing about it is based on my doubt that Jim Vance and Cap would undertake such a momentous endeavor without the approval of the Old Man.

Coleman Hatfield, in *Tale of the Devil,* vacillates on the reason for the raid on the McCoy home. Hatfield says, "Anse knew that the Hatfields might be able to end the feud if Randal McCoy was killed because Anse thought that Randal was the source of the continuing trouble."[7] Hatfield and Spence say also, "It is my understanding that there was no intention to kill the women."[8] He does not say that the purpose of the raid was to silence potential witnesses, as so many feud writers claim.

One may say that the purpose of the raid was not to kill women, or one may say the purpose of the raid was to silence potential witnesses, but one cannot rationally say both these things, simply because the most damaging potential witness at Ran'l McCoy's house was his wife, Sally. Sally could testify that the McCoy boys were in the physical custody of the Hatfields shortly before they were murdered. If the purpose was to remove potential witnesses, the gang would have surely stopped off on the way to Ran'l's house and tried to kill Preacher Anse Hatfield, whom everyone on both sides knew was as damaging a potential witness as anyone, including Sally McCoy.

If it was intended as a murder raid, it makes Devil Anse look like both a bloodthirsty murderer and a bumbling fool. That is why writers end up all over the lot. Some say Anse had nothing to do with the raid; some say he planned it but was either too sick or too chicken to lead it. None of them makes a very strong case, and neither explanation make sense to anyone other than either a Hatfield partisan, who wants to prove Anse innocent, or to a McCoy partisan, who wants to show him to be a butcher or a coward — or both.

Coleman Hatfield says the group went to Ran'l's place on New Year's Eve, but thought they had lost the element of surprise, and returned home. Then "...they returned the next night *with the intention of kidnapping Randal McCoy.*"[9] (Italics mine)

That statement by Coleman Hatfield supports what I have always believed was the real purpose of the raid, but I had not seen any writer say it until *Tale of the Devil* was published. If Ran'l McCoy could be spirited over the river, just like the Phillips posse was doing to Hatfields in the opposite direction, there was a chance to end the whole affair without any more bloodshed — and at very little expense.

Once in West Virginia, Ran'l could be indicted for any number of serious crimes, even though he was probably innocent of any crime, because, as everyone knows, you can indict a ham sandwich. It would have been easy to indict Ran'l for kidnapping the men who were sitting in the Pikeville jail. Once Ran'l was safely tucked away in the Logan jail, negotiations for an exchange could have begun.

Ran'l McCoy brought to West Virginia alive and executed by Anse would mean the end of everything for Anse. Ran'l McCoy alive and indicted and held without bail in Logan might give Anse the bargaining chip he needed to spring his boys from the Pikeville jail and end the conflict. Although I believe that was Devil Anse's plan, I don't' believe it would have succeeded. I don't believe anything short of giving up his land would have stopped Dils and company.

In his book that came after *Tale of the Devil*, Hatfield drops the idea of killing Ran'l as a possible reason for the raid, and says only that the raid was "to kidnap Old Randall McCoy,"[10] and for that I salute Mr. Hatfield.

In the very next sentence Hatfield lapses into exonerating his ancestors by shifting blame, saying, that Devil Anse opted out of leading the raid because he was against it, and, besides, at forty-nine, he was too old. So, he turned it over to Jim Vance, who was sixty-three!

For decades before *Tale of the Devil* was published, I had told everyone I discussed it with that I thought the purpose was to kidnap Ran'l and set up an exchange because a murder raid never made sense to me. This is easier to defend than any of the previous writers' explanations.

If Devil Anse wanted to eliminate potential witnesses or simply to remove Ran'l McCoy, he would never have sent a group to Ran'l McCoy's house because that was both unnecessary and dangerous to the perpetrators. Ran'l McCoy's house was surrounded by heavy forest land. Any of Devil Anse's family above the age of ten could shoot straight enough with a rifle to have killed Ran'l and/or Sally from the woods, without ever being exposed to the view of a witness. Ran'l and Sally both showed themselves many times a day, while they did their daily chores. A sniper shoots one, and when the other comes to the aid of the fallen spouse, the deal is sealed. Then the sniper mounts his horse and beats it back to West Virginia, unobserved.

Since killing the potentially dangerous McCoys from ambush would have been both easy and relatively safe, the only conceivable reason for the Hatfields to approach the house directly is to physically lay hands on someone in the house. Devil Anse's purpose for the raid was to kidnap Ran'l and hold him hostage, pending an exchange for the Hatfields being held in the Pikeville jail.

Under the leadership of the probably inebriated Jim Vance, aided by the young and emotional Cap Hatfield and the almost surely inebriated Johnse Hatfield, the raid was a bloody disaster that cost two young people their lives and cost Devil Anse most of what he had worked a lifetime to build. It is impossible to conceive a greater catastrophe for Devil Anse than to be seen as the murderer of two young people who had never done him any harm, and who were only defending their home from bullets and fire when they were cut down.

The movie has Johnse reminding Jim Vance of Devil Anse's order to take Ran'l alive, but Vance tells Johnse that Ran'l will never surrender. Vance then ensures a bloodbath by yelling to Ran'l, "Your final day has dawned." Had he followed orders, he would have yelled something like: "Ran'l McCoy, you are under arrest. Surrender yourself and submit to lawful West Virginia authority and save your family from possible harm." One certainly wouldn't expect a man to meekly surrender after being told *twice* that he would be killed.

As the raiders approached the McCoy home, Johnse, who either lost his nerve or was drunk, fired a shot, taking the element of surprise away from the raiders, and Ran'l and Calvin returned fire.

Jim Vance then went into attack mode. Calvin had a Winchester rifle and Ran'l his double-barreled twelve gauge shotgun, and they fought a pretty good fight. Had Vance not been able to fire the house, there might have been a much smaller party on the way back to West Virginia.

With the house ready to fall in on their heads, Calvin and Ran'l decided to make a run for it. Continuing its denigration of the character of Ran'l McCoy, the movie has him abandoning his family early and running into the woods unarmed. Once safely hidden, he begins to pray, while his family is subjected to a fiery attack. This is really a bit too much, but at least the script is consistent where Ran'l is concerned. He is a religious fanatic early and a drunken blasphemer late — and a coward throughout.

In the movie, both Johnse and Cottontop shot at the fleeing Ran'l, but they didn't tell Vance and the others that the quarry had flown. Cap goes to the back of the house and talks to Cottontop, but Cottontop still doesn't tell him that Ran'l got away.

Calvin was shot in the head and killed as he ran from the house. According to Pricy Scott, who saw the two bodies at Jim McCoy's house the following day, Calvin was shot in the head, the bullet passing through from side to side. This means that someone in the raiding party was a good enough marksman to hit a man in the head while the target was running laterally across his field of vision, with only the light from the fire and the full moon. That certainly doesn't resemble Dean King's Hatfields, who couldn't hit three men riding abreast from thirty feet above the road.

Ran'l escaped into the woods after shooting either two or three of the attackers.[11] He most likely ducked behind the house, and ran for the woods, where the fire light was not as good as it was in the direction taken by Calvin.

"But he ran and hid," some may say. Yes, Ran'l ran and hid, but only when the burning house was ready to fall in on his entire family. He did not hide in the hog pen, as so many writers claim. The very idea is preposterous. There is absolutely nothing he could have done that would have drawn the attention of the attacking gang as much as jumping in among a bunch of squealing hogs.

There is no way that Ran'l McCoy would have been alive and free on the second day of January, 1888, if he had jumped into his hog pen. After the New Year's raid, Ran'l moved to the town of Pikeville, where he operated a ferry and never had a hog pen again.

The Hatfields chose not to follow Ran'l, knowing that he had a shotgun and knew every inch of that area. If they had followed him, he would probably have reduced the membership in the gang considerably.

While the house was burning, Ran'l's thirty-year-old crippled daughter, Alifair, who was trying to get to the well for water to fight the fire, was shot and killed. Her mother, Sally, was clubbed senseless by either Jim Vance or Johnse Hatfield (or both) while trying to reach her dying daughter.

According to Truda McCoy, Cap killed Alifair,[12] but I think the movie has it right; it was Ellison "Cottontop" Mounts, the man who was hanged for the crime in 1890. Mounts' last words on the scaffold convince me of his guilt.

If the raid had been intended to kill all the McCoys, as many writers say, then none of the survivors would have been left alive. If the purpose had been to silence witnesses, then surely Jim Vance would have delivered a coup de grace to the unconscious Sally McCoy, who was the only person at the scene who could place any of the Hatfields with the slain boys just before they were killed.

The fact that the raiders withdrew, leaving several family members alive, when they saw that Ran'l had escaped, strengthens my belief that the purpose was to kidnap him. Had the goal been his death, I believe the gang would have followed him into the woods.

Given that the raiders withdrew after they learned that Ran'l had escaped, leaving several survivors, it logically follows that the purpose of the raid was to either kill or kidnap Ran'l McCoy. If Ran'l had exited the house with his hands raised when the first shot was fired, he would have either been killed—if I am wrong about the raid's purpose—or taken to West Virginia as a prisoner if I am right..

I believe that Devil Anse thought Ran'l would indeed surrender in order to save his family. Who knows whether he might have given himself up if Vance had knocked on the door—or kicked the door open—and told him that if he came along no one would be hurt? Johnse fired his rifle and all hell broke loose and the result was a bloody fiasco.

I agree with Truda McCoy — Devil Anse planned the raid. I agree just as fully with those who don't believe Anse knew anything about a *murder raid*, whose object was to kill some or all of the McCoy family, because until he got the report from the returning raiders, I believe that Anse thought it was a *hostage-taking raid.*

Whether I am right or wrong about the raid's purpose, Devil Anse is responsible for the two murders that night, just as if he had pulled the trigger, because he was in command. His great mistake was to send killers to do a kidnapping, and it didn't work. For that, he is accountable.

---

1  Charles Gillespie, in his confession, said that Johnse Hatfield clubbed Sally.

2  King Dean, *The Feud*, 177-78.

3  King, Dean, 73-4.

4  Other than moonshining, of course, for which Devil Anse was indicted ten times.

5  McCoy, *The McCoys*, 215, n. 15.

6  *Pittsburgh Times,* October 16, 1888.

7  Hatfield and Spence, *Tale of the Devil*, 171.

8  Hatfield and Spence, *Tale of the Devil*, 170.

9  Hatfield and Spence, *Tale of the Devil*, 169.

10  Hatfield, Coleman, *The Feuding Hatfields and McCoys*, 41.

11  Rice, Otis, *The Hatfields and the McCoys*, 121.

12  McCoy, *McCoys*, 143–44.

# CHAPTER 18.

# CHASING HATFIELDS

The disruption of the church service to capture three of the Hatfield gang we see in the movie never happened. The brothers' surname was Mayhorn, not Mahon, and they were both sons-in-law to Wall Hatfield.

In the movie, we see the posse surrounding a shack containing Lark Varney and French Ellis. The incident ends with Lark Varney dead and French Ellis captured. In reality, Lark Varney was captured unharmed and held in jail until after the habeas corpus hearing in Louisville. French Ellis was never caught; he lived another fifty years before he was buried in Devil Anse's graveyard.

The involvement of Dan Cunningham is not mentioned in the movie. If some of the time spent showing Ran'l's psychological deterioration had been spent on Cunningham, it would have been good television. The significance of Cunningham's involvement is clear when you consider that Frank Phillips, with a forty-man posse, captured five Hatfields (Wall surrendered), whereas Dan Cunningham, with only Treve Gibson as a partner, captured three. Counting his capture of Johnse ten years later, Cunningham actually captured four of the Hatfield gang.

Cunningham, himself a feudist and sometime Deputy US Marshal, coal company gun thug and mass murderer, was just the man to hunt for bounty in feud country. First he went after McCoys in Kentucky. After Jim McCoy got the drop on him, foiling

Cunningham's attempt to arrest him, Old Dan concentrated on the Hatfields.[1]

Cunningham went to Virginia, hunting another man wanted for murder, and ran into Charles Gillespie near his Tazewell County home.[2] Cunningham lay in ambush beside a mountain trail and got the drop on Gillespie, who surrendered without a fight. He took Gillespie first to Charleston, then to Ironton, Ohio, and finally to Pikeville. Gillespie confessed in all three places.[3] For his cooperation, Gillespie was granted a continuance and not tried with the others. In May, 1890, he escaped from the Pikeville jail and was never heard of again.[4]

Cunningham ran into Alex Messer, who was purported to have twenty-seven notches on his gun, in a saloon. The detective engaged Messer in friendly conversation and conned Messer into inviting him to Messer's place, where Cunningham got the drop on him and cuffed him.[5]

The taking of Ellison Mounts was a little more difficult, as Mounts engaged Cunningham and his partner in a gunfight, during which the partner, Treve Gibson, was shot in the leg.[6] Of course, this would not have fit the movie's story line, which has Ellison as a frail teenager.

Strangely enough, the self-proclaimed fearless pursuer of the Hatfields never got Cap or Anse. Cunningham, who survived both of the top Hatfield feudists, never seemed to be able to find Cap, even though he ran a store for years, had a law office in Logan, and served for years as a Deputy Sheriff, with murder warrants outstanding and a sizeable reward on his head. The same goes for Anse, who visited Logan regularly for nearly forty years. Cunningham, who succeeded in capturing three of Anse's gang by trickery, and without violence, except in the case of Mounts, never succeeded in taking either of the two Big Boys.

Cunningham bragged much about his bravery, as do his apologists to this day. I say that Cap Hatfield and his father being able to walk the streets of Logan without fear of the big bad bounty hunter speaks louder than the Cunningham boasting. As with Anse and Cap, Cunningham never attempted to collect the bounties on those

McCoys who were known to be hard men to handle. After Jim got the drop on Cunningham, he wanted nothing at all to do with Jake, Lark and Bud, the fearsome sons of Asa Harmon McCoy. It goes without saying that Cunningham wanted no part of Frank Phillips, upon whose head was the biggest bounty of all.

Old Dan was thoroughly embarrassed when he went to Logan to hunt the *Old Man*. In January, 1889, Cunningham showed up in Logan, bragging that he would take Devil Anse and Cap the same way he had taken the other feudists. Cunningham was said to have set Devil Anse's barn on fire, causing the loss of a valuable horse and much grain and tack.[7] Old Dan talked too much, though, and Devil Anse used his bragging around town as the basis for swearing out a peace warrant.

When Cunningham made his foray into the Island Creek stronghold of Devil Anse, the old guerilla-turned-deputy sheriff, served the peace warrant and arrested Cunningham. Devil Anse, Cap and a couple of others marched the bounty hunters more than ten miles on foot to the Logan County jail. To add insult to injury, the detectives were said to have been forced to carry a Hatfield on each of their backs across every stream they traversed on the way to jail.[8]

I include this episode because, once again, it fits the character of the practical joker, Devil Anse. It is something I think he would certainly do, given the chance.

In one of the newest additions to the legend, Dean King says that a bounty hunter got the drop on Devil Anse while hunting in the woods. Devil Anse drew his gun and killed the bounty hunter before the bounty hunter could pull his trigger. According to King, Devil Anse was able to do this because the bounty hunter was distracted while *reading Devil Anse his rights!*[9]

So, King wants his reader to believe that, sixty-plus years before the Miranda decision required a policeman to read the rights to a criminal suspect, a bounty hunter chose to do so in the wilds of West Virginia. Readers who watch *Dog, the Bounty Hunter* on cable TV know that a bounty hunter doesn't even read the Miranda rights to a person they capture in 2013, but King says they did it for Devil Anse in the 1890s. This ridiculous story of a bounty hunter reading Anse his rights in the West Virginia woods in the 1890s is touted by King as one of his major finds during his four years of intensive research[10]

One week after the murder raid on the McCoy home, Jim Vance paid his account in full. Frank Phillips, at the head of a posse of more than thirty men, three quarters of whom were *not* McCoys, caught Jim Vance and Cap, with only Jim's wife, Mary Vance, as backup, and came out on top in a 1–0 shutout. Cap and Mary escaped, but Jim Vance was seriously wounded and unable to get to his feet. Bad Frank Phillips came up and shot him in the head at point-blank range.[11]

The movie does a creditable job on Vance's actual killing, but it also shows Cap killing at least two of the raiders when, in fact, no one except Jim Vance was killed that day.

Our movie shows Frank Phillips sitting at a table in a hotel lobby, interviewing the scum of Pikeville for possible inclusion in his posse, but Altina Waller tells us that, "a stunning 40 percent of Cline's new recruits were wealthy... They represented, in fact, most of the elite of Pikeville."[12] Who, other than Colonel John Dils could have enlisted that much of the Pikeville elite in an expedition into the home ground of the feared Hatfield gang?

One week after the murder of Jim Vance, Phillips led his posse into West Virginia again, after telling everyone that he would bring Anse and Cap back to Pikeville next time. There he met a group of West Virginians, Devil Anse among them, in what is known as the Battle of Grapevine.

The Battle of Grapevine was a battle between two posses, one led by Frank Phillips and the other by Logan County Constable John Thompson. Of course, the movie has Devil Anse in command of the West Virginia contingent, and Ran'l McCoy with the Kentucky forces.

The Battle of Grapevine was inconclusive, with neither side scoring a knockout, but the Kentucky side actually won on points, as the West Virginians retired from the field.

Ran'l McCoy was not a member of the Phillips posse, as stated plainly by Governor Buckner in his letter to Governor Wilson:

"Old Randolph McCoy was not with this raiding party, as has been represented by your Excellency, but was at the time in Pikeville, Kentucky, as the citizens of that place *will all testify.*"[13] (Italics mine)

In reality the skirmish amounted to very little, with Bud McCoy wounded on the Kentucky side and Deputy Bill Dempsey, who had no prior connection to the feud, killed by Frank Phillips. The killing of Deputy Dempsey was another case where Phillips murdered a wounded man at point-blank range. Dempsey's first day as a feudist was also his last.[14]

Dean King once again goes far beyond the realm of reality with his description of the killing of Bill Dempsey. King says:"Bad Frank drew his pistol... Bad Frank abruptly put the barrel of his pistol up to Dempsey's neck... Bad Frank discharged the gun; the blast severed Dempsey's head from his neck.[15] Everyone who knows anything about ballistics and gunshot wounds knows that this is an utter impossibility. No one ever blew someone's neck completely in two with a pistol shot, and no one ever will, but it is now a part of "feud history."

In the movie scene of the battle, we see Cottontop Mounts taken into custody by Frank Phillips. In the movie, Mounts, who is just a little boy, behaves like a little boy as he is captured. In reality Mounts was captured about eight months later by the bounty hunter, Dan Cunningham. Mounts, who was twenty-four years old and over six feet tall, put up a hell of a fight, shooting Cunningham's partner, Treve Gibson, in the leg before he was subdued.[16]

Altina Waller's discussion of the Battle of Grapevine —entitled *The Battle for Grapevine Creek*— is outstanding. She gives the reader more facts in this chapter than all previously written books combined. Of course Waller does not give the details that King claims to possess, but a historian never claims to know things that are unknowable, such as the mental process of Jim McCoy as he went into battle.

According to King, Jim McCoy rode a quarter of a mile ahead of the rest of the posse as they approached the battlefield at Grapevine. Given the topography of that location, if Jim McCoy were that far ahead of the posse, he would have been completely out of sight of his company. Here, again, King adds something to his story which makes the subject look stupid.

King says that after Jim McCoy had fired only one shot, and before the remainder of the posse had even entered the fray, "the cold air became luminous with gun smoke."[17]

Waller says: "One has to wonder if Devil Anse, as he realized a fight was about to begin, thought it ironic that this first real pitched battle between the two sides took place at the very place where the feud began. It was undoubtedly his lawsuit against Perry Cline for the possession of Grapevine Creek, begun some sixteen years before, that had brought about this confrontation."[18]

Waller obviously agrees with what I say about the last phase of the feud:: "Thus, the Tug Valley and Pikeville regions of Pike County had been at odds since the Civil War; this new "war" in the guise of a feud could be interpreted as an extension of that struggle...."[19] The "new war" Waller refers to is what she calls "the second phase of the feud," which refers to the events occurring during the time of the Phillips raids in December, 1887 and January, 1888.

This fight was between the elite of Pikeville and Devil Anse Hatfield. It ended when Anse surrendered his land. Only a quarter of the Kentucky gang were McCoys, split almost evenly between those who were seeking revenge for the killing of the three boys on Election Day, 1882, and those who were seeking revenge for the war-time killing of Asa Harmon McCoy in January 1865.[20] The remaining three fourths represented the modernizing Pikeville elite, which was interested only in exploiting the riches of the Valley, and didn't give a hoot in hell for Hatfields or McCoys.

In reality, Devil Anse did not give up his land and move away from Tug River because of Ran'l McCoy. The specter looming over Grapevine Creek in January, 1888 was not only Frank Phillips, who was, in fact, a man to be feared. The threat Devil Anse faced at that time was Phillips plus four men who had not joined Ran'l after his sons were killed in 1882. They were men whom Frank Phillips alone was able to lead into battle for the first time in December, 1887 — Jim McCoy, whom Truda McCoy said was "the bravest of them all," and the three sons of Asa Harmon McCoy, Jake, Lark and Bud.

Each of the three sons of Asa Harmon McCoy was at least equal to Cap Hatfield in a fight. The reality of Devil Anse's situation in January, 1888 was that if he didn't move out of Tug Valley, there was a real possibility that he would have been either killed or brought to Pikeville for trial. Life under continuous pressure from a large, well-financed and equipped posse headed by those five men was not acceptable to Devil Anse, so he capitulated.

The West Virginia posse was badly outnumbered at the Battle of Grapevine, but had the Pikeville posse been composed only of merchants and bankers, the home team would probably not have been forced from the field.

The West Virginians were unable to sustain the battle because in addition to having Frank Phillips and the *fighting McCoys*, the Kentucky crew also had the firepower.[21] The Kentucky boys, with the money of Pikeville's financial elite behind them, were equipped with new Winchesters, whereas most of the West Virginia boys carried single-shot breechloaders and a few old flintlocks. This differential in firepower between new, repeating rifles and old single-shots worked at Grapevine just like it worked for Custer at Gettysburg — and against him at the Little Bighorn. Yes, Custer was outgunned at the Little Bighorn. His troopers carried single-shot Springfields, whereas over a hundred of the Indians had six-teen-shot Henry repeaters.

Mutzenberg says that the advantage in arms was with the Hatfields, saying, "In this battle the Hatfields fought with the best rifles that money could procure, heavy caliber Colts and Winchester rifles. The Kentuckians were armed less perfectly, about half of them using rifles and shotguns of the old pattern. Phillips and two others, only, fought with repeating rifles. It was due to this superiority in armament that the Kentuckians suffered such heavy losses in horses and wounded men."[22]

This claim is among the most nonsensical of statements in a book that is replete with nonsense. Does anyone believe that, after months of planning, a group of Pikeville bankers and merchants backed by Colonel Dils, invaded West Virginia armed with obsolete weapons? If we believe Mutzenberg, we believe that the Pikeville posse, after months of planning and with the support of virtually every wealthy man in Pikeville, went into battle with ancient weapons, while the hastily assembled West Virginia posse was armed with the latest weapons. That is nonsense.

Immediately after the battle of Grapevine, Devil Anse ordered twenty-five new Winchester rifles and ten thousand rounds of ammunition.[23] The new ordnance was never used because two weeks after the battle of Grapevine, Devil Anse sold his Grapevine land to a land speculator[24] who later flipped it to a group of Philadelphia financiers known as the Torpin Group, who then leased it to US Steel. Johnse Hatfield became a company policeman for US Steel.

By spring 1888, Anse had relocated to Main Island Creek, in the Guyandotte River Valley. The illiterate Devil Anse did not have a ceremonial gathering, where he read an eloquent statement, as the movie shows. He just packed up and left.

The feud did not end as so many other feuds of that era ended, with one or both the leaders dead or in prison. It ended when Devil Anse gave up his land.

1  McCoy, Truda, *The McCoys,* 197-98.
2  Cunningham, Dan. *Horrible Butcheries,* 37.
3  Rice, 98-9.
4  Rice, 113.
5  Rice, *The Hatfields and the McCoys,* 99.
6  *Ibid.*
7  Jones, 152.
8  Jones, 151-152.
9  King, *The Feud,* 307.
10  , King, *The Feud,* xi.
11  Rice, 69.
12  Waller, *Feud,* 191.
13  Mutzenberg, *Famous Feuds,* 44.
14  Waller, *Feud,* 186.
15  King, Dean, *The Feud,* 211.

16  Rice, *The Hatfields and the McCoys,* 99.

17  King, *The Feud,* 208.

18  Waller, *Feud*, 185.

19  *Ibid.*

20  Waller, *Feud*, 258-9.

21  Hatfield and Spence, 178.

22  Mutzenberg, *Famous Feuds,* 39.

23  Hatfield and Spence, *Tale of the Devil,* 178–79.

24  Waller, *Feud*, 198.

# CHAPTER 19.

# THE TRIALS

The History Channel folks missed out big time by not showing the trials of the Hatfields as they actually were. The trials, with all the maneuvering that accompanied them, would have been great TV drama. The trial of Wall, who was tried separately, had everything a courtroom drama needs.

With Devil Anse gone from the Valley and nine Hatfields in jail in Pikeville, the fight then moved to the courts. West Virginia Governor Wilson was incensed by what he deemed to be kidnapping of West Virginia citizens and took a personal interest in the case. The governor was at the counsel table as a habeas corpus petition was heard in federal court in Louisville. The court refused to rule, saying it had no jurisdiction over a case involving a contest between two sovereign states.

The court of appeals denied the petition for habeas corpus, and West Virginia appealed it to the Supreme Court, which ruled that the Hatfields could be arrested in Kentucky, even though they had been brought there illegally.[1]

When Wall was in Louisville for his habeas corpus hearing, A.J. Ferguson, Pike County prosecutor, told the newspapers that Wall had five living wives and thirty-three children. Wall denied it, of course. It is probably true that he sired four children by a woman not his wife, the previously mentioned Sarah (Mounts) Christian. Sarah was the daughter of Margaret Cline Mounts, and therefore a first cousin to Perry Cline. The Cline family historian says that it is true.[2]

This woman, by whom Wall sired four children, was married to a man named Dan Christian, the adopted (though informally) son of Devil Anse Hatfield.[3]

As my research leaves me at least four wives and twenty-nine children short of what Mr. Ferguson said Wall had, I will say that the prosecutor was probably exaggerating. Of course Dean King supersizes even the prosecutor's exaggeration early in his book, while he is laying the foundation for his story of a violent and immoral people. Without citing any source at all, King says: "Wall who was rumored to have seven wives and fifty-five children..."[4] This is one of dozens of gratuitous and un-sourced calumnies leveled against Tug Valley people by King as he constructs his mythical decades-long blood feud between bloodthirsty and amoral clans.

The critical ruling in the case came when the Federal court ruled that the Hatfields were kidnapped without the state of Kentucky sanctioning the kidnapping. Truda McCoy says that Governor Buckner did, in fact, sanction the raids but that the McCoy faction later denied it to protect the governor.[5] Since the admission of such an egregious deception is an admission against interest for Truda McCoy, I credit it as being most likely true. Had the taking of the Hatfields in West Virginia been an official act of the state of Kentucky, there would have been no alternative but for the court to turn them loose.

This means that someone in Pikeville was powerful enough not only to get the governor to seek extradition and post rewards, but also to sanction an illegal invasion of a neighboring state.

Wall Hatfield was completely taken in by the Dils/Cline cabal. Even though he was denied bail, he was allowed to be a trusty and had the run of the town. Of course, he never went anywhere without an officer shadowing him, as there was no way the Pikeville gang would take a chance on losing their prize catch. They smothered Wall with kindness, to the point where he obviously thought he had friends in high places in Pikeville. Talk about a setup!

We know he talked to Dils, because he said that Dils had offered to post bail for him, up to fifty thousand dollars.[6] Of course Dils, who controlled the courts, knew there would be no bail, so it is quite possible that he did make such an offer, knowing it would not be needed. Anyone who thinks Colonel Dils would actually have ponied up fifty five thousand dollars to guarantee Wall Hatfield's appearance for trial is a potential customer for a nice bridge in Brooklyn.

When his trial opened, none other than lawyer Perry Cline represented Wall. In payment of Cline's fee, Wall signed over to him the land he had bought from Devil Anse — some of the land Anse had taken from Cline.[7] The actions of both Wall Hatfield and Perry Cline are puzzling. We will never know why Wall chose Cline as his lawyer, or why Cline took the case.

Truda McCoy said that Cline assured Ran'l that he was looking after Ran'l's interests while serving as lawyer for Wall and his sons-in-law, and I think she was right.[8] Perry Cline didn't even make use of the very important fact that Wall had voluntary subjected himself to Kentucky law, which a good lawyer might have been able to convince a jury, even a prejudiced one, was the action of an innocent man, and possibly have gotten Wall off with an accessory conviction. But he got life, of which he served only about six months, before he was buried on the grounds of the Kentucky state penitentiary at age fifty-five.

Wall's thinking seems to have been confused from the time he offered to surrender. Surely a man wouldn't subject himself to a trial, if he were not convinced he would be exonerated, but Wall should have known that he could be convicted as an accessory to multiple murders, even in a fair trial. His own testimony showed him to have been an active accessory to the crime. He obviously didn't know that and thought that because he was not on the Kentucky side of the river — and no testimony placed him there — he was not guilty.[9]

When the totality of Wall's feud-related activities is considered, it is quite possible that he fully intended to have the three McCoys tried before Preacher Anse in the event of Ellison's death. Wall could very well have testified truthfully when he swore that he had tried to save the boys' lives, in which case he believed that all he had to do was convince a jury of that, and he would be exonerated.

Some say that having Perry Cline as his lawyer convinced enough of the jury that the entire power structure was somehow on Wall's side to cause them to give him life instead of death. I say that, given the testimony where no witness placed Wall Hatfield on the Kentucky side of the Tug River when the boys were shot, he would have fared no worse had he saved his money and defended himself. No Pike County jury would hang a man for murder on the basis of the testimony in this case. They didn't hang Messer who, according to the testimony, was at the forefront of the shooters, so they definitely wouldn't have hanged Wall under any circumstances. Truda McCoy was right — Perry Cline was never on Wall's side.

While I don't think Wall was ever in danger of hanging, I don't think it was possible for him to be acquitted after Sally McCoy testified. Sarah (Sally) McCoy, Ran'l's wife is the feud's most tragic figure. How she held up as well as she did is a mystery to me.

Her testimony in Wall's trial was heart-rending: "I am the mother of Tolbert, Farmer (sic) and Randolph McCoy. They are dead...Wall had a double barrel shot gun laying across his lap...I was talking, praying and crying for my boys...I heard Wall say that if Ellison Hatfield died, he would shoot the boys as full of holes as a sifter bottom....I fell on my knees and began praying, begging and crying for my children."[10]

Feud writers search in vain for a hero in the feud story, but their efforts always fall short of the mark. There were no heroes, but there was a heroine — Sally McCoy. Sally McCoy at the schoolhouse on Mate Creek, pleading for the lives of her sons; Sally McCoy dragging her battered body through the snow in an effort to reach her dying daughter on January 1, 1888; and Sally McCoy giving her heart-rending testimony on the witness stand in 1889; these all leap out to me as heroic actions.

The women—other than Roseanna-- get little press, because, except for Sally's wounding and her poignant testimony they don't figure in the public story. But, for readers who don't know how things worked in the hills back then, I suggest two short scenes from two movies:

First, in: "My Big Fat Greek Wedding," the mother said "Your father is the head of the house, but I am the neck that turns the head." If you understand that, then you know exactly what Levicy Hatfield and Sally McCoy did in their homes.

Then you see the neck doing its work in the scene in Costner's movie when Ran'l was at Devil Anse's house, while his three sons were prisoners there. Ran'l asked if he could see the boys and Devil Anse quickly answered, "No." Then he asked if Sally could see them, and Anse was stumped--it was a moral dilemma for him. He thought for a few seconds, then turned and looked at Levicy. Levicy gave the slightest positive nod of her head, and Anse turned immediately and told Ran'l that Sally could come. The neck had turned the head, as it usually did in those mountain homes when a moral issue was to be decided.

Sally McCoy was the only witness in the case of Ellison Mounts. When asked if she saw Ellison Mounts kill her daughter, Alifair, Sally answered, "No."[11]

Truda McCoy wrote that when Sally McCoy gave that answer, Perry Cline, who wasn't even involved in the case, jumped up and shouted an objection, which the judge sustained. McCoy wrote that Cline then said, "Sally McCoy swore a lie," at which time general pandemonium broke out, with Ran'l trying to get at Cline for calling Sally a liar.[12] Cline told Ran'l, "Hush, Ran'l. We have to hang someone."[13]

My great, great uncle, Ransom Hatfield attended the trial, along with his father, Preacher Anse, who was a principal witness against some of the Hatfield defendants. Uncle Ransom did not remember exactly what was said by the various people in the courtroom, but he said that pandemonium broke out in the courtroom when Sally answered that she did not see Mounts kill Alifair, so Truda McCoy's version is probably pretty close to the truth.

With three full confessions in hand, the jury sentenced Mounts to death, in spite of the testimony by the prosecution's key witness that she did not see Mounts kill Alifair.

**Ellison "Cottontop" Mounts — <u>Vera Kay Fink Hankins</u>**

The Kentucky Court of Appeals, in a perfunctory decision barely a page in length, affirmed the death penalty for Mounts.[14]

The movie has Perry Cline representing Mounts, but that was wrong. Mounts had a court-appointed lawyer named Connolly.

We also see Wall being sentenced along with three others, when, in fact, Wall was tried separately.

Wall appealed his life sentence, and the court of appeals upheld the verdict. One might get the impression that Wall didn't receive a fair hearing before the court of appeals by reading the court's words: "...when reaching the spot where they were to carry into execution their murderous intent, they surrounded their victims[15] for the purpose of having a shooting match, and, cocking their guns, blew the top of the smaller boy's head off, shot Tolbert some fifteen times and Pharmer eleven times, and then made the night hideous by hooting as the owl, in contempt, doubtless, of the law, and those who administer it."[16]

It is obvious from the record that the Pikeville crowd meant to hang Uncle Wall, if possible. Facing the reticence of any jury to hang a man who was not present when the crime was committed, Wall's prosecutors took the path most likely to secure a conviction; they made Wall the leader of the lynch mob! Devil Anse, whose name the court misspells the only two times it is used, was a minor character in the scenario constructed by Wall's prosecutors.

The strategy worked so well that the appeals court actually believed that Wall Hatfield, and not Anse, was the leader of the Hatfield gang. The court said that the execution party was "under the leadership of Valentine Hatfield,"[17] and referred to Wall as "the presiding judge of this murderous clan."[18]

One might wonder how anyone other than Devil Anse Hatfield could ever be considered the leader of the Hatfield gang, but the power of the mass media can imprint just about anything into the minds of the public--and the minds of appeals court judges.

John Spears, writing in the New York Sun during the time when Wall Hatfield was awaiting trial in the Pikeville jail, wrote: "Then the voice of Wall Hatfield, from the Virginia side, was heard saying: 'Take aim. Fire!'"[19] Spears has Wall Hatfield — not Devil Anse — giving the Hatfield firing squad the order to fire. He has Wall giving the order from across the river — *in Virginia*! Spears, writing in New York, did not even know which state Wall Hatfield was in; yet he claimed to know his exact words.

The claim that anyone other than Devil Anse gave that order is ludicrous on its face, but Devil Anse was not in jail awaiting trial. Thus we see a man who is writing a story in New York City, and who does not even know how to spell the names of any of the three victims, nor the state in which they were held prisoner, able to reach the members of the Kentucky Court of Appeals with a patent lie. We know that Spears influenced that court because the court repeatedly — *nine times* — referred to the State of Virginia as the state where the boys were held prisoner and where Wall was when they were shot.

Wall Hatfield in charge of the execution and giving the order to fire *from Virginia* appears in only two places in all feud related writings — John Spears reportage and the Kentucky Court of Appeals decision in Wall Hatfield's case. The inescapable con-clusion is that the writings of John Spears had a significant effect upon the Kentucky Court of Appeals. This was almost surely the work of Cline and company. John Spears had no reason to reverse the roles of the Hatfield Brothers, and I don't believe that he did. I think Spears wrote what he was told, and he was told that lie for the express purpose of poisoning the atmosphere around the trial of Wall Hatfield.

It is quite obvious from this language that the majority of the court of appeals would have hung Wall had they been deciding the punishment. The last paragraph of the decision says: "...the jury in inflicting the punishment by imprisonment for life *'has tempered justice with mercy'*" (italics in the original).[20]

Wall was also sorely mistreated by Dean King. An elected mag-istrate in Logan County, West Virginia, and a well-respected man, he was referred to as "Uncle Wall" by people on both sides of the Tug River. According to the trial testimony, even the three McCoys he was convicted of killing called him "Uncle Wall."

While King has colorful descriptive nicknames for almost all the major characters, including many, such as "Deacon" Ellison Hatfield and "Crazy" Jim Vance which were not the common mode of address for them during their lifetimes, he strips Uncle Wall of the avuncular moniker by which Wall was known by virtually everyone in the valley. In fact, the *only* nickname for any of the characters that can be found in the sworn trial testimony is Uncle Wall Hatfield.

King makes a special effort to deprive Uncle Wall of his moniker, saying that John Wallace Hatfield was known as Uncle Wall, to distinguish him from the real Uncle Wall—Valentine Hatfield.[21] This John Wallace Hatfield was, as King says, *twenty years old* at that time. While several respected men of middle age and above were referred to in the Tug Valley as "Uncle" — Wall Hatfield and Jim McCoy being prime examples — no one of the tender age of twenty was ever tagged with that moniker.

All of the prisoners who had been captured by Frank Phillips' posse got life terms. Of the three captured by Dan Cunningham, Mounts was hanged, Alex Messer got life, and Charles Gillespie, who turned state's evidence, got a continuance, escaped from the Pikeville jail in May 1890, and was never heard of again.[22]

Ellison "Cottontop" Mounts, whose sentence was not tempered with mercy, was hanged in Pikeville on February 18, 1890. He was the last man so honored in Pike County. His last words were not, "They hornswoggled me with love," as we see in the movie. His last words were "The Hatfields made me do it."

The springing of the trap-door on Ellison Mounts was the last act of violence in the "Hatfield and McCoy feud." Although a few bounty hunters continued to bother the Hatfields periodically, all of them survived into the 20th century. I believe that there are at least a few unmarked graves on West Virginia hillsides containing the bones of bounty hunters who went looking for Hatfields and found them—but there is no proof.

Two of the men active on the Kentucky side of the 1887-8 violence died violently during the 1890s. Bud McCoy, the son of Asa Harmon who was wounded at the Battle of Grapevine was killed in an argument with a cousin, Pleasant McCoy, in 1892. Bad Frank Phillips, the scourge of the Hatfields, was shot in the thigh by his friend and former deputy, Ransom Bray, in 1898. His leg was amputated in an attempt to save his life, but Bad Frank suffered for two weeks and then succumbed to gangrene.

With Devil Anse secreted in the hills of Island Creek, all that remained of the feud was Ran'l McCoy, telling his sad story to passengers on the Pikeville ferry.

The modernizers had accomplished their immediate goal of removing the "feud" as an impediment to the exploitation of the Valley's riches. Their ultimate goal, which was to convert the independent sons of the hills into docile wage slaves, would take much longer.

---

1  Mahon v. Justice, 127 US 700.

2  Cecil Cline, *The Clines and Associated Families,* 74.

3  Hatfield and Spence, *Tale of the Devil,* 92.

4  King, 5. Of course King does not tell us why rumors are part of a "True Story," nor does he give even a hint of the source of his "rumor."

5  McCoy, *McCoys,* p. 227.

6  Rice, *The Hatfields and the McCoys,* 85.

7  Waller, *Feud,* 229.

8  McCoy, *McCoys,* 199.

9  Waller, *Feud,* 229.

10  *Plyant Mayhorn v. Commonwealth of Kentucky, Case #19601,* p.7-7. KDLA

11  McCoy, *McCoys,* 201.

12  For the courtroom scene I have both the word of Truda McCoy, as cited, and that of Ransom Hatfield to me personally.  Uncle Ransom attended the trials with his father, Preacher Anse, who testified.

13  McCoy, *McCoys,* 201–02.

14  11 *Kentucky Law Reporter* 311.

15  I seriously doubt the Hatfields were dumb enough to form a circle and then start shooting.

16  11 *Kentucky Law Reporter* 470.

17  11 KLR 471.

18  *Ibid.*

19  Spears, *Mountain Feud,* 14.

20  11 *KLR* 472

21  King, *The Feud,* 118.

22  Rice, *The Hatfields and the McCoys,* 113.

# CHAPTER 20.

# WEIGHING THE BALANCE

## Violence is never the Answer

A favorite pastime of most who read about the feud is ascribing blame to one side or the other. Of course the exercise is utterly futile in the supersized versions, because most of the violence is random and mindless, reflecting nothing but defective character and/or stupidity in the participants. The violent episodes which actually happened can be assessed, and the result of that assessment is unsatisfactory to partisans of either side.

The most important thing to me is that, in every case, the use of violence proved ultimately to be damaging to the initiator. Because I ascribe the death of Asa Harmon McCoy to the Civil War, and I consider the hog trial and the killing of Bill Staton to be non-feud related because they did not involve Devil Anse Hatfield, the arrest of Johnse Hatfield by the McCoys was the first aggressive action by either party.

The arrest of Johnse on a charge of carrying a concealed weapon, which many of the men in the Valley were also guilty of every day, was not a simple effort on the part of the McCoys to preserve law and order. It was, rather, payback for Johnse allowing Roseanna to return home pregnant and still a McCoy.

This action led directly to the only armed face to face confrontation between the two families until the 1888 New Year's raid. It was the only time Devil Anse Hatfield, himself, ever had a face-to-face armed confrontation with Ran'l McCoy's family. By taking their prisoner and humiliating them in the process, Devil Anse contributed to the animosity felt by the McCoy brothers when they went to the election the following year, which led to the death of Anse's brother, Ellison.

When the McCoy boys butchered Ellison Hatfield on Election Day, 1882, they guaranteed themselves the vengeance of Devil Anse, which led to their slayings in the paw paw grove. Devil Anse's lynching of the three brothers caused him to have to live the rest of his life under indictment for murder and subject at all times to arrest and trial for the crimes.

When Cap Hatfield and Tom Wallace entered the home of Bill Daniels, and physically assaulted one or two of his womenfolk, they aroused the enmity of Jeff McCoy which led to his killing, and insured the appearance of Bill Daniels as a witness against their kinsmen and comrades in the later trials.

When Jeff McCoy went to the home of Cap Hatfield to get Tom Wallace and shot into the cabin where Cap's wife lay ill in bed, he brought about the angry vengeance that Cap wrought upon him on the bank of the Tug.

The killing of Jeff McCoy by Cap Hatfield neutralized Devil Anse's years-long effort to quiet the Kentucky passions and keep the indictments against him and his cohort on the back burner. It also gave the Dils/Cline group some small basis for asserting to the governor that there was, indeed, a feud in Pike County that required action on the governor's part.

The illegal invasions of West Virginia by the Frank Phillips posse brought on all the violence and bloodshed of the second phase of the feud, in 1887-8. While every writer notes the illegality of the execution of the three sons of Ran'l McCoy, no one seems to realize that the Phillips raids were of the same ilk. The raids were crimes under the laws of both states, and were applications of extra-legal violence which usurped the proper authorities.

Those who damn Devil Anse for his extra-legal killing of the three McCoys who killed his brother, while approving the extra-legal kidnappings and killings by the Kentucky posse, are being inconsistent, to say the least.

The Phillips raids led directly to the worst crimes of the entire decade — the burning of the McCoy home and the killing of two of Ran'l's children and the maiming of his wife. The New Year's raid on the McCoy home cost Ran'l McCoy two children and his home, and it was also the most destructive event that happened to Devil Anse Hatfield.

Looking back at the historical record, we see that even though the Hatfields killed more McCoys, the major events usually featured first action by the McCoy/Kentucky side followed by reaction by the Hatfields. With the exception of the visit by Cap Hatfield and Tom Wallace to the Daniels home, which initiated the sequence that culminated in the killing of Jeff McCoy, the McCoy/Kentucky side was the aggressor each time. This is stated solely for historical clarity, and not to justify the Hatfield retaliation, which was harsh in the case of the paw paw executions, and obviously extreme in the case of the New Year's raid. Although the Hatfield retaliations may be considered extreme, they could have been prevented if the McCoy/Kentucky side had simply refrained from the actions which provoked the Hatfield reaction.

The lesson of the feud is that violence is never a satisfactory way to settle inter-personal or inter-family differences. Stripped of all the "filler material" in the supersized versions of the feud story, the futility of seeking solutions through violence is clear. Of course the dozens of apocryphal stories in the supersized versions are all just random and senseless manifestations of the savagery of an immoral people, and therefore teach us nothing; moreover, they are lies.

Here is where the contrast between Costner's film and the supersizer books must be drawn. Kevin Costner is not traveling around the country claiming to be an expert on the feud and telling people that his movie is "The True Story." He took real historical figures and made an entertaining movie loosely based upon history, producing an entertaining six hour drama that delivered the message. While the movie is terrible on historical detail, the basic lesson comes through clearly. That is real art!

## A People Devalued

As the reader now knows, I believe that there was a purpose for sending the New York reporters to our area instead of to the other parts of Kentucky where much larger feuds were underway. The purpose was to present the people of the Tug Valley as semi-savage barbarians, thus rendering the taking of their mineral riches more palatable to the American public.

When I saw the TV movie, closely followed by books by two best-selling authors, all of which revived and reinforced the image of the violent and dissolute hillbilly seen in the reportage of the New York reporters in 1888, I sensed something afoot. I fully expected soon to see reports about the destructive effects of modern mineral-extraction processes upon the environment and the people.

Colgate Professor Jeff Bary says: ""As a result of *devaluing the people* that live in this region of our country, we've justified the exploitation of this region," said Bary. "The coal industry comes in and strips all the trees off the top of the mountain and blasts off the top with a lot of dynamite."[1](*Italics mine*)

Below is a photo of the mountaintop removal at Kayford Mountain, West Virginia.

The "feud story" is all about *devaluing the people.* It started out that way in 1888 and continues in the best-selling books of the present. After all, who gives a damn if violent and amoral people are robbed, displaced or poisoned?

The article continues with: "Bary said that in addition to devastating the landscape, mountaintop removal releases heavy metals that pollute the air and water supplies of the region."

The process of hydraulic fracturing in the Marcellus Shale formation, which underlies more than 90% of West Virginia, is now gathering momentum. I will go out on a limb and predict that there is more bad news coming soon. If we hear that the "fracking" has filled the water supply with poisonous and/or radioactive wastes, we will know why "the feud" became such a hot subject for the media complex in 2012-13.

The Dean King book has laid the groundwork well, as a reading of the readers' comments on the various reviews of the book show.

In the reviews on Amazon, we see:

"If one was to wander the hills of this frontier state, and that's what it was, one had to be armed to the teeth, not only against bandits, but against property owners (if they caught a stranger wandering on their land, even in innocence, they were very likely to be shot)."—Alistair Browne

We see here that King's book has convinced this reader that mountain people of the nineteenth century, who were among the world's most friendly to strangers, were actually the polar opposite.

In another review, by a retired Lieutenant Colonel, we see that King has successfully brought T. C. Crawford's image up to date: "The breadth of this feud spans for decades in some of the rawest and wildest parts of Eastern America that *are still, in many ways, the same today*. It also shows how the scars of the War Between the States affected close friends and families in their different beliefs, and in some cases is still true today. Mr. King's anecdote in the forward is a case in point where *he drew gunfire during his terrain walks in the area* because he had the wrong guides (i.e. forest rangers vice (sic) Hatfield guide)." –Richard Jeffries (*Italics mine*)

King has brought it up to the present, by convincing this retired Colonel that if he brings his teen-aged daughter or granddaughter to the Tug Valley today, he may be shot at—especially if he is in the company of uniformed law officers.

Recent writers have done their work exceedingly well. It is now up to serious scholars to refute them. This book is a start.

---

1 http://news.colgate.edu/2013/09/professor-jeff-bary-hopes-multidisciplinary-series-sheds-light-on-mountaintop-removal-mining.html#more-11426

# BIBLIOGRAPHY

Addington, Luther F. *The Story of Wise County, Virginia*. Wise: Centennial Committee and School Board of Wise County, 1956.

Alther, Lisa. *Blood Feud: The Hatfields and the McCoys: The Epic Story of Murder and Vengeance*. Guilford: Lyons Press, 2012.

Bailey, Rebecca J. *Matewan Before the Massacre, PhD Thesis*. Morgantown: West Virginia University Department of History, 2001.

Caudill, Harry M. *Night Comes to the Cumberlands*. Boston: Little, Brown, 1963.

—. *Theirs Be the Power: The Moguls of Eastern Kentucky*. Urbana: Universithy of Illinois, 1983.

Cline, Cecil Lee and Harry Dale. *The Clines and allied Families of the Tug River Region of Kentucky and West Virginia*. Louisville: Gateway Press, 1998.

Cunningham, Daniel. "The Horrible Butcheries of West Virginia, in West Virginia History, Vol. XLVI, 1985-86, pp25-43." (1986).

Donnelly, Shirley. *The Hatfield-McCoy Reader*. Parsons, WV: McClain Printing Company, 1971.

Ely, William. *The Big Sandy Valley: A History of the People and Country from the Earliest Settlement to the Present Time*. Catlettsburg: Clearfield, 1887 .

Hatfield, Coleman C., and Spence, Robert Y. *The Tale of the Devil*. Chapmanville: Woodland Press, 2012.

Hatfield, Coleman C., with Davis, F. Keith. *The Feuding Hatfields & McCoys*. Chapmanville: Woodland Press, 2012.

Hatfield, G. Elliott. *The Hatfields*. Paintsville: East Kentucky Press, 1974.

Hatfield, L. D. *The True Story of the Hatfield and McCoy Feud*. New York: Cosimo Classics, 2012.

Hatfield, Phillip. *The Other Feud: William Anderson "Devil Anse" Hatfield in the Civil War*. Self published, 2010.

Hutton, T.R.C. *Bloody Breathitt: Power and Violence in the Mountain South, (PhD Thesis)*. Nashville: Vanderbilt University, 2009.

Jones, Virgil C. *The Hatfields and the McCoys*. Chapel Hill: University of North Carolina, 1948.

King, Dean. *The Feud: The Hatfields & McCoys: The True Story*. New York: Little, Brown and Company, 2013.

Klotter, James C. *Kentucky: Portrait in Paradox, 1900-1950*. Frankfort: Kentucky Historical society, 1996.

—. *William goebel: The Politics of Wrath*. Lexington: University of Kentucky, 2009.

Klotter, James C.. *Kentucky Justice, Southern Honor and American Manhood*. Baton Rouge: LSU Press, 2003.

McCorkle, William A. *Recollections of Fifty Years in West Virginia*. New York: Putnam's Sons, 1928.

McCoy, Samuel. *Squirrel Huntin' Sam McCoy: His Memoir and Family Tree*. Pikeville: Pikeville College Press, 1979.

McCoy, Truda Williams. *The McCoys: Their Story*. Pikeville: Preservation Council Press, 1976.

McKnight, Brian D. *Contested Borderland: The Civil War in Appalachian Kentucky and Virginia*. Lexington: University of Kentucky, 2006.

Mutzenberg, Charles G. *Kentucky's Famous Feuds and Tragedies*. New York: R.F. Fenno, 1917.

Osborne, Randall and Weaver, Jeffrey C. *The Virginia State Rangers and State Line*. Lynchburg: H.E. Howard, 1994.

Pearce, John Ed. *Dayh of Darkness: The Feuds of Eastern Kentucky*. Lexington: University of Kentucky Press, 1994.

Preston, John David. *The Civil War in the Big Sandy Valley of Kentucky, 2nd Ed.* Baltimore: Gateway Press, 2008.

Pritchard, James M. "The Devil at Large. In Virginia at War, 1863, pp55-84. Davis, William C. and Robertson, James I, eds." Lexington: University of Kentucky, 2009.

Rice, Otis K. *The Hatfields and the McCoys.* Lexington: University of Kentucky Press, 1982.

Scalf, Henry P. *Kentucky's Last Frontier.* Pikeville: Pikeville College Press, 1972.

Spears, John r. *The Hatfields and the McCoys: The Dramatic Story of a Mountain Feud.* Lexington, KY: Create Space, 2013.

Sutherland, Daniel E. *A Savage Conflict: The Decisive Role of Guerillas in the American Civil War.* Chapel Hill: University of North Carolina, 2009.

Swain, G. T. *History of Logan County, West Virginia.* Logan: G.T. Swain, 1927.

Taylor, Paul E. *Bloody Harlan.* Baltimore: Jniversity Press of America, 1989.

Turner, Carolyn clay, and Traum, Carolyn Hay. *John C.C. Mayo, Cumberland Capitalist.* Pikeville: Pikeville College Press, 1983.

Waller, Altina. *Feud: Hatfields, McCoys and Social Change in Appalachia, 1860-1900.* Chapel Hill: University of North Carolina, 1988.

Waller, Altina. "Feuding in Appalachia: Evolution of a Cultural Stereotype." Pujdup, Bkillings and Waller, eds. *Appalachia in the Making: The Mountain South in the Nineteenth Century.* Chapel Hill: Universityh of North Carolina Press, 1995. 347.

Ward, Geoffrey C. *Before the Trumpet: Young Franklin Roosevelt.* New York: Konecky & Konecky, 1985.

Weaver, Jeffrey C. *Bushwhackers' Paradise: the Civil War in Wise and Buchanan County, Virginia.* Saltville: Twin Commonwealth Press, 1993 .

Wright, William T. *Devil John Wright of the Cumberlands.* Pound: William T. Wright, 1932.

# INDEX

Made in the USA
Charleston, SC
06 December 2013